Integration of Natural Language and Vision Processing

(Volume IV)

Recent Advances

Edited by

Paul Mc Kevitt

Dept. of Computer Science, University of Sheffield, U.K.

Reprinted from *Artificial Intelligence Review*
Volume 10, Nos. 3–4, 1996

Kluwer Academic Publishers
Dordrecht / Boston / London

Library of Congress Cataloging-in-Publication Data

Integration of natural language and vision processing / edited by Paul Mc Kevitt.
p. cm.
"Reprinted from Artificial Intelligence Review".
Includes bibliographical references.
(acid-free paper)
1. Natural language processing (Computer science) 2. Computer vision. I. Mc Kevitt, Paul.
QA76.9.N38I55 1995
006.3'5--dc20
95-12

ISBN-13: 978-94-010-7268-7 e-ISBN-13: 978-94-009-1716-3
DOI: 10.1007/978-94-009-1716-3

Published by Kluwer Academic Publishers,
P.O. Box 17, 3300 AA Dordrecht, The Netherlands.

Kluwer Academic Publishers incorporates
the publishing programmes of
D. Reidel, Martinus Nijhoff, Dr W. Junk and MTP Press.

Sold and distributed in the U.S.A. and Canada
by Kluwer Academic Publishers,
101 Philip Drive, Norwell, MA 02061, U.S.A.

In all other countries, sold and distributed
by Kluwer Academic Publishers Group,
P.O. Box 322, 3300 AH Dordrecht, The Netherlands.

Printed on acid-free paper

Table of Contents

Artificial Intelligence Review **10**: 155–158, 1996.

About the Authors

Guy J. Brown is a lecturer in Computer Science at the University of Sheffield. He received a BSc in Applied Science from Sheffield Hallam University in 1988, and a PhD in Computer Science from the University of Sheffield in 1992. He has studied computational models of hearing since 1989, and also has research interests in speech perception, music perception and auditory virtual reality.

Anthony Cohn is a Reader in Automated Reasoning in the Division of AI, School of Computer Studies at the University of Leeds. He leads a research group working on Automated Reasoning with a particular focus on qualitative spatial reasoning. He holds a number of grants in the area, and has published widely. He has been Chairman of the UK AI Society AISB and also of the European Coordinating Committee on AI. He was Programme Chair of the European AI Conference ECAI94.

Paul Duchnowski was born in 1965 in Warsaw, Poland and emigrated to the United States in 1979. He received his Bachelor's, Master's and Doctor of Science degrees in Electrical Engineering, all from the Massachusetts Institute of Technology in 1987, 1989, and 1993, respectively. His ScD thesis investigated a new structure for automatic speech recognition motivated by models of human speech cue integration. He is currently conducting post-doctoral research in the Laboratory for Interactive Systems at the University of Karlsruhe, Germany. For professional purposes, he is interested in automatic speech recognition, speech processing, human and machine multimodal communication, and other probabilistically describable phenomena.

John Gammack was born in 1960 in Scotland, also on the north west Celtic fringe of the EU. He is currently a Senior Lecturer in the Department of Computing and Information Systems, at the University of Paisley, where he specialises in psychological, philosophical and social aspects of information systems in organisations. He completed his PhD in Experimental Psychology at the University of Cambridge, England in 1988 following a combined honours degree in Psychology with Computing Science at the University of Stirling, Scotland. He has published widely in the areas of knowledge elicitation, management information systems and organisational decision support. His current research is funded for 3 years under the UK government's Department of Trade and Industry CSCW programme and concerns the provision of software environments to support constructive and dialogical processes in distributed design teams.

John Gooday is a Research Fellow in the Qualitative Spatial Reasoning Group at the University of Leeds. He holds a BSc in physics from University College London, an MSc in computing from Imperial College and a PhD in nonmonotonic temporal reasoning from the University of Exeter. His research interests centre on applications of logic to commonsense reasoning, in particular spatial, temporal and nonmonotonic reasoning.

Peter Hall is a Lecturer in Computer Science at the Victoria University of Wellington, New Zealand. He was awarded his PhD in 1993 from the University of Sheffield, UK. His Master's degree in Computer Graphics comes from Middlesex Polytechnic, UK (1989). Peter's BSc degree, gained in 1983, is in Physics and was obtained from Leeds University, UK. Between his BSc and his PhD Peter has spent six years working in the software industry. His research interests are in Computer Vision and Computer Graphics. Both areas reflect his broader interests in fine Art, visual communication, visual perception, and cognition.

Bernhard Jung received his Diploma (MSc) in Computer Science in 1992 from his hometown University of Stuttgart, in southern Germany. His academic background further includes a minor in computational linguistics and, at the University of Missouri, St. Louis, USA, the general study of philosophy. At present, he is employed with the Collaborative Research Centre SFB 360 "*Situated Artificial Communicators*" at the University of Bielefeld where he works for the CODY project and pursues his doctorate (PhD) in Artificial Intelligence. His current research generally concerns knowledge processing in situated agents and specifically addresses the integration of structural and spatial knowledge representation and reasoning. Prior research activities lie in machine learning (University of Stuttgart), natural language processing (LILOG Project, IBM Germany), and model-based configuration and failure analysis (FAW Research Institute for Applied Knowledge Processing, Ulm, Germany). Bernhard Jung's other interests include multi-agent systems, virtual reality, multimedia, and cognitive systems.

Stefan Manke was born in 1966 in Bonn, Germany. Currently he is a PhD student in the Computer Science Department at the University of Karlsruhe, Germany, where he has also got his Master's degree in Computer Science in 1991. His research interests are on-line handwriting recognition and the integration of speech recognition and lipreading. He is also interested in multi-modal systems and neural networks.

Paul Mc Kevitt is 32 and from Dún Na nGall (Donegal), Ireland on the Northwest of the EU. He is a Visiting Professor of Language and Vision computing at the Aalborg University in Denmark, EU and a British EPSRC (Engineering and Physical Sciences Research Council) Advanced Fellow in the Department of Computer Science at the University of Sheffield, England, EU. The Fellowship, commenced in 1994, and releases him from his tenured Lectureship (Associate Professorship) for 5 years to conduct full-time research on the integration of natural language, speech and vision processing. He is currently pursuing a Master's Degree in Education at the University of Sheffield. He completed his PhD in Computer Science at the University of Exeter, England in 1991. His Master's Degree in Computer Science was obtained from New Mexico State University, New Mexico, USA in 1988 and his Bachelor's Degree in Computer Science from University College Dublin, Dublin, Ireland, EU in 1985. His primary research interests are in Natural Language Processing including the processing of pragmatics, beliefs and intentions in dialogue. He is also interested in Philosophy, Multimedia and the general area of Artificial Intelligence.

Naoyuki Okada is a Professor of artificial intelligence at Kyushu Institute of Technology, Iizuka Japan. His research interest is in the development of agents with integrated intelligence: language association with mind, symbol grounding in perception or motion, fusion of intellect and emotion, and integrated processing of multi-media. He has actively published unique papers in these areas. He was leader of the working group of systematizing science of knowledge subordinate to Science Council of Japan. Okada is trustee of Japanese Society for Artificial Intelligence, consulting editor of Pragmatics & Cognition, and president of PACLING (Pacific Association for Computational Linguistics).

Raman Rajagopalan is 31, is married and has one daughter. He was born in Urbana, Illinois, USA in 1964, completed his early scholing in India, and returned to the USA (Memphis, Tennessee) in 1972. He completed his Bachelor's degree in Electrical Engineering from Memphis State University in 1981 and his Master's degree in Electrical Engineering from the University of Illinois at Urbana-Champaign in 1984. Afterwards, he joined IBM Corporation in Houston, Texas

(1984–91), and later completed a Master's degree (1988) and a Doctoral degree in Computer Science (1995) at the University of Texas at Austin. While studying at the University of Texas, he held a research position with the EDS corporation (1992) and a consultant position with the Texas Department of Human Services (1994–195). He joined Intel Corporation in Portland, Oregon in 1995 as a Systems Engineer, where he is currently working on Object-Oriented Modeling and Programming projects in the Finance domain. His primary research interests are in Qualitative Reasoning, with emphasis on Spatial Reasoning, and in the integration of multimedia input to a knowledge base.

Gert Rickheit is Professor of Linguistics and Psycholinguistics in the Faculty of Linguistics and Literary Studies at the University of Bielefeld, Germany. He studied Linguistics, Psychology, Philosophy and Literary Sciences at the Universities of Braunschweig and Bochum and obtained his PhD at the University of Bochum. His main research is in the field of Psycholinguistics. As initiator and speaker of the Research Group "*Coherence*" from 1986 to 1991 he carried out research into the coherence processes in speech production and reception. Together with his colleagues he developed experimental and simulative methods which are applied in research into human language processing. He was also one of the initiators of the nationwide programme "*Cognitive Linguistics*", which was financed by the Deutsche Forschungsgemeinschaft from 1987 to 1995, in which projects on research into human language processing were also supported. He has been speaker of the Collaborative Research Centre SFB 360 "*Situated Artificial Communicators*" since 1993.

Neil Todd obtained a BSc degree in Theoretical Physics from the University of Exeter in 1982. After working as a Research Assistant with Henry Shaffer in the Department of Psychology at Exeter he was awarded a PhD in the Psychology of Music in 1989. Between 1989 and 1991 he was a Science and Engineering Research Fellow in Information Technology at Exeter. Between 1991 and 1993 he was a Medical Research Council Research Fellow in Cognitive Science at the Departments of Music at City and Sheffield Universities. He is currently a Lecturer in Psychology at the Unviersity of Manchester. His research interests include: the production and perception of expressive musical performance; the analysis and synthesis of rhythm in music, speech and bioacoustic signals; music, motion and affect; and, controversially, the vestibular system. He is a practising jazz bass player and composer in the jazz idiom. He has recently had premiered a composition for String Nonet.

Graziella Tonfoni presently teaches Natural Language Processing and Computational Linguistics at the University of Bologna, Italy. She has been Visiting Scholar at the following American Universities and Research Institutes: Massachusetts Institute of Technology, Harvard University, Bolt Beranek and Newman. In addition, she has given seminars and lectures in many other American and European Universities and Research Centers. She is the Author of CPP-TRS (Communicative Positioning Program-Text Representation Systems). CPP-TRS is an innovative methodology for enhancing communication effectiveness and an iconic language for text preplanning and preprocessing. Dr. Tonfoni is also the designer of CPP-TRS existing applications and the author of 17 books. She was given an award as the Outstanding Woman in Research in Rome in 1984.

Minh Tue Vo was born in 1966 in South Vietnam and moved to Montreal, Canada in 1982. He is currently working towards his PhD in Computer Scienc at Carnegie Mellon University, Pittsburgh, U.S.A. He obtained his Bachelor's degree in Computer Engineering from University of Waterloo, Waterloo Canada in 1990 and his Master's degree in Computer Science from Carnegie Mellon in 1993. His research interests include neural network systems and multimodal human-computer interfaces.

Ipke Wachsmuth has held the chair of Knowledge-Based Systems/Artificial Intelligence in the Faculty of Technology at the University of Bielefeld, Germany for the past seven years. His academic background is in mathematics and computer science. He holds a Master's degree in mathematics (Dipl.-Math.) obtained in 1975 from the Technical University of Hanover, Germany, where he also obtained his PhD (Dr.rer.nat) in 1980 for research in cellular automata synchronization, and a Habilitation degree in Computer Science which he obtained from the University of Osnabrück, Germany, in 1989 for research on knowledge base organization. Before coming to Bielefeld, he held faculty and project leader positions in the Department of Mathematics/Computer Science and the Linguistics Department at the Unviersity of Osnabrück, Germany. He was also assistant professor in the Department of Mathematical Sciences at Northern Illinois University in 1981–83 and research fellow in the LILOG group at IBM Germany, Stuttgart in 1986–88. Prof. Wachsmuth has a strong multidisciplinary commitment and has published in the fields of cellular automata, cognitive learning research, intelligent tutoring systems, natural language understanding, technology assessment of AI, expert systems, and large knowledge bases. A sabbatical leave from the University of Bielefeld in 1992/93, spent with the Scientific Visualization Group at the German National Research Center for Information Technology (GMD) at Bonn-Sankt Augustin, led him into computer graphics and virtual reality. His current research activities cover virtual environments, dynamic knowledge representations and multi-agent techniques in the context of human-machine communication. Among many other professional services, Ipke Wachsmuth chaired the 19th Annual German Conference on Artificial Intelligence in 1995 and was recently re-elected to the executive board of the Collaborative Research Centre SFB 360 "*Situated Artificial Communicators*".

Alex Waibel received the BSc degree from the Massachusetts Institute of Technology in 1979, and his MSc (Electrical Engineering and Computer Science) and PhD (Computer Science), in 1980 and 1986, from Carnegie Mellon University. Since 1986 he has been with the Computer Science faculty at Carnegie Mellon, where he now serves as Senior Research Scientist directing the JANUS speech translation project and the INTERAC Multimodal Interfaces Project. He holds joint appointments in the Center for Machine Translation, the Robotics Institute and the Computational Linguistics Department at Carnegie Mellon. Since 1991 he is a University Professor of Informatik at Karlsruhe University, Germany, where he directs the Laboratory for Interactive Systems. Professor Waibel has lectured and published extensively in the areas of speech recognition and synthesis, neurocomputing, machine learning, machine and speech translation and multimodal interfaces. He is one of the founders of C-STAR, and co-directs Verbmobil, both large consortia aimed at international cooperation for multilingual human-human communication. His 1989 paper on Time-Delay Neural Networks was awarded the IEEE Signal Processing Society's Senior paper award in 1995, and the ATR best paper award in 1990.

Artificial Intelligence Review **10:** 159–163, 1996.

Editorial

Integration of natural language and vision processing: Recent advances

There is a recent move towards integration of Natural Language and Vision Processing (NLP and VP) in the field of Artificial Intelligence (AI) (see Denis and Carfantan 1993, Dennett 1991, Mc Kevitt 1994a, 1994b, Pentland 1993, and Wilks & Okada (in press)). This issue is the sixth of a Special Volume to focus on the Integration of Natural Language and Vision Processing, the others concentrating on computational models and systems, intelligent multimedia, and theory and grounding representations. The focus here is *recent advances* and hence we have papers on recent theories, models and systems. Issues consist of site descriptions, papers and book reviews, and here we have one site description, nine papers and one book review.

First, we have a site description by Gerd Rickheit and Ipke Wachsmuth. Then there are two papers on theoretical issues. Antony Cohn and John Gooday present a logical approach to representing and reasoning about space where they provide a formal language called Regional Connection Calculus (RCC). RCC can express concepts such as regions being inside, partially inside, or outside each other. The logic takes care of *vague regions* where boundaries are not well defined or not precisely known. RCC also involves representing how regions change with time. They show how RCC can be used to provide a formal description of the syntax and semantics of *Pictorial Janus*, a concurrent visual language. Such visual languages suffer from the problem of having no properly specified formal semantics so that proofs of program correctness are virtually impossible. Graziella Tonfoni presents Communicative Positioning Program-Text Representation Systems (CPP-TRS) which is both a methodology and a language that she claims can apply to any communicative context. The methodology (CPP) identifies invisible aspects of communication and the meta-language (TRS) complements natural language. The intended application of CPP-TRS is the creation of a visual news processing environment. CPP-TRS contains icons which are not intended to be a substitute for words or sentences but to represent visually what natural language does not convey naturally. The CPP-TRS system is able to support the user with a set of visual tools that are suited to structuring text and communicating effectively. CPP-TRS can be used in a way which is non-transparent or transparent to the reader of the text.

Next, we have a number of papers on computational models and application systems. Naoyuki Okada discusses the integration of vision, language and motion in the AESOPWORLD project at Kyushu Institute of Technology. He presents a model of mind consisting of nine domains such as recognition-understanding, planning-creation, action-expression and so on. Vision and motion are connected and controlled by planning. The system simulates the protagonist of "the Fox and the Grapes" and his mental and physical behaviour are shown by graphic displays, the voice generator, and the music generator which express his emotional states. Peter Hall and myself look at the integration of natural language and vision processing for the interpretation of angiograms or X-rays of human blood vessels. The idea is that 3-D vision reconstruction techniques can be applied to angiograms and can reconstruct a model of the vasculature of an individual. Medical reports are produced by doctors on an individual's vasculature and NLP can be applied to these to aid the reconstruction process. A medical report usually specifies the location of a lesion on the vasculature and applying NLP to the report can aid the vision system to locate lesions more effectively.

Neil Todd and Guy Brown look at computational models of music. They investigate the visualisation of rhythmic structure and stress how theories in auditory processing of rhythmic signals have enabled the construction of a robust algorithm for recovery of rhythmic grouping structure. The algorithm works for both music and speech. This theory was inspired by the theory of edge detection in vision (see Marr 1982). The output of the algorithm is visualised in the form of what is called a *rhythmogram* and they look at different levels of rhythmic structure from individual phonemes to a complete poem. So, here we see that researchers do not only have visions for language but also visions for music and parallels between music, language and vision are discussed in Ó Nualláin (1995) and Vgotsky (1962).

John Gammack and myself investigate the maximisation of communication between the user and computer. We point out that a philosophy of interface design where the computer analyses the intentions of users through verbal and nonverbal media will result in optimum communication. We give examples of Operating System CONsultant (OSCON), a computer program which can analyse users' intentions in language, and a recent experiment on cross-cultural emotions in faces. Waibel et al. investigate integration of speech, gesture and pointing, eye-gaze, lip motion and facial expression, handwriting, face recognition, face tracking, and sound localization for human-computer interaction. There has been an upsurge in development of machines which can analyse human behaviour as has been exemplified by the recent workshops at IJCAI-93 on *Looking at People* (see Pentland 1993) and at IJCAI-95 on *Entertainment and AI/Alife* (see Kitano et al. 1995). Raman Rajagopalan discusses an efficient method for integrating text and graphical input to a knowledge base. He points out that, while pictures focus on spatial information in a compact form, text concentrations on the non-spatial properties of objects. The difficult task of coordinating the processing of this information is to establish the relationship between object references in the text and objects in diagrams (conference). He presents the *Picture Semantics* description language for associating contextual information with objects provided directly in diagrams. Finally Ipke Wachsmuth & Bernhard Jung discuss verbal interaction in virtual design and assembly as part of project SFB360. In the CODY project ((COncept DYnamics) they develop a knowledge representation scheme for dynamic object conceptualization in assemblage. A toy airplane can be assembled from building blocks on a virtual assembly bench.

Steven Pinker's book, *The Language Instinct*, reviewed here, focusses on an issue which will be crucial for language and vision integration. If language and vision systems are to be successful then will have to be able to learn names for new objects and actions and how to express new visual concepts in language forms. Also, visualisation of concepts from language and symbolic forms will be important. As I scan the papers here once more I see a number of names which keep reoccurring: Marr, Minsky, Okada, Pentland, and Waibel.

The articles here are in response to a call by Masoud and myself which went out in December '93. I note that the USA, Japan and the EU (Germany, Britain, Italy) are well-reflected showing up the fact that language and vision integration is a truly international issue. All of the papers have been reviewed by at least one reviewer other than myself and have been subsequently revised. Reviewers, Rajiv Chopra, Andrew Csinger, Andrew Fano, Antony Galton, John Gooday, Niall Griffith, Hans-Helmut Nagel, James Spohrer, and Yuri Tijerino are to be thanked for the time and effort they have put into this process and I shall not say which reviewers reviewed which papers! The development of this sixth (and other) issue(s) on language and vision would not be possible without Bill George (Desk Editor, Editorial Department), Polly Margules (Kluwer Inhouse Editor, Humanities and Social Sciences), Melanie Willow (Journals Editorial Office), and Masoud Yazdani (The Founding Editor of *AI Review*), and they are to be thanked for all their cooperation. Melanie and Bill have worked very hard with authors and reviewers to enable this to happen.

That's the papers for this final issue which should give some feel for recent advances in language and vision integration. I hope you enjoyed reading the previous five issues.

The analysis of intentions is not only important for interpreting the actions of agents in visual environments but also for determining what agents mean when they use words. That is, words have meanings which people intend them to have. Cognitive Sciences (CS) and Computer Science (CS) are converging on Information, Intentions and Integration and we propose the following formula for future development:

$$CS = I \times I \times I = I^3.$$

Lexicons and AI programs of the future will have, in conjunction with flat semantic representations for word senses, spatial representations, pictures and sounds and these will all be useful for multimedia interfaces and Super-InformationHighways. Metaphors and new uses will easily be derived from analogical mappings between spatial relations and pictures. Such are our words on visions for language.

Slan leat,

Paul Mc Kevitt*
Dún Na Gall (Donegal)
Ireland, EU

and

EPSRC Advanced Fellow in Information Technology
[1994–2000]
Department of Computer Science
University of Sheffield
England, EU.

April, 1996

Notes

* Paul Mc Kevitt is currently funded for five years on an Engineering and Physical Sciences Research Council (EPSRC) Advanced Fellowship under grant B/94/AF/1833 for the Integration of Natural Language, Speech and Vision Processing.

References

Denis, M. & Carfantan, M. (eds.) (1993). *Images et langages: multimodalité et modelisation cognitive*. Actes du Colloque Interdisciplinaire du Comité National de la Recherche Scientifique, Salle des Conférences, Siège du CNRS, Paris, April.

Dennett, Daniel (1991). *Consciousness Explained*. Harmondsworth: Penguin.
Kitano, Hiroaki, Bates, Joseph & Hayes-Roth, Barbara (1995). *Entertainment and AI/Alife*. IJCAI-95 Workshop at The 14th International Conference on Artificial Intelligence (IJCAI-95), Montreal, Canada, August.
Marr, David (1982). *Vision*. New York: Freeman.
Mc Kevitt, P. (1994a). Visions for Language. In Proceeding of *The Workshop on Integration of Natural Language and Vision Processing*. Twelfth American National Conference on Artificial Intelligence (AAAI-94), Seattle, Washington, USA, August, 47–57.
Mc Kevitt, P. (ed.) (1994b). Proceedings of *The Workshop on Integration of Natural Language and Vision Processing*. Twelfth American National Conference on Artificial Intelligence (AAAI-94), Seattle, Washington, USA, August.
Ó Nualláin, Seán (1995). *The Search for Mind: A New Foundation for Cognitive Science*. Norwood, New Jersey: Ablex Publishing Corporation.
Pentland, Alex (ed.) (1993). *Looking at People: Recognition and Interpretation of Human Action*. IJCAI-93 Workshop (W28) at The 13th International Conference on Artificial Intelligence (IJCAI-93), Chambéry, France, EU, August.
Vgotsky, V. (1962). *Thought and Language*. Cambridge, Mass.: MIT Press.
Wilks, Y. & N. Okada (eds.) (in press). *Computer Language & Vision Across the Pacific*. Norwood, NJ: Ablex.

Artificial Intelligence Review **10:** 165–170, 1996.

Collaborative Research Centre "Situated Artificial Communicators" at the University of Bielefeld, Germany

G. RICKHEIT & I. WACHSMUTH
SFB 360, University of Bielefeld
D-33501 Bielefeld, Germany
E-mail: rickheit@nov1.lili.uni-bielefeld.de
ipke@techfak.uni-bielefeld.de

Abstract. The Collaborative Research Centre "Situated Artificial Communicators" (SFB 360) is employed in modelling that which a person performs when, with a partner, he cooperatively solves a simple assembly task in a certain situation. Acoustic perception of the spoken word, visual perception of the partner and the objects and processes involved in the situation, understanding of that perceived, the formulation of own utterances, e.g. instructions to the partner, and the planning and performance of actions belong to these intelligence abilities. The theme of the Collaborative Research Centre SFB 360, in which Linguistics, Cognitive Science and Artificial Intelligence are closely entwined, is unique in this form. The scientific headquarters at the University of Bielefeld, in North Rhine Westphalia, Germany, has succeeded in entering a field of research which, in the trend of the growing importance of intelligent information systems, is a decisive factor for technical innovation.

Key words: man-machine communication, artificial intelligence, situatedness, cognitive robotics, speech and vision integration

1. Research and Method

The Collaborative Research Centre "Situated Artificial Communicators" started in the middle of 1993, after approval by the Deutsche Forschungsgemeinschaft. In our research, we examine, on the one hand, which characteristics and abilities of man, referred to here as *natural communicator*, justify his behaviour in solving an assembly task with a partner being described as *intelligent*. On the other hand, we attempt to transmit and implement the insight gained on the principles of intelligent behaviour for the construction of artificial systems, i.e. computer programmes or robots. Our long-term aim is that such *artificial communicators* take on the role of a human partner in the accomplishment of assembly tasks. Short-term, artificial communicators allow a close examination of the intelligence abilities of man. We are not conscious of several abilities which we demonstrate in every-day life as they come automatically to us. It is only when we try to replicate these artificially that we realise which intelligent abilities are necessary for the accomplishment of an assembly task.

In an assembly situation, the following intelligent abilities of man are necessary, i.e. that he (or she)

- acoustically perceive his partner, i.e. *hears*,
- visually perceive the situation, that is the partner, the objects and the on-going procedures and actions, i.e. *sees*,
- cognitively process that perceived, i.e. *understands*,
- formulate his own utterances, i.e. *speaks*, and
- plan and carry out his own actions, i.e. *grasps*, *moves* or *mounts* objects.

The fact that all these abilities are produced in a certain situation, i.e. that man is thereby *situated*, drastically limits his fundamental possibilities: the spoken word can only have certain meanings, as it refers to the actual situation; only certain own utterances are possible, as they must refer to both the task to be solved and the situation; for this reason, only certain actions are possible. In this way, situatedness is a prerequisite for a more exact examination of the intelligence abilities of man as well as for the transmission of the insights gained to artificial systems. In the foreseeable future, we will have to depart from the vision of the universally employable robot and aim at specialised robots for limited tasks.

The remarkable thing about the abovementioned intelligence abilities of man is that he can produce these even when the information available, i.e. what he has seen or heard, is incomplete or garbled. This ability is defined as *robustness*. Many artificial systems, robots or computer programmes suffer from the very fact that they are not comparatively robust. This characteristic in man, therefore, is of great interest to our research. This characteristic originates, in part, from the fact that humans can relate information from various sources, i.e. that which they have seen or heard, and process the whole *integrated.* Disorder or incompleteness in the spoken word can be counterbalanced by that which is seen and vice-versa. Apart from this, that which is spoken can contain directions to look more closely (*active vision*). In the same way, we use properties, which we perceive in objects, e.g. their colour, their form, their size and their position, in order to refer to these objects in speech. This is the reason, for example, why we refer to an object as *the small red screwdriver in the tool box.*

As the situatedness of natural and artificial communicators plays a decisive role in the overall concept of the Collaborative Research Centre, it was necessary to select a reference situation, which touches all projects (cf. Figure 1). This situation can be defined as follows: two communicators must cooperatively construct an *object.* One, the *instructor*, has a diagram and instructs the other, the *constructor*, in such a way that the constructor, with the help of the spoken directions, can carry out the necessary actions as unproblematically as possible. Such an object can be a *model aeroplane*, which is to be constructed from the components of a wooden building kit. In this way, it is possible to make the situation to be described sufficiently interesting, but also sufficiently controllable and practically manageable. The ability to control is necessary, because our knowledge on the abilities of man in such a situation is still very fragmentary. Controlled experiments must be carried out, as man is to serve as the model for the machine constructor. The practical manageability is necessary, because the technical means, e.g. for recognition of the spoken word or for understanding a situation based on a diagram, are still a long way short of the abilities of man. In spite of this, our research group aims at constructing concrete, but limited artificial systems in a step by step procedure. Processes must be developed which will enable cooperation between different specialised systems for individual intelligent abilities.

2. Themes and Projects

The Collaborative Research Centre currently comprises ten projects in four thematic fields.

In the thematic field A *Speech and Visual Perception* three projects examine how an artificial communicator can receive, process and understand acoustic and visual information via sensors, i.e. microphone and camera. Here, knowledge of the most varied form is used, which must be organised in a certain manner and brought into relation to each other (Project A1). It must further be clarified how, based on the raw data of the image, i.e. information on the individual image pixels, objects can be identified and defined by the others (Project A2). Studies are being carried out on the processing of the spoken

Figure 1. Assembly situation (fictitious) with human instructor and one-arm robot constructor with articulated hand, receiving speech and vision input via microphone and camera (by kind permission from SFB 360 Project D3 "System Integration")

word: what contribution words such as *so*, *yes*, *nope*, *ehm* etc., intonation and speech melody make towards comprehension in a directional dialogue (Project A3).

In the thematic field B *Perception and Reference* four projects examine how the optically available information on the one hand and the spoken information on the other are to be put into relation with each other. Only in this manner can an artificial communicator correctly identify an object on hand of a spoken formulation such as *the small red screwdriver in the tool box* (Project B3) or select an appropriate formulation, so that his partner knows, which object is meant (Project B2). Experiments on how humans refer to objects with formulations and how they link between speech and image processing in a technical sense are a prerequisite for this (Project B1). Processes of active vision or "looking more closely" are examined with the help of a computer/camera system for recording eye movements (Project B4).

In the thematic field C *Knowledge and Inference* one project examines how the knowledge, of which communicators avail, allows certain conclusions in a given situation. Our investigations examine how the connection between a word and an object, which we wish to refer to by the word, can continually alter in an on-going assembly task. For example, a wooden disc from the assembly kit is first referred to as a disc and later as the wheel of an aeroplane, or some composite object may be named an undercarriage (Project C1).

In the thematic field D *Speech-Action Systems* two projects examine the question of according to which principles the integration of individual intelligence abilities occur. To achieve this, two complementary procedures are examined. On the one hand, for situations, which are even more limited than those already described, we try - in one step - to bridge the gap between the understanding of an utterance and the resulting action (Project D1). On the other hand, based on the systems in the other projects, it is attempted to collate the functional units and to examine the performance capacity of differents forms of the collation through computer experiments (Project D3).

Further projects, prepared to expand the thematic fields C and D in the next funding period, will take on the themes of the cognitive representation of natural-language directions, the coordination of syntax in spoken discourse, and speech-action systems which are based on multiple sensor input.

3. Principal Investigators, SFB 360

The Collaborative Research Centre is supported by the Deutsche Forschungsgemeinschaft. Principal investigators, as of the funding period 1993-96, are the following scientists from the University of Bielefeld, Faculty of Technology and Faculty of Linguistics and Literary Studies:
Hans-Jürgen Eikmeyer, Dafydd Gibbon, Walther Kindt, Franz Kummert, Henning Lobin, Dieter Metzing, Stefan Posch, Gert Rickheit (speaker), Hannes Rieser, Helge Ritter, Gerhard Sagerer (co-speaker), Hans Strohner, Ipke Wachsmuth.

4. Report Series (ISSN 0946-7572)

Reports from SFB 360 can be ordered by writing to:

Administration, SFB 360
University of Bielefeld
P.O. Box 100131
D-33501 Bielefeld, Germany

or by emailing to:

anke@SFB360.Uni-Bielefeld.DE (Anke Bodzin)

The WWW homepage for SFB 360 is

http://www.techfak.uni-bielefeld.de/sfb/

More general information, abstracts of reports, and an ftp-server address for postscript versions of reports can be accessed from this WWW page. A selection of further references is given below.

References

G.A. Fink, N. Jungclaus, H. Ritter, and G. Sagerer. A communication framework for heterogenous distributed pattern analysis. In *Proc. International Conference on Algorithms and Architectures for Parallel Processing*, pages 881–890, Brisbane, 1995.

D. Gibbon. Empirical and semiotic foundations for prosodic analysis. In U.M. Quasthoff, editor, *Aspects of Oral Communication*, pages 441–479. De Gruyter, Berlin, 1995.

A. Maßmann and S. Posch. Mask-oriented grouping operations in a contour-based approach. In *Proc. 2nd Asian Conference on Computer Vision*, volume III, pages 58–61, Singapore, 1995.

J.-T. Milde. A hybrid control architecture for a simulated robot manipulator. In *Proceedings of the 13th IASTED International Conference on Applied Informatics*, pages 370–373, 1995.

R. Moratz, H.J. Eikmeyer, B. Hildebrandt, F. Kummert, G. Rickheit, and G. Sagerer. Integrating speech and selective visual perception using a semantic network. In *1995 AAAI Fall Symposium on Computational Models for Integrating Language and Vision*, Cambridge, MA, (to appear).

U. Naeve, G. Socher, G.A. Fink, F. Kummert, and G. Sagerer. Generation of language models using the results of image analysis. In *Proc. 4th European Conference on Speech Communication and technology*, pages 1739–1742, Madrid, Spain, 1995.

H. Strohner, L. Sichelschmidt, and I. Duwe. Focus in resolving ambigous reference. In P. Bosch and R. van der Sandt, editors, *Focus and Natural Language Processing*, pages 629–638. IBM Scientific Centre/Institute for Logic and Linguistics, Heidelberg, 1994.

B. Velichkovsky, M. Pomplun, and H. Rieser. Attention and communication: Eye-movement-based research paradigms. In W.H. Zangemeister,. H.S. Stiehl, and C. Freksa, editors, *Visual Attention and Cognition*. Elsevier, Amsterdam, 1995. (in press).

I. Wachsmuth and B. Jung. Dynamic conceptualization in a mechanical-object assembly environment. *This volume 10(3-4).*

Artificial Intelligence Review **10:** 171–186, 1996.

Using Spatial Logic to Describe Visual Languages

J.M. GOODAY & A.G. COHN
*Division of Artificial Intelligence, School of Computer Studies, University of Leeds, Leeds LS2 9JT England**
Email: {*gooday,agc*}*@scs.leeds.ac.uk.*

Abstract. Visual computer languages exploit the natural language of diagrams and pictures to provide a simple and intelligible approach to programming. Unfortunately, it is difficult to provide them with a formal syntax and semantics. In this paper we show how the RCC spatial calculus can be used to provide an unambiguous, formal description of such languages by systematically describing the syntax of Pictorial Janus.

Key words: visual programming languages, spatial languages

1. Introduction

Computer programming would be much simpler if programming languages were somehow close to natural language. Unfortunately, specifying algorithms and data structures unambiguously requires a degree of formality not usually associated with natural language and thus reconciliation between the two is hard to imagine. However, there is another form of 'natural' language – the language of diagrams. Simple, stylised, pictures are readily understood (and reproduced) by people regardless of the spoken language they use. This simple, universal form of communication is the basis of visual programming languages. Rather than forcing users to write in a rigid, artificial textual language they allow programs to be constructed in terms of the more natural and flexible language of diagrams and drawings. These drawings are then animated to illustrate the way in which the program is executed.

Although visual programming languages may be easier for human users to cope with than traditional computer languages, specifying their syntax and semantics for implementation/program verification purposes is hard. This is because first order logic, the traditional formalization tool, does not include a spatial vocabulary that could be used to describe diagrammatic representations.

In this paper we show how a spatial calculus – RCC[1] (Randell et al. 1992, Cohn et al. 1994) – can be used to formally described visual languages.

In particular, we use RCC to construct a semantics for the Pictorial Janus language.

2. An Overview of Pictorial Janus

Pictorial Janus (Kahn & Saraswat 1990) is a visual form of the concurrent constraint-based language Janus (Saraswat et al. 1990). Concurrent languages are particularly suited to representation in pictorial form as diagrammatic information makes the relationships between the various processes easy to see. Janus itself is a simple, general purpose language in which a network of asynchronous program agents may be linked by channels along which data and information about channel access rights can be passed. Agents may contain one or more rules which can be used to process incoming messages. Computation in Janus involves selecting appropriate rules to apply to the inputs of an agent and replacing the agent with the chosen rule. To determine which of an agent's rules to apply, Janus uses a matching process analogous to that found in many Herbrand languages (Prolog, GHC, Strand, etc.). A successful rule match results in the inputs and outputs of the agent becoming the inputs and outputs of the rule, which then replaces the agent itself – this process is called reduction. Rules may contain calls to other agents or even recursive calls to their parent agent.

The syntax of Janus can be entirely represented in pictorial form, which makes it an ideal basis for a visual programming language. Figure 2 shows the Pictorial Janus syntax for constants and functions. A constant consists of a closed contour (the shape is irrelevant) containing a number or string (i.e. what the constant represents) and a single internal port. The internal port[2] is represented by another closed contour abutting the constant but wholly inside it and acts as a handle for the entire object. Ports cannot themselves contain any elements. Functions are represented by closed contours containing a label and an internal port together with any number of external ports. In this case we have illustrated a list constructor-function, cons, which normally takes two arguments and thus requires two external ports. The final part of the figure shows how the cons function can be used to build up a list.

A Pictorial Janus agent is a closed contour containing rules, a call arrow to another agent contour, or a label. It may have any number of external ports but no internal ports. A rule is defined in exactly the same way as an agent but with the additional requirement that it must be contained within an agent. Agents may communicate via channels: directed curves linking two ports (an arrow is used to indicate directionality). Finally, links are undirected curves joining two ports.

The semantics of the language, as described in (Kahn & Saraswat 1990), are somewhat ambiguous. However, the computational model is relatively straightforward. The first picture of Figure 3 shows a simple append program in Janus, together with data in the form of two linked lists.

In Janus the execution of a program is achieved by allowing agents to 'reduce' asynchronously. Reduction consists of three steps: (1) Matching – the agent's rules are checked against its current inputs in order to determine which, if any, are applicable. Matched rules are then expanded to exactly overlap the agent; (2) Commit – matched elements 'dissolve' leaving behind a new configuration; (3) Link shrinkage – any remaining links are shrunk to zero length and remaining elements are scaled.

Figure 3 demonstrates the reduction steps that result from applying the append program to two single element list (a). In the first reduction cycle the recursive (lower) rule is matched and expands to take the place of the append agent (b). The commit stage sees the matched rule/agent contours and other matched elements dissolve leaving a new append agent together with a number of links. Finally, (c) the remaining links are shrunk to zero length, effectively transferring the first element of the lower list to the output. At this point the new append agent is expanded. In the next reduction cycle the base-case (upper) rule of the new append agent is matched with the remaining input (e). Once again, the matched elements are dissolved (f) and the links contracted (g). Reduction is halted as the (irreducible) answer list is all that remains.

3. An Overview of the RCC Qualitative Spatial Logic

The RCC spatial logic, originally developed to facilitate spatial reasoning within Artificial Intelligence (AI) domains, is loosely based upon Clarke's (Clarke 1981, 1985) 'calculus of individuals based on connection', and is expressed in the many sorted logic LLAMA (Cohn 1987). The most distinctive feature of Clarke's 'calculus of individuals', and of our work, is that extended *regions* rather than points are taken as fundamental. Informally, these regions may be thought of as infinite in number, and 'connection' may be any relation from external contact (touching without overlapping) to spatial or temporal identity. Spatial regions may have one, two, three, or even more than three dimensions, but in any particular model of the formal theory, all regions are of the same dimensionality. Thus, if we are concerned with a two-dimensional model the points at which these regions meet are not themselves considered regions. We introduce a sort symbol REGION to denote the set of all regions.

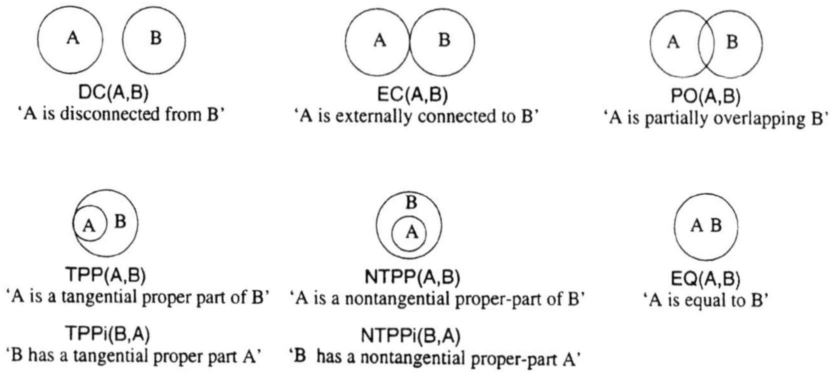

Figure 1. RCC base relations.

The basic part of the formal theory assumes a primitive dyadic relation: C(x, y), read as 'x connects with y' (where x and y are regions). Two axioms are used to specify that C is reflexive and symmetric. C can be given a topological interpretation in terms of points incident in regions. In this interpretation, C(x, y) holds when the topological *closures* of regions x and y share at least one point. In this paper (though not in our work as a whole) we make the assumption that all regions are topologically closed (i.e. include their boundaries).

Using the relation C, further dyadic relations are defined. These relations are DC (is disconnected from), P (is a part of), PP (is a proper part of), EQ or $\doteq$ (is spatiotemporally identical with), O (overlaps), DR (is discrete from), PO (partially overlaps), EC (is externally connected with), TPP (is a tangential proper part of), and NTPP (is a nontangential proper part of). The relations P, PP, TPP and NTPP have inverses (here symbolised Pi, PPi, TPPi and NTPPi. Of the defined relations, the set DC, EC, PO, TPP, NTPP, EQ, TPPi and NTPPi form a jointly exhaustive and pairwise disjoint set of 'base relations' shown in Figure 1.

We draw the reader's attention to the distinction between C(x, y) (x connects with y) on the one hand and O(x, y) (x overlaps with y) on the other. In the latter case, but not necessarily in the former, there is a REGION which is a part of both x and y.

The complement of a REGION, and the sum, product (or intersection) and difference of a pair of REGIONs are also defined. Here, we will use infix arithmetic operators to denote these functions (e.g. + denotes the sum of two REGIONs and − their difference). The product of two REGIONs may not always be a REGION: if the two do not overlap, this product is an object of the sort Null (spatial and temporal REGIONs belong to distinct subsorts of the sort REGION). Similarly, if two REGIONs are EQ, then $(x - y)$ is of sort Null, as is the complement of the universal REGION, Us. An additional axiom is used to ensure that every REGION has at least one NTPP; this has the consequence that space is indefinitely divisible. There are therefore no 'atoms' – REGIONs which cannot be subdivided – in the current version of the theory, although there are several possible ways in which they could be added to it, as discussed in Section 5 of (Randell et al. 1992).

Given the ability to construct the sum of two arbitrary REGIONs it is easy to see that REGIONs can be divided into two kinds depending on whether there are topologically connected (i.e. in one piece) or disconnected (in more than one piece). Such scattered REGIONs may be used to model, for example, a cup broken into several pieces. We therefore define a monadic predicate CON(x) to distinguish the former kind of REGION. We also define a predicate Maxpart(y, x) which is true when y is a maximal connected (i.e. CON) REGION of x.

4. Axiomatising the Syntax of Janus

We will now show how each of the program elements of a Janus program can be precisely captured in the spatial logic. The quotes in italics are all from (Kahn & Saraswat 1990).

The spatial logic is a logic for talking about REGIONs. Clearly, the REGIONs of interest in the present situation are those corresponding to the various individual picture elements that make up a Janus program. Thus we assume that a picture is made up of primitive features: *character strings, lines, directed lines* and *closed curves*. Each of these corresponds to a REGION, the area actually occupied by the lines composing each of feature in the first three cases (lines in a real diagram have non zero thickness of course), and the area enclosed by the curve in the final case.

One important point to note when reading the axioms and definitions below is that we are assuming a sorted logic where we have a sort, which we will call PPES (Primitive Picture Elements) which is disjoint from the sort REGION of pure spatial REGIONs which is already assumed in the previous descriptions of the logic (e.g. Randell et al. 1992). The intended inhabitants of the PPES sort are sets of the strings, lines, directed lines and closed curves in the picture under consideration. A PPES which denotes a singleton picture element, we will call a PPE which is a subsort of PPES. Given a picture at a particular time we can identify a particular spatial REGION with each PPES: thus we can imagine a transfer function which maps PPES to REGIONs. However, we will not yet make this transfer function explicit but will assume that terms denoting PPES are automatically coerced to terms of sort REGION when required, i.e. when they appear as arguments to the predicates of the spatial logic such as PP, TPP, EC, DC etc.[3] The REGION denoted by the coercion of a PPES is of course the same as the REGIONs denoted by the individual PPEs comprising the PPES. One reason why we want to distinguish PPES from REGIONs is that when animating a Janus program, the various PPES will transform, and, for example, possibly becoming coincident – however we will still want to distinguish the two PPES, although they may denote identical REGIONs – imagine two accetate sheets overlaid on an overhead projector: lines may coincide as the sheets move relative to each other, but the lines remain distinct.

We also need to introduce a sort JPES (Janus Program Elements) whose intended inhabitants are sets of agents, rules, and the other program structures of Janus. These are all PPES, i.e. JPES is a subsort of PPES. A JPES which denotes a single primitive Janus Program structure, we will call a JPE which is a subsort of JPES. In the axioms and definitions below all the variables are implicitly restricted to range over the sorts for which the formula is well sorted, as in the sorted logic LLAMA (Cohn 1987). As an aid to readability, a variable name is annotated with a * when it ranges over JPES or PPES. This approach requires that we specify the allowable sorts of all the function and predicate symbols. The topological predicates (P, TPP, $\doteq$, Maxpart etc) all require REGIONs for all their arguments. For the other predicates we will specify their sort constraints as we introduce them, with the following notation: **sort**: $\alpha(\tau_1, \ldots, \tau_n)$. For specifying the argument and result sorts of functions, we will use the notion: **sort**: $\alpha(\tau_1, \ldots, \tau_n) \Rightarrow \tau_{n+1}$.

Each of the different kind of PPEs (i.e. Line, Dline, String, Ccurve, String) is a subsort of PPE. In order to distinguish the beginning and the end of directed lines, we introduce two functions, start and end which denote REGIONs and effectively divide a directed line into two.

sort: start(DLINE) $\Rightarrow$ REGION
sort: end(DLINE) $\Rightarrow$ REGION
$\forall(x)$ [TPP(start(x), x) $\wedge$ TPP(end(x), x) $\wedge$ (start(x) + end(x) $\doteq x$)
$\wedge$ DR(start(x), end(x))].

This is also an appropriate point to state explicitly exactly what the sorts JPE and PPE encompass (we will occasionally use the (sort) predicate JPE(x) and PPE(x) explicitly in order to coerce a variable to the appropriate sort).

JPE(x) $\equiv_{def}$ Agent(x) $\vee$ Port(x) $\vee$ Rule(x) $\vee$ Constant(x) $\vee$
Function(x) $\vee$ Link(x) $\vee$ Channel(x) $\vee$ Callarrow(x)
PPE(x) $\equiv_{def}$ Ccurve(x) $\vee$ Dline(x) $\vee$ Line(x) $\vee$ String(x).

One important question which we do not address here fully is the question of parsing a picture into a finite set of PPEs. In general a picture will be ambiguous. For example, one rule of the append program (Figure 3) has a line crossing the circle, effectively dividing it into two. We could either parse the picture as just described, or as two externally connected part-circles with an externally connected line. There are many ways such ambiguities could be eliminated; the shape conventions for particular kinds of Janus primitives assumed by (Kahn & Saraswat 1990) will often disambiguate, as indeed will observing the order in which the picture elements are actually drawn as (Kahn & Saraswat 1990) also note. However we will not address this issue further here and simply assume the entire picture has been parsed as represented by a set of Line, Dline, Ccurve and String propositions. Of course the inability to make sense of a picture though the axioms below would be a reason to reject the particular parse and try another.

In the next subsections we define all the Janus Program elements (JPES): agents, rules, etc.

4.1. *Ports*

"*A port is a closed contour with nothing inside*".

> **sort**: Port(JPE)
> $\mathsf{Port}(port) \equiv_{def} \mathsf{Ccurve}(port) \wedge \neg\exists(y)\ [\mathsf{PPE}(y) \wedge \mathsf{PP}(y, port)]$.

Two kinds of ports are distinguished: internal and external ports. We define binary predicates for each of these two concepts since these notions are relative to another JPE.

> **sort**: Iport(JPE, JPE)
> **sort**: Eport(JPE, JPE)
> $\mathsf{Iport}(port, x) \equiv_{def} \mathsf{Port}(port) \wedge \mathsf{TPP}(port, x)$
> $\mathsf{Eport}(port, x) \equiv_{def} \mathsf{Port}(port) \wedge \mathsf{EC}(port, x)$.

It is necessary to ensure that the only PPEs that can overlap ports are other ports. In particular, one internal port may overlap one external port. This occurs when, for example, a constant is attached to an external port of a function: the internal port of the constant is overlaid onto the external port of the function (see Figure 2). The following axioms enforce this.

$$\begin{aligned}
&\forall(port, w)\ [\mathsf{Iport}(port, w) \rightarrow \\
&\quad \neg\exists(y)\ [\mathsf{PPE}(y) \wedge y \not\doteq port \wedge (\mathsf{PO}(y, port) \vee y \doteq port)] \vee \\
&\quad (\exists(y, z)\ [\mathsf{Eport}(y, z) \wedge \\
&\qquad\qquad \forall x\ [(\mathsf{PPE}(x) \wedge y \not\doteq port \wedge (\mathsf{PO}(y, port) \vee y \doteq port)) \rightarrow \\
&\qquad\qquad\quad x = y]])]
\end{aligned}$$

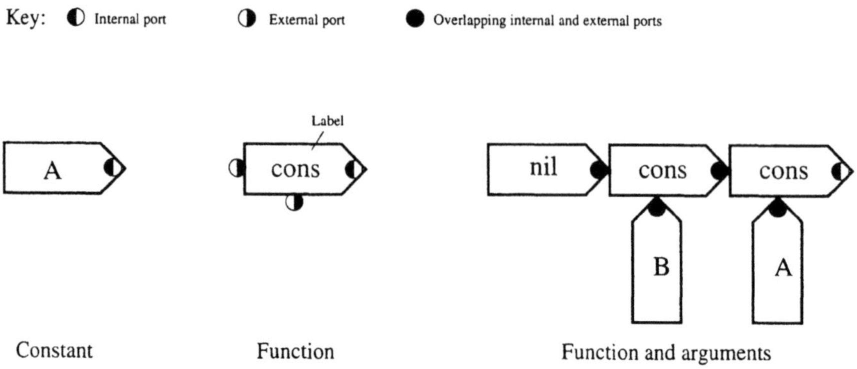

Figure 2. Constants and functions in Pictorial Janus.

$$\begin{aligned}&\forall(port, w)\ [\mathsf{Eport}(port, w) \rightarrow\\ &\quad \neg\exists(y)\ [\mathsf{PPE}(y) \wedge y \not\doteq port \wedge (\mathsf{PO}(y, port) \vee y \doteq port)] \vee\\ &\quad (\exists(y, z)\ [\mathsf{Iport}(y, z) \wedge\\ &\qquad\qquad \forall x\ [(\mathsf{PPE}(x) \wedge y \not\doteq port \wedge (\mathsf{PO}(y, port) \vee y \doteq port)) \rightarrow\\ &\qquad\qquad\quad x = y]])].\end{aligned}$$

Two further axioms are necessary to ensure that a port can only be an external port for one particular JPE or an internal port for one particular JPE. Note that this does not prevent a port from being both an internal port for one JPE and an external port for another. This is the case in Figure 2 – each of the overlapping ports can be parsed as either an internal port of one JPE or an external port of the other. In practice, we would simply take the results of one parse and ignore the other as the two are essentially isomorphic.

$$\forall(port, x)\ [\mathsf{Eport}(port, x) \rightarrow \neg\exists(y)\ [x \neq y \wedge \mathsf{Eport}(port, y)]]$$
$$\forall(port, x)\ [\mathsf{Iport}(port, x) \rightarrow \neg\exists(y)\ [x \neq y \wedge \mathsf{Iport}(port, y)]]$$

Some JPEs may have more than one external port; a set of external ports will denote a multipiece REGION all of whose maximal subparts are external ports.

sort: Eports(JPES, JPE)

$$\mathsf{Eports}(ports^*, x) \equiv_{def} \forall(subpart)\ [\mathsf{Maxpart}(subpart, ports^*) \leftrightarrow \mathsf{Eport}(subpart, x)]$$

4.2. *Constants*

"A constant has a closed contour, an internal port, no external ports, with a string or number inside".

For simplicity, we assume here that numbers are strings. It will be convenient to be able to easily identify the contour, the internal port and perhaps the label. Therefore we will define both a rank one and a higher rank predicate for such structures.

sort: Constant(JPE)
sort: Constant(JPE, JPE, PPE)
Constant(*const*) $\equiv_{def}$ $\exists$(*iport, label*) [Constant(*const, iport, label*)]
Constant(*contour, iport, label*) $\equiv_{def}$ Ccurve(*contour*) $\wedge$
Iport(*iport, contour*) $\wedge$ String(*label*) $\wedge$ P(*label, contour*) $\wedge$
$\neg\exists$(*eport*) [Eport(*eport, contour*)] $\wedge$
($\forall$(*port*) [Iport(*port, contour*) $\rightarrow$ *port* = *iport*] $\vee$
$\exists$(*port*$'$, *x*) [Eport(*port*$'$, *x*) $\wedge$ $\forall$(*port*) [Iport(*port, contour*) $\rightarrow$
(*port* = *iport* $\vee$ *port* = *port*$'$)]]).

Note that we make sure that the set of PPEs that form the constant includes the port and the string, not just the contour, in order to make sure that when we want to 'delete' a constant (as part of the procedural semantics) we will delete all of it not just the contour. Similar considerations will motivate the definitions of the other JPEs below.

4.3. *Functions*

"*A function has a closed contour, one internal port, some external ports and a label*". As with constants, we define both a rank one and a higher rank predicate.

sort: Function(JPE)
sort: Function(JPE, JPE, JPES, PPE)
Function(*func*) $\equiv_{def}$ $\exists$(*contour, iport, exports**, *label*)
[Function(*contour, iport, eports**, *label*) $\wedge$
func $\doteq$ *contour* + *eports**]
Function(*contour, iport, eports**, *label*) $\equiv_{def}$ Ccurve(*contour*) $\wedge$
Eports(*eports**, *contour*) $\wedge$ String(*label*) $\wedge$ P(*label, contour*) $\wedge$
Iport(*iport, contour*)] $\wedge$
($\forall$(*port*) [Iport(*port, contour*) $\rightarrow$ *port* = *iport*] $\vee$
$\exists$(*port*$'$, *x*) [Eport(*port*$'$, *x*) $\wedge$
$\forall$(*port*) [Iport(*port, contour*) $\rightarrow$
(*port* = *iport* $\vee$ *port* = *port*$'$)]]).

Collectively, we will call functions and constants, functors.

sort: Functor(JPE)
Functor(*x*) $\equiv_{def}$ Function(*x*) $\vee$ Constant(*x*).

4.4. *Links*

"A link is an undirected curve whose end points terminate at ports".

> **sort**: Link(JPE)
> **sort**: Link(JPE, JPE, JPE)
> $\mathsf{Link}(link) \equiv_{def} \exists(port1, port2)\ [\mathsf{Link}(link, port1, port2)]$
> $\mathsf{Link}(link, port1, port2) \equiv_{def} \mathsf{Line}(link) \wedge$
> $\quad \mathsf{EC}(link, port1) \wedge \mathsf{EC}(link, port2) \wedge \mathsf{Port}(port1) \wedge$
> $\quad \mathsf{Port}(port2) \wedge \mathsf{DC}(port1, port2).$

The condition $\mathsf{DC}(port1,\ port2)$ ensures that two different ports are involved. Notice that a link does not include its terminating ports.

4.5. *Channels*

"A channel is a directed curve whose end points terminate at ports".

> **sort**: Channel(JPE)
> **sort**: Channel(JPE, JPE, JPE)
> $\mathsf{Channel}(chan) \equiv_{def} \exists(port1, port2)$
> $\quad [\mathsf{Channel}(chan, port1, port2)]$
> $\mathsf{Channel}(chan, port1, port2) \equiv_{def} \mathsf{Dline}(chan) \wedge \mathsf{Port}(port1) \wedge$
> $\quad \mathsf{Port}(port2) \wedge \mathsf{EC}(\mathsf{start}(chan), port1) \wedge$
> $\quad \mathsf{EC}(\mathsf{end}(chan), port2) \wedge \mathsf{DC}(port1, port2).$

Again, notice that a channel does not include its terminating ports. We should also impose the condition that a link or channel ECs only two ports:

$$\forall(link, port1, port2, port3)\ [[[\mathsf{Link}(link, port1, port2) \vee \mathsf{Channel}(link, port1, port2)] \wedge \mathsf{Port}(port3) \wedge \mathsf{EC}(link, port3)] \rightarrow [port3 = port1 \vee port3 = port2]].$$

4.6. *Rules*

"A rule has a closed contour, no internal ports, and any number of external ports (distinguished from agents by being inside an agent)". We assume here that every rule has at least one external port.

Because we wish our definitions to be well founded (not mutually recursive), we will define the notion of a *template* and later add additional axioms which fully characterise the properties which rules have over and above a 'template' (see Section 4.10).

sort: Rule(JPE)
sort: Template(JPE, PPE, JPES)
sort: Rule(JPE, PPE, JPES, JPE)
Rule(*rule*) $\equiv_{def}$ $\exists$(*contour, eports*, agent*)
[Rule(*rule, contour, eports*, agent*)]
Rule(*rule, contour, eports**)$\equiv_{def}$Template(*rule, contour, eports**)$\wedge$
$\exists$(*rule′, contour′, eports′**)
[Template(*rule′, contour′, eports′** $\wedge$ PP(*rule, rule′*)]
Template(*rule, contour, eports**) $\equiv_{def}$ Ccurve(*contour*) $\wedge$
Eports(*eports*, contour*) $\wedge$ *rule* $\doteq$ *eports** + *contour*) $\wedge$
$\neg\exists$(*iport*)Iport(*iport, contour*).

In order to avoid confusion and possible ambiguity, rules should of course not overlap:

$\forall$(*rule*1, *rule*2) [(Rule(*rule*1) $\wedge$ Rule(*rule*2) $\wedge$ O(*rule*1, *rule*2)) $\rightarrow$
*rule*1 = *rule*2].

We also define a predicate to test if sums of disconnected REGIONs are rules.

sort: Rule(JPES)
Rules(*x**) $\equiv_{def}$ Rule(*x**) $\vee$
$\exists$(*y, z**) [*x** $\doteq$ *y* + *z** $\wedge$ Rule(*y*) $\wedge$ Rules(*z**)].

4.7. *Call arrows*

"*A call arrow is a directed curve from inside an agent contour to the contour of another agent*".

Actually it is clear that "another agent" may actually be the same agent, in order to allow for recursive agents. This can be seen readily by inspecting sample programs in the Janus papers, e.g. the program for append depicted in Figure 3.

sort: Callarrow(DLINE, JPE, JPE)
Callarrow(*arrow, agent*1, *agent*2) $\equiv_{def}$ Dline(*arrow*) $\wedge$
Template(*agent*1) $\wedge$ Template(*agent*2) $\wedge$
NTPP(start(*arrow*), *agent*1) $\wedge$ [TPP(end(*arrow*), *agent*2) $\vee$
EC(end(*arrow*), *agent*2)].

Again, for reasons to avoid possible mutual recursion, the definition of Callarrow does not actually refer to agents, but a separate axiom is included:

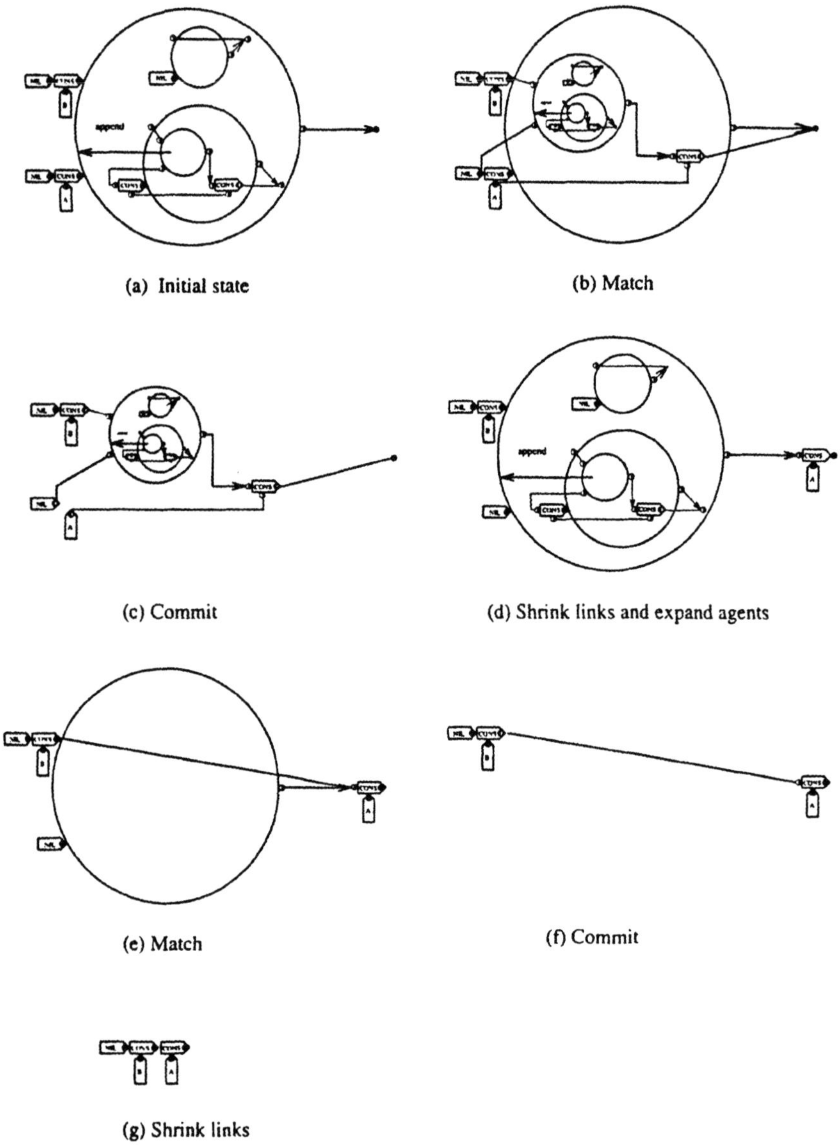

(a) Initial state

(b) Match

(c) Commit

(d) Shrink links and expand agents

(e) Match

(f) Commit

(g) Shrink links

Figure 3. Execution of append.

$$\forall(arrow, agent1, agent2)\ [\mathsf{Callarrow}(arrow, agent1, agent2) \rightarrow (\mathsf{Agent}(agent1) \wedge \mathsf{Agent}(agent2))].$$

Note that we have to allow a call arrow to TPP or EC the pointed to agent depending on whether it touches the agent from the inside or out. Normally one could expect that it would TPP in a recursive situation but EC otherwise, and we could indeed insist on this in the definition, but the original paper describing Janus does not.

4.8. *Agents*

"An agent has a closed contour with either rules, a call arrow or a label inside, no internal ports and any number of external ports".

sort: Agent(JPE)
sort: Agent(JPE, PPE, JPES, JPES)
Agent(*agent*) $\equiv_{def}$ $\exists$(*contour, ports*, rules**)
  [Agent(*agent, contour, ports*, rules**)]
Agent(*agent, contour, ports*, rules**) $\equiv_{def}$
  agent $\doteq$ *ports** + *contour* $\wedge$ Ccurve(*contour*) $\wedge$
  Eports(*ports*, agent*) $\wedge$ $\neg\exists$(*iport*) [Iport(*iport, contour*)] $\wedge$
  ((PP(*rules*, contour*) $\wedge$ (Rules(*rules**) $\vee$ String(*rules**))) $\vee$
   $\exists$(*arrow, agent*2) [Callarrow(*arrow, agent, agent*2)]).

4.9. *Messages*

Messages are the term structures which form arguments to rules and agents. Given an external port of a rule or agent we will want to know what the message there is. The definition of Message below 'finds' the constant or function attached to the external port in question, along with all other constants or functions externally connected to it. If there is no message we will adopt the convention that the port is the 'message' (to avoid problems of null messages). Messages might also be output messages taking the form of a channel, so we need to allow for this in the definition below.

sort: Message(JPE, JPES)
sort: Messages(JPES, JPES)
Message(*port, message*) $\equiv_{def}$ Port(*port*) $\wedge$
  [*message* = *port* $\wedge$ $\neg\exists$(*z*)[Iport(*port, z*)] $\wedge$
   $\neg\exists$(*c, port'*) Channel(*c, port, port'*)] $\vee$
  [$\exists$(*port'*)Channel(*message, port, port'*)] $\vee$
  [$\exists$(*x, ports*, messages**)
    [Function(*x*) $\wedge$ Eports(*ports*, x*) $\wedge$ Iport(*port, x*) $\wedge$
    Messages(*ports*, messages**) $\wedge$ *message* $\doteq$ *x* + *messages**] $\vee$
  [Constant(*message*) $\wedge$ Iport(*port, message*)].

The definition of Messages takes the form of four mutually exclusive disjuncts. The first handles the case of the empty message; the second the case when the message is a channel; the third is the complicated recursive case when the message is a function which will have sub messages attached to its own external ports; the final case handles messages which are Janus constants. The recursive case uses an auxiliary predicate Messages since a function may have more than one external port and therefore more than one attached sub message. This predicate either recognizes that there is only one sub message, or (in its second disjunct) recursively tests that a message is attached to each port. Note that the second argument of Message (and therefore Messages) will be of sort JPE (a subsort of JPES) rather than JPES when the message is a constant, channel or empty message).

$$\begin{aligned}&\mathrm{Messages}(ports^*, messages^*) \equiv_{def}\\ &\quad \mathrm{Message}(ports^*, messages^*) \vee\\ &\quad \exists(port, message, p^*, m^*)\ [\mathrm{Port}(port) \wedge ports^* \doteq port + p^* \wedge\\ &\qquad messages^* \doteq message + m^* \wedge \mathrm{Message}(port, message) \wedge\\ &\qquad \mathrm{Messages}(p^*, m^*)].\end{aligned}$$

4.10. *Ensuring a complete analysis*

We need to ensure that every PPE is taken account of. The following axiom ensures this.

$$\forall(x)\ [\mathrm{PPE}(x) \rightarrow \exists(y)\ [\mathrm{JPE}(y) \wedge \mathrm{P}(x, y)]].$$

There are other global consistency checks we should make. All ports should be attached directly or indirectly to an agent, functor, or rule.

$$\begin{aligned}&\forall(x)\ [\mathrm{Port}(x) \rightarrow \exists(a)\ [[\mathrm{Agent}(a) \vee \mathrm{Functor}(a) \vee \mathrm{Rule}(a)] \wedge\\ &\quad [\mathrm{P}(x, a) \vee \exists y\ [(\mathrm{Channel}(y) \vee \mathrm{Link}(y)) \wedge \mathrm{EC}(y, x) \wedge \mathrm{EC}(y, a)]].\end{aligned}$$

All rules should be part of an agent.

$$\forall(rule)\ [\mathrm{Rule}(rule) \rightarrow \exists(agent)\ [\mathrm{Agent}(agent) \wedge \mathrm{P}(rule, agent)]].$$

5. Further Work

Thus far we have only shown how RCC could be used to specify the visual syntax of Pictorial Janus; however, equally interesting and important, is the task of formalizing the procedural semantics of the language. Here we give only a flavour of our intended approach. Clearly some temporal primitives have to be introduced. The predicates already defined above now need to take an extra argument to specify when they hold true. We can avoid looking at every possible change in the spatial relationship between two REGIONs (program elements) because RCC includes axioms that effectively make predictions about what changes in relation might occur assuming that translation and deformation is continuous (e.g. DC cannot be followed directly by PO without an intervening EC).

We can view computation as proceeding through a cycle of different states that loosely correspond to the match, commit and link shrinkage steps of Janus described in Section 2. Each state will contain its own particular set of extra constraints on spatial relationship changes. For example, during the matching state the axiom that specifies that rules must be proper parts of agents is relaxed so that a rule can expand to become EQ to its surrounding agent. A Janus program runs through these program state cycles until no further changes in spatial relationship can be made – i.e. all the agents are fully reduced and the program has run to completion.

6. Final Comments

We have described how a spatial logic, originally developed for representing and reasoning about physical systems can be used to provide a formal description of the Pictorial Janus visual programming language. We believe that not only is this development quite natural, but also it is very important to have formal specifications of visual programming languages, just as any other programming language. The approach may also provide an approach to the prototyping of visual languages.

Of course, one route to provide such a formal specification is via a textual language as Kahn and Saraswat propose, so that Pictorial Janus is translated to (textual) Janus and then a semantics given to the language. Which is the more desirable will depend on many things. For example if the actual implementation of Pictorial Janus is in terms of textual Janus then this latter route might be rather appropriate. However, it is clear that the implementation need not take this approach and in such situations it seems perhaps unnecessarily cumbersome to take this route rather than the more direct approach we have presented. Moreover, turning away from Janus in particular, one could imagine some other visual language for which there was no textual variant and in such situations it would arguably be obviously best to take the direct approach. If the user of the visual language does not think in terms of an underlying textual language, then a semantics which does not involve a textual language is better.

Notes

* The support of the EPSRC under grants GR/G 36852, GR/H 78955 is gratefully acknowledged. This work has also been partially supported by a CEC ESPRIT basic research action, MEDLAR II, 6471. We gratefully acknowledge discussions with Ken Kahn and Vijay Saraswat when Tony Cohn visited Xerox Parc in 1991 and with Volker Haarslev in Hamburg in 1995.

[1] RCC stands for either 'Region Connection Calculus' or 'Randell, Cohn and Cui' depending on one's viewpoint.

[2] We will colour ports black in all figures for clarity.

[3] The only possible confusion would arise with the equality predicate, since we will want not only to equate REGIONs but also PPES, without coercing the latter. In order to handle this we will use two different equality symbols, the standard = for the latter case, and $\doteq$ for the former.

References

Allen, J. F. (1981). An Interval-Based Representation of Temporal Knowledge. Proceedings of *The 7th IJCAI*.

Clarke, B. L. (1981). A Calculus of Individuals Based on 'Connection'. *Notre Dame Journal of Formal Logic* **23**: 204–218.

Clarke, B. L. (1985). Individuals and Points. *Notre Dame Journal of Formal Logic* **26**(1): 61–75.

Cohn, A. G. (1987). A More Expressive Formulation of Many Sorted Logic. *Journal of Automated Reasoning* **3**: 113–200.

Cohn, A. G., Gooday, J. M. & Bennett, B. (1994). A Comparison of Structures in Spatial and Temporal Logics. In Casati, R., Smith, B. & White, G. (eds.) *Philosophy and the Cognitive Sciences*: Proceedings of *The 16th International Wittgenstein Symposium*, Hölder-Pichler-Tempsky: Vienna.

Cui, Z., Cohn, A. G. & Randell, D. A. (1992). Qualitative Simulation Based on a Logical Formalism of Space and Time. Proceedings of The *AAAI-92*, 679–684. AAAI Press, Menlo Park: California.

Kahn, K. M. & Saraswat, V. A. (1990). Complete Visualizations of Concurrent Programs and Their Executions. *Technical Report Tech. Rpt. SSL-90-38 [P90-00099]*, Xerox Palo Alto Research Center, Palo Alto, California.

Randell, D. A., Cohn, A. G. & Cui, Z. (1992). Naive Topology: Modelling the Force Pump. In Struss, P. & Faltings, B. (eds.) *Advances in Qualitative Physics*, 177–192. MIT Press.

Randell, D. A., Cui, Z. & Cohn, A. G. (1992). A Spatial Logic Based on Regions and Connection. Proceedings of *The 3rd Int. Conf. on Knowledge Representation and Reasoning*, 165–176. Morgan Kaufmann: San Mateo.

Saraswat, V. A., Kahn, K. M. & Levy, J. (1990). Janus – A Step Towards Distributed Constraint Programming. Proceedings of *The North American Logic Programming Conference*, MIT Press.

Artificial Intelligence Review **10:** 187–208, 1996.

A Visual News Processing Environment

GRAZIELLA TONFONI*
University of Bologna, Istituto di Glottologia, Via Zamboni, 16 – 40126 Bologna, Italy
E-mail: Tonfoni@cs.unibo.it

Abstract. CPP-TRS (Tonfoni 1989–94) is both a methodology and a language. Through the methodology (CPP – Communicative Positioning Program) those invisible aspects of communication are identified and represented by the meta-language (TRS – Text Representation Systems), which complements natural language. CPP–TRS is a new paradigm which applies to any communicative context.

Icons in CPP-TRS are not intended to represent words or sentences in order to substitute them; they are rather intended to represent visually what natural language does not convey naturally. The improvement of communication is a challenge of the present and the future: CPP-TRS is designed explicitly for it.

The CPP-TRS system thus is able to support the user with a set of visual tools, that are specifically suited to structuring text and communicating effectively.

The same tools can support communication very effectively in situations where ambiguity can highly compromise the final result.

The system may be used in a way that is either opaque or transparent to the reader of the text.

Key words: visualized communication, text-design, tools for writing, tools for reading, visualized texture of information

1. Introduction

CPP-TRS (Communicative Positioning Program-Text Representation Systems) (Tonfoni 1989–94) is a visual language which is based on a system of 12 canvases, 10 signals and 14 symbols and a further set of visual dynamic schemes. CPP-TRS is based on the fact that every communicative action is the result of a set of cognitive processes, and the whole system is based on the concept that the writer can enhance communication by visually planning and organizing therefore increasing the visual perception of a text. Based on a very simple syntax, CPP-TRS is capable of representing meaning and intention as well as communicative function visually. CPP-TRS is an unambiguous, fast and effective system for reinforcing natural language. It complements natural language by adding certain important elements that are not represented by natural language itself. These elements include communicative intention and communicative function of the text expressed by the writer, as well as the role the reader is supposed to play. The communicative intention and function of a text in current news writing as well as the reader's role are invisible because neither specific words nor punctuation convey them sufficiently and unambiguously; they are therefore opaque. As a meta-language, CPP-TRS can be applied to different news typologies both in a transparent and an opaque way.

2. Visualization

Relevant research has been conducted in visualization. Mc Kevitt (1994) and Srihari (1995) show the main trends and applications in the field of integration of linguistic and visual information. Beardon (1993) carefully analyzes the differences between the study of natural language and the design of an iconic language. Yazdani (1991) describes an intelligent language tutoring environment. The specific nature of CPP-TRS is now being described. The CPP-TRS system consists of two consistently integrated parts. CPP is the methodological component of the system: the CPP methodology enables the reader to understand the writer's position towards certain news. It is a complete program that provides visual schemes, models and tools aimed toward organizing information effectively. TRS is the visual language component. It is strictly integrated with the CPP methodology, and is the corresponding way of representing those cognitive processes and communicative actions, which have been previously identified by CPP.

As to be able to plan an Integrated Environment for supporting News Processing (Packaging – Filing – Storing – Retrieving and Delivery) based on CPP-TRS, it is absolutely important to think about different tools having different purposes and different users. Users are newswriters, commentators and readers.

The keyrole is played by the User, whom I would like to define as the Chooser of those different tools which are available, according to his/her own needs and preferences.

3. A Cognitive Punctuation System

A CPP-TRS based keyboard is one of the various applications of CPP-TRS and it is specifically intended to support the writer and the commentator in processing news with the whole visual system, which is being introduced as an addition to the current system of punctuation and smoothly integrated with it.

CPP-TRS constitutes a visual representation system that is as consistent as the system of punctuation. The punctuation system in written language represents and complements aspects of oral language, such as pauses and intonation, that enable the proper interpretation of written texts.

The CPP-TRS visual language is not any different than the punctuation system since it represents visually those elements, like communicative intention, communicative function and the reader's role, that are invisible but so important as to be able to process, understand, file and retrieve news. CPP-TRS is both a conventional and natural meta-language that makes explicit from the beginning what otherwise is left to arbitrary interpretation. Making language more explicit by adding visual conventions does enhance the final understanding of news without compromising it or leaving it to arbitrariness and randomness.

4. Textual Canvases

CPP-TRS directs both the news writer and the commentator toward starting from a global perspective, reflecting on the intention and function of each incoming news item. The first software tools for writing which are being provided is a set of "canvases" which are visual stimuli and global representations of communicative actions. Canvases are visual schemes that describe various communicative processes in action and they are specifically intended to support the reader identify different news typologies.

Just as an artist chooses a canvas with an appropriate texture, a writer needs to decide how much *texture* the text will have. The texture of text has to do with the density of information conveyed by it and it depends on the particular communicative purpose of the text. Before actually structuring the text, a writer prepares to write by thinking about text as an open possibility. Text can be written from a multitude of perspectives and points of view, with many different focuses, intentions, and organizational considerations. Each way of writing text enables a different viewing of it and it is a continuous invitation for the writer to *redraw* it.

The canvases picture how a writer can capture and organize thoughts into texts that have specific communicative purposes. Canvases help a writer reflect on and visualize what he is doing as he prepares for and begins writing.

Canvases are the first tool that visually represent simple concepts related to words and sentences. They are available in software. Let us now analyze some of them in a more detailed way.

4.1. *Canvas for Word Explosion and Word Chaining*

Word Explosion (Figure 1) – This canvas is for brainstorming, and a writer can use it at the beginning of the writing process. It enables a writer to free

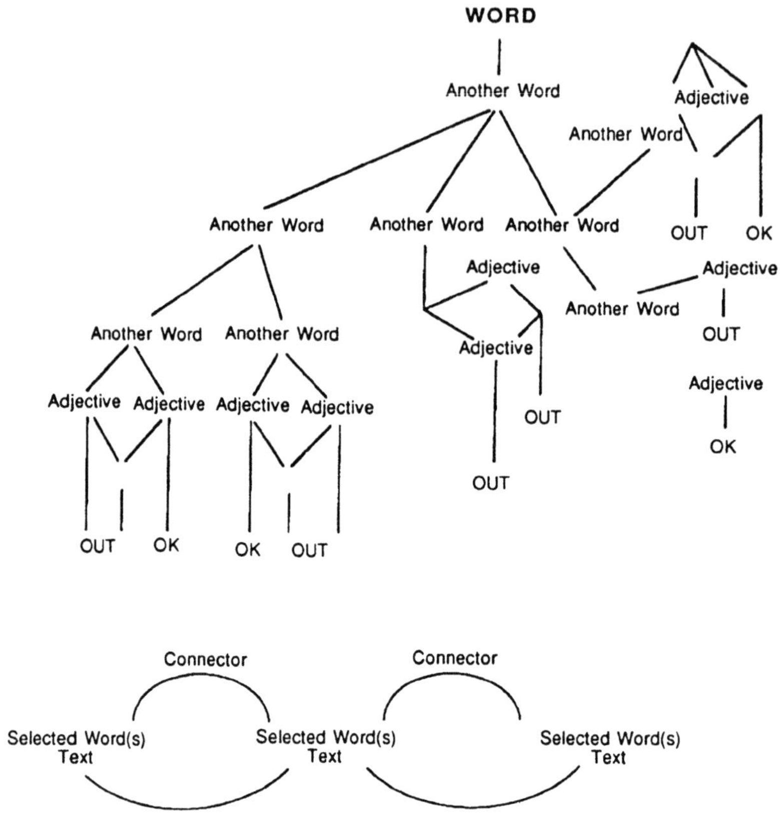

Figure 1. Canvas for Word explosion and Word Chaining.

his/her mind from preconceived ideas about what he/she is going to write about. It facilitates the cognitive process of free association. *Word Chaining* – This canvas depicts how a writer can put together a group of words from a word explosion so that they form a logical, linear chain. The word chain that results from this process can be a group of sentences, paragraphs, or even larger parts of a text.

4.2. *Canvas for metaphor creation*

This canvas (Figure 2) illustrates that a metaphor begins with two word explosions: one for the source word and one for the target word. The source word is a word that the writer starts with, and the target word is one that he chooses in transferring a new meaning to the source word. The writer explodes both the source and target words, selects a word from each, and then

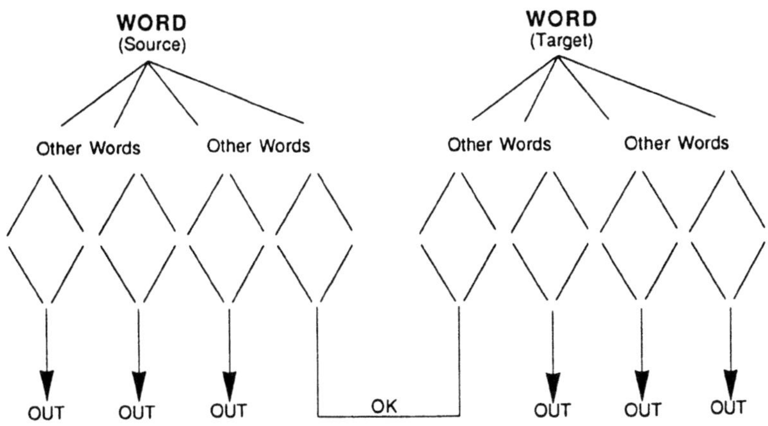

Figure 2. Canvas for metaphor creation.

draws a *bridge* between them. Once the writer links the words by establishing the bridge, he creates a metaphor.

4.3. *Canvas for pattern recognition and analogies in stories*

This canvas (Figure 3) shows how a writer can create a scheme that represents the logical structure of a story by focusing on certain words and parts that link it together. Once the story is visually represented, it becomes easy for the writer to replicate its structural patterns to create other analogous stories.

4.4. *Canvas for global narrative text planning*

This canvas (Figure 4) represents a visual scheme for globally planning narrative text. A canvas such as this enables a writer to sketch out a long story that may encompass a number of events, protagonists, and possible outcomes. It opens up the possibilities of many different ways to develop the story, and it aids in checking its coherence.

4.5. *Canvas for local narrative text planning*

This five-part canvas (Figure 5) helps a writer plan and analyze the details of a narrative text. It visually represents how a writer can examine the backward and forward links from a narrative concept, evolve a story in different ways from a particular point, use temporal and causal connectors to link narrative concepts, and reconstruct the story differently by changing its sequence.

Figure 3. Canvas for pattern recognition and analogies in stories.

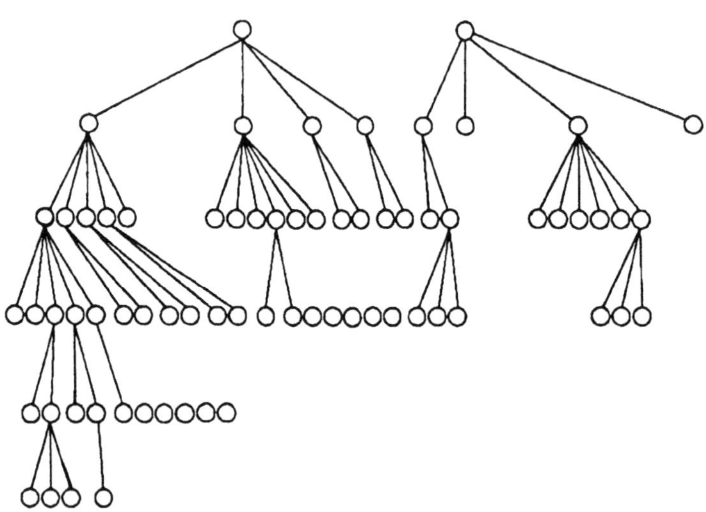

Figure 4. Canvas for global narrative text planning.

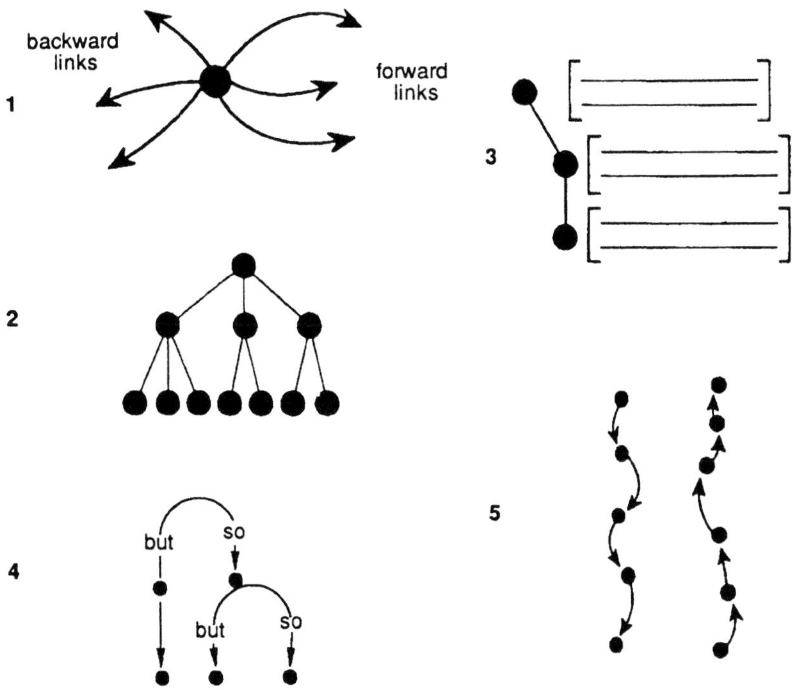

Figure 5. Canvas for local narrative text planning.

4.6. *Canvas for analogous story planning*

This canvas (Figure 6) is a visual aid for planning or finding other stories that are analogous to a particular story. It depicts the ways that two stories can be analogous. They can be partially analogous, which means they are either initially, intermediately, or finally analogous. Two stories can also be totally or globally analogous.

4.7. *Canvas for explanatory text drawing*

This canvas (Figure 7) presents visual schemes for planning and organizing a text that teaches the reader about a topic exhibiting a logical progression or some causal or temporal development. The first visual scheme in this canvas resembles a traditional outline and shows the logical progression of the text, starting with a title and flowing down through the division and development of a set of paragraphs. The second scheme provides an alternative to a strictly logical progression of paragraphs, and it instead focuses on identifying and maintaining the topic and developing text that more readily keeps the reader's attention.

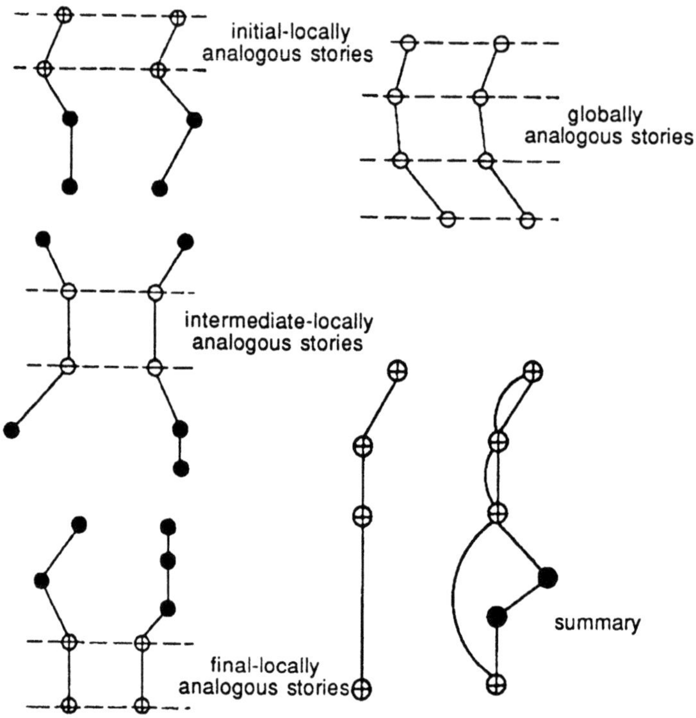

Figure 6. Canvas for analogous story planning.

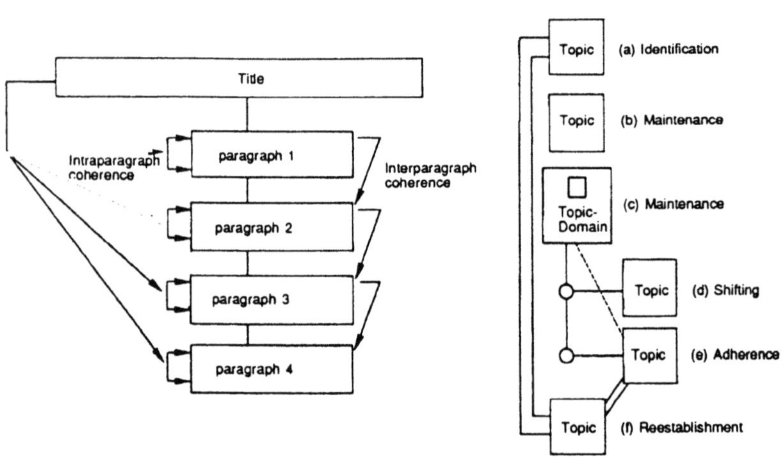

Figure 7. Canvas for explanatory text drawing.

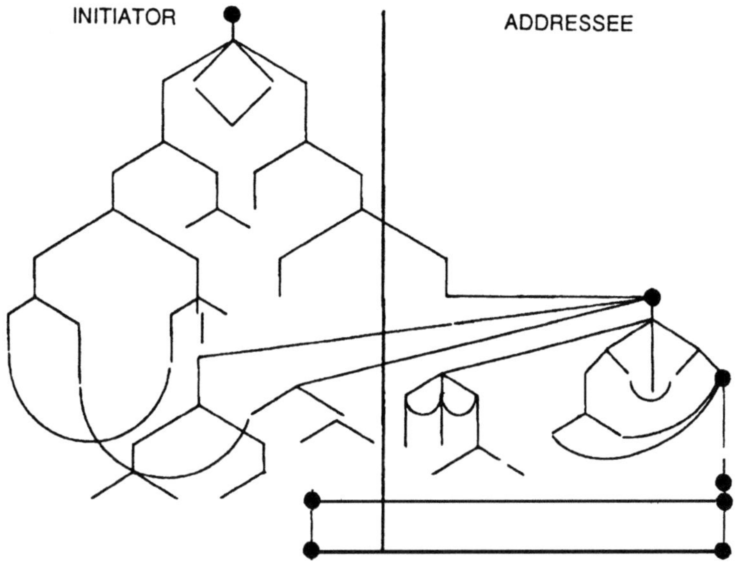

Figure 8. Canvas for dialog-conversation.

4.8. *Canvas for dialog-conversation*

This canvas (Figure 8) is for planning a conversation, recording its rhythm, and tracking its evolution. It is divided by a vertical line into two spaces: the left space records the contributions of the initiator of the conversation, while the right space records those of the addressee. The lines flowing down through the initiator's and addressee's spaces trace the dynamics of the dialog as it progresses. The process of planning and drawing a conversation on the canvas has the effect of slowing it down so that it stays focused and is directed toward some goal. It also enables a detailed, written reconstruction of the conversation.

4.9. *Canvas for collective text perception*

This is a two parts canvas (Figure 9). The first part helps a writer visualize a particular type of collective writing called *collage writing*. Collage writing may be done by a group of people that collectively endeavor to create a story, explanatory text, or any other text by piecing together their individually written contributions. The second part of the canvas represents *mosaic reading*. Mosaic reading shows how different readers can read the same text in different ways. In mosaic reading, a small group of people summarize the same text and then compare how their summaries differ.

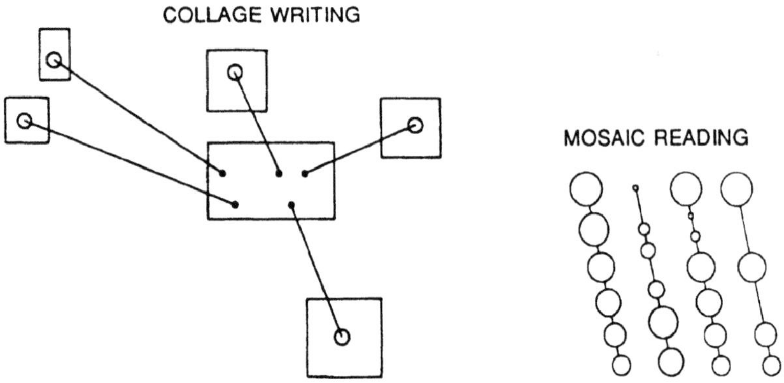

Figure 9. Canvas for collective text perception.

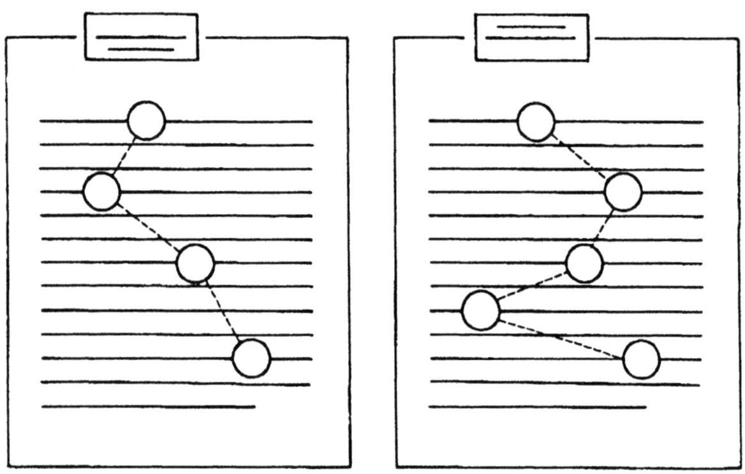

Figure 10. Canvas for text rotation.

4.10. *Canvas for text rotation*

This canvas (Figure 10) concerns writing texts that carry the *same* message to readers that have differing information needs and backgrounds. For instance, a writer may «rotate» a letter, resume, or sales brochure to accommodate the particular perspectives and expectations of different readers. When a writer rotates text, he concentrates on presenting information in ways that take account of the reader's viewpoint and that facilitate the reception of his message.

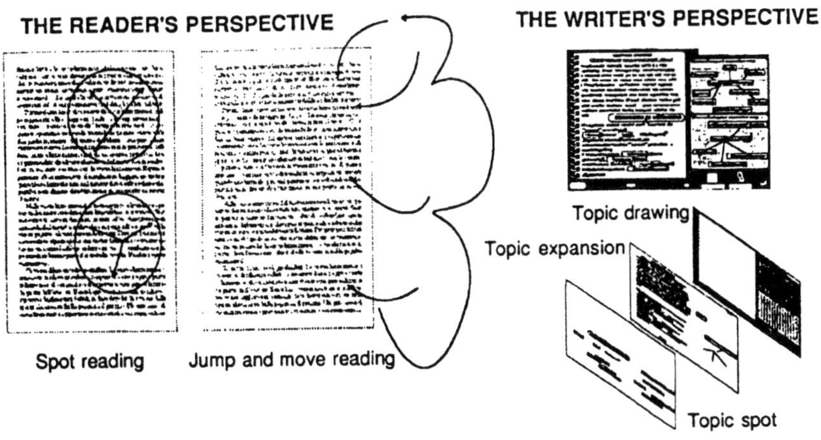

Figure 11. Canvas for hypertext.

4.11. *Canvas for hypertext*

Hypertext (Figure 11) is particularly suited for «hands-on» explanatory texts such as instruction manuals or procedural guides. It is a nonlinear text that is intended to be read and accessed at different levels according to the reader's needs. When a writer creates a hypertext, he is providing a structure that enables readers to find the level of detail or explanation that they need, to understand the information conveyed. The canvas for hypertext illustrates how a writer can structure text to facilitate readers with differing information needs.

4.12. *Canvases for fresco talking*

A fresco is an appropriate visual metaphor for group conversations. Because of the large size of frescoes and the time constraints imposed by the materials, fresco painting was a highly cooperative activity. The oral dimension of collective communication exhibits this same characteristic. What has to be done verbally is constrained by a limited period of time so that all the group members must interact effectively and cooperate to achieve the common goal (Figure 12).

4.13. *Canvas for tapestry writing*

Tapestry is a rich metaphor because it visually carries certain characteristics akin to collective writing. The weaving in tapestries, for example, has a range of densities – from fine to course. The density of a tapestry corresponds to the quantity of a collectively written text (Figure 13).

Figure 12. Canvas for fresco talking.

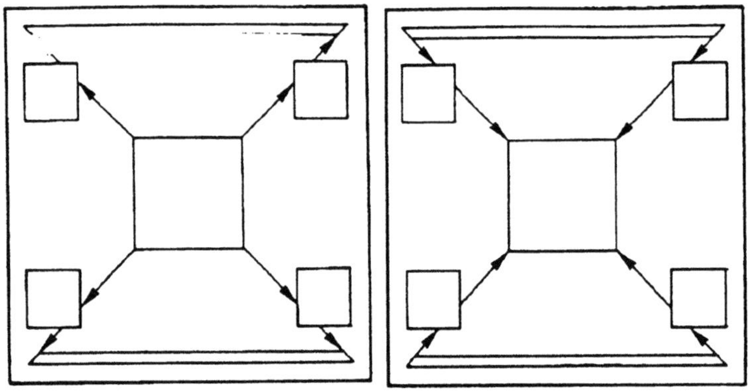

Figure 13. Canvas for tapestry writing.

4.14. *Canvas for collective writing*

Like tapestry making, is moreover a complex activity that must be planned. There are four tapestry canvases that visually model and facilitate group interactions for collective writing. Each visual model shows a different approach or attitude toward collective writing (Figure 14).

Figure 14. Canvas for collective writing.

Once the news reader has got a global view of what and how he/she is focusing on, he/she can then proceed to a more detailed structuring of each news item. For this CPP-TRS provides visual signs and symbols, which are part of the keyboard.

5. Textual signs

The textual signs give a writer additional possibilities for explicitly expressing his/her communicative intention to readers. They tell readers on a global level what the text is about even before they begin reading the language of the text. These signs are therefore more immediate and less abstract than the visual symbols.

The set of geometric signs for shaping text are as follows:

For a story and information
Square

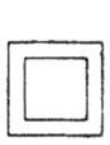
For a text analogous to another text and a case analogous to another case
Frame

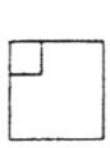
For a summary and reduced information
Square within a square

For ideas or concepts that emerge from reading a text and information kernels extraction
Grouped Semicircles

For a memory text and a subject-related information
Triangle

For a global idea or general concept that emerges from reading a text and general information focussing
Circle

For an idea or a particular concept and/or information extraction
Semicircle

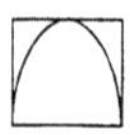
For adding an alternative development to a story or additional information
Inscribed Arcs

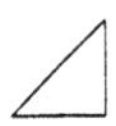
For a comment and explicitly subjective positioning toward information
Right Triangle

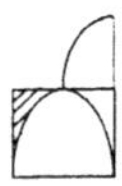
For opening up an information space for a new alternative or specific information expansion or revision
Opened Text Space

6. Textual Symbols

Symbols in CPP-TRS (Tonfoni 1989–94) enhance the communication and cooperation between the writer and readers of text. These symbols raise the semantics of text by making its meaning explicit. By using these symbols a writer makes more apparent to himself and to his readers what he is trying to accomplish in the text he writes.

There are two kinds of visual symbols. The first kind characterizes the style or type of text, while the second kind facilitates an interaction between the writer and readers of text.

Describe: From Latin «describo» meaning write around. It means giving as much information as you want starting from a point, the middle point of the spiral and proceeding by expanding the spiral; there is no need to follow any logical-chronological order; the spiral may be small or large. It depends on how much information is being presented.

Define: From Latin «definio», put limits. It means giving just some information, the relevant one, about a certain point, the middle point of the square by drawing the meaning territory; there is no need to follow any logical-chronological order, but there is a need to select and choose just some relevant information to be kept within the square.

Define is describe under certain constraints; like in any dictionary, where definition of a word or a concept implies choosing what is relevant to be written in order to understand the specific meaning.

Narrate: It means presenting facts and events by following a logical and chronological order; there are points following each other on a line. The longer the story is, the more of them you may add. Arrows mean the logical reading direction of facts and events. If the story becomes longer and more articulated, some more points are being added on the right side and the line becomes longer and longer.

Point out: It means getting a point, which is a specific event or fact, out of a narrative which is a story, focusing on that, adding more information, therefore expanding it.

The visual symbol represents the specific point which is being chosen and expanded within a chain of facts and events. Within a story it may represent the need for further information and details just about a part of it.

Explain: from Latin «explano» – unwrap, open up. It means representing facts in a cause and effect order; I may start from the original cause and get down progressively to a set of effects or proceed from effects going back to the original cause. This is why the symbol, which is a graphic representation of a procedural description, works in two ways and opposite directions: from up down and from down up respectively.

Regress: from Latin «regredior», go back. Regression here means giving more information about a certain item within a chain of information.

The visual symbol represents the item focusing process and the in depth information expansion process, which is being activated just about that point.

Inform: from Latin «informo» – put into shape, shape up. It means packaging just some information.

The visual symbol is double-faced: you have to read it left to right or right to left.

First Phase (1): from large into tight – it means informing synthetically; departing from a large data-base proceeding toward a synthesis (central point). Second Phase (2): from tight into large – it means informing analytically; departing from a limited set of data (central point) proceeding toward a more analytical data search.

Because of their strong visual impact, symbols (1) and (2) respectively, are being used to represent the concepts of synthesis and analysis in general and may be added to the other symbols as well (define – describe – explain, etc.).

Reformulate: from Latin «reformo – reformulo» – change shape and shape again. It means changing attitude toward information packaging: from explaining into describing or defining or informing etc.

It practically means substituting a cognitive attitude with another, a visual symbol with another one.

The visual symbol means «change», «substitute».

Express: from Latin «exprimo» – push out, press out.

It means giving personal and emotional opinions about facts. This is the most subjective mode of information packaging, bound to personal experiences like «I like/I dislike» or «I feel/I don't feel good».

The visual symbol represents a visual territory which is open and subject to modification according to personal opinions: some kind of amoeba-like shape.

There is a second kind of symbol called the turn-taking symbol. A writer can place turn-taking symbols within text to facilitate a dialog with the readers of text. These symbols explicitly tell readers how the writer wants them to interpret the text and when it is their turn to actively take part in modifying it.

The turn-taking symbols are the following:

Major scale / This symbol signals readers that what follows should be read exactly as written.

Minor scale \ This symbol invites readers to modify the marked off portion of the text.

Open or unsaturated rhythm — This symbol indicates to readers that the writer considers the text to be incomplete. It invites readers to get into that portion of text and add more information if they can.

Tight or saturated rhythm — This symbol indicates to readers that the writer considers the text as complete.

Vee-like insertions — The insertion symbols are used in combination with the text-style symbols to explicitly identify the style of text. For example, when used in combination with the describe symbol, they indicate to readers that the portion of text between them is a description.

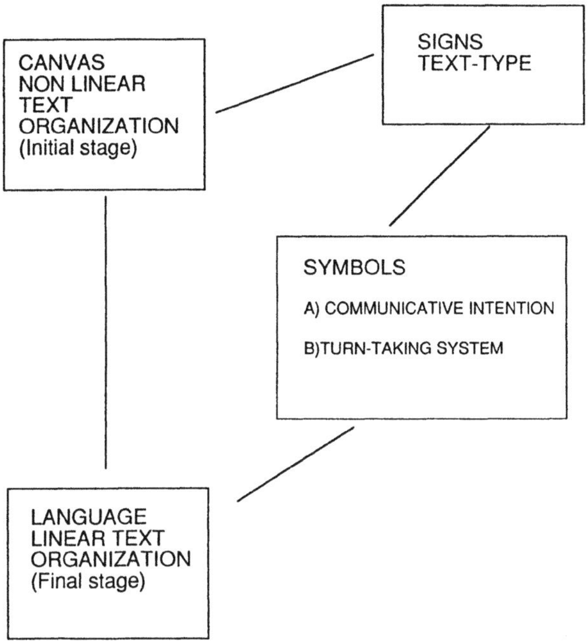

Figure 15. Visual text perception.

The CPP-TRS approach differs radically from any traditional approach which leads the news reader toward just organizing text linearly, by stringing together words and sentences first.

7. Visual Text Perception

In CPP-TRS (Tonfoni 1989–94) the news reader will be able to process and make transparent those aspects that are most difficult to grasp and therefore to transmit just using natural language by explicitating visually communicative intention, function and turn-taking.

In a CPP-TRS perspective the traditional process of reading a text has been reversed. Instead of starting with words, the news writer and commentator must first plan on the global intention, next redesign the structure of the news, and finally select the appropriate symbols. This approach avoids the pitfalls of the traditional approach by making communicative intention and function explicit.

The CPP-TRS system is explicitly aimed toward supporting the news writer with the wide set of visual tools which have been presented and are now shown in Figure 15, that are specifically suited to structuring text and communicating effectively.

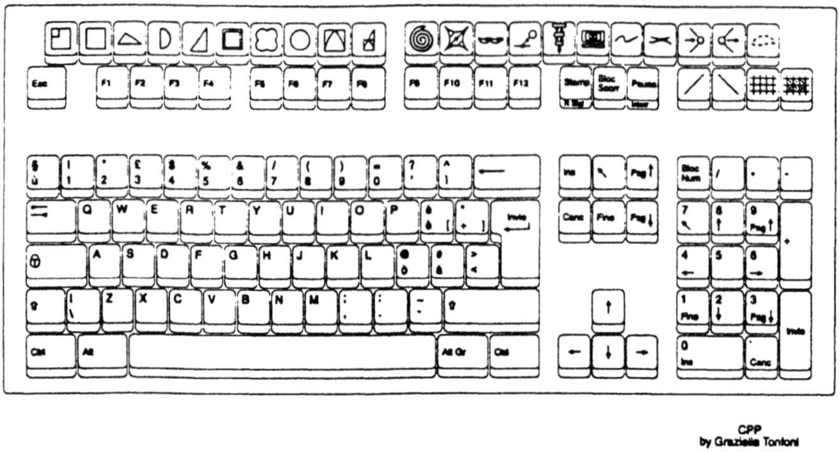

Figure 16. CPP-TRS news processing keyboard.

More specifically we can add that CANVASES are dynamic diagrams for Communicative Problems Definition.

SIGNS are global control icons for Communicative Type and Function of a text.

SYMBOLS are local control icons for Communicative Intention of sentences or paragraphs. The same tools can support oral communication very effectively especially in the course of the interviewing process, which is aimed toward acquiring knowledge to be then turned into news or integrating news with newcoming information.

The system may be used in a way that is either opaque or transparent to the reader of the news. The transparent use of the CPP-TRS system has the visual representation of signs and symbols in the text so that they can be seen and processed by the reader as a visual language complementing natural language. This will of course be very much related to the kind of training the writer and commentator have been previously exposed to.

Each verbal category within the news will be complemented by a visual symbol, which represents the specific information packaging mode which is being associated to the corresponding verbal category.

The CPP-TRS System will work like some kind of traffic-control signs system where the news reader can alternate and change some information packaging way by substituting it with another one. This is actually very useful to be able to store and file relevant information by alternating differing ways of packaging, according to the different styles and personalized information needs.

Let us now have a look at the CPP-TRS News Processing Keyboard (Figure 16) which has the signals and symbols in it.

In text-production by using CPP-TRS the text is to be packaged by the writer and commentator so as to increase understanding by sending out visually and unambiguously communicative intention as well as communicative function.

In text-reception by using CPP-TRS the text is to be reshaped as to be filed and retrieved by carrying out interpretation visually. By increasing the mastering of CPP-TRS anybody should be able to use it as naturally as the punctuation system with any language.

CPP-TRS will stay with the user (which I have previously defined as chooser) just after some learning and training because it is natural: it makes visible what happens all the time to anybody who is using language to communicate.

There is no need to explain all the time, which is the difference between  and , such difference has actually been acquired by listening to different ways of pausing and comparing them.

The same way works for CPP-TRS acquisition: the chooser will have to pay some specific attention to what other individuals do with language, and what he/she personally does too so as to be able to recognize the difference between  (describe) and  (define).

As an example we can identify two parts of the present article which we can also complement with the transparent use of both symbols.

Let us consider a few paragraphs, which have been previously presented and let us complement with a corresponding symbol as to represent communicative intention:

 CPP-TRS (Communicative Positioning Program – Text Representation Systems) by Graziella Tonfoni is an easy visual language which is based on a system of 12 canvases, 10 signals and 14 symbols. Based on a very simple syntax, CPP-TRS is capable of representing meaning and intention as well as communicative function visually.

 CPP-TRS is an unambiguous, fast and effective system for reinforcing and/or substituting natural language in human-machine interaction and in E-mail systems.

CPP-TRS is a communicative traffic control system aimed toward facilitating message production-delivery and interpretation.

Like any language, by knowing the syntax an indefinite number of sentences can be generated and, based on the syntax, processed and understood in a fast, unambiguous and easy way.

CPP-TRS allows the user to generate any kind of message proceeding from very simple instructions toward more complex explanations.

8. A Visual Consensual System

The punctuation system is a consensual system for representing visually pauses and intonation in written language. As we have already seen, CPP-TRS is a consensual system for representing invisible aspects of natural language visually. Let's now go through a simple example of how you can actually shape up a text in a transparent way by using CPP-TRS. The newswriter is preparing for giving some information about a recently published book and he wants to operate on different levels. He will first of all create some space for general information by pressing the corresponding keyboard element . He will also produce a summary and will therefore press the corresponding keyboard element . He will also introduce some personal comment and will therefore press the corresponding key-board element .

Here is a CPP-TRS based transparent text according to the previously identified choices.

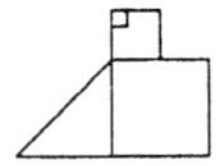

Like in music, with CPP-TRS a text can be controlled both on a global and on a local level as to facilitate the interpretation process. By receiving this visual information, the reader will be able to get the general structure of the text before going into a more detailed examination of single paragraphs and sentences.

9. Conclusions

As it has been illustrated, the CPP-TRS based News Processing Keyboard is aimed toward providing the writer and commentator with a whole set of tools for structuring news items and filing them effectively.

The transparent use of CPP-TRS leaves the visual message of signs and symbols in the text so that they can be read by the reader as a visual language. The transparent use presupposes that the reader has learned the system. A few hours of user training will allow any reader to speed up and control any communication process, which he/she may either initiate or respond to.

The text may also be turned back to its original and linear form: this will allow the reader to have different versions for the same text, some transparent and some not. It will be the reader's decision to decide what to choose or maybe how to alternate them all, according to his/her preferences. The text will still be available in different forms showing the process of information organization.

Interactivity may also be added to the system: writer, commentator and the reader as well may decide to add or modify the text, but they will do it transparently so as to be able to trace back and recognize what has been done and have it visible for anybody who will get it.

As we have seen, the iconic representation applies to an interpretation level of content structuring and could be highly compatible with other iconic languages working at a content level, by covering those specific aspects which are hard to convey as pointed out by Kay (1990).

To conclude: in text-production a significant increase of understanding will be achieved by sending visually and unambiguously communicative hints to trigger «intended guessing».

CPP-TRS may therefore be defined as a metalanguage; by acquiring and mastering it anybody will be able to use it naturally as the punctuation system in any communicative situation, without having to put constraints and restrictions on context of possible use as happens with sublanguages.

CPP-TRS will be naturally acquired after some learning and training, because it is just the visual representation of what happens all the time to anybody, who is either producing or interpreting a text, means using natural language for communicative purposes.

Acknowledgments

I would like to thank Paul Mc Kevitt and Masoud Yazdani for their comments on the present paper. I am indebted to Marvin Minsky for having been open, receptive and supportive to my new ideas and to my CPP-TRS methodology and language.

I would also like to thank James Richardson, Technical Writer, for having expertly helped me edit an English summarized version of my three previously published Italian books on CPP-TRS.

Note

* Author of CPP-TRS© and CPP-TRS© Applications Designer.

References

Beardon, C. (1993). Computer-Based Iconic Communication. In Ryan, K. & Sutcliffe, R. (eds.) *AI and Cognitive Science '92*, 263–76. Springer-Verlag, London, 1992.

Kay, A. (1990). User Interface: A Personal View, In Laurel, B. (ed.) *The Art of Human-Computer Interface*. Addison-Wesley: Reading, Mas.

Mc Kevitt, P. (1994). Visions for Language. Proceedings of *The Workshop on Integration of Natural Language and Vision Processing*. Twelfth American National Conference on Artificial Intelligence (AAAI–94), Seattle, Washington, USA.

Srihari, R. K. (1994–95). Computation Models for Interpreting Linguistic and Visual Information: A Survey. *Artificial Intelligence Review* **8**: 349–369.

Tonfoni, G. (1991a). *La Scrittura multimediale: Tecniche di progettazione e design testuale* (Multimedia Writing: Textual Design and Architecturing), Treviso, Pagus.

Tonfoni, G. (1991b). *La Communicazione aziendale come arte visiva* (Business Communication as Visual Art), Treviso, Pagus.

Tonfoni, G. (1992). *Partitura, solfeggio, movimento: Note di esecuzione di scrittura* (Partition, Solfeggio, Movement: Notes on the Execution of Writing), Treviso, Pagus.

Tonfoni, G. (1994a). *Abitare il testo* (Living Text), Treviso, Pagus.

Tonfoni, G. (1994b). *Writing as A Visual Art*, Intellect, Oxford.

Tonfoni, G. (1994c). *CPP-TRS: On Using Visual Cognitive Symbols to Enhance Communication Effectiveness*, ISMCR-94, Topical Workshop on Virtual Reality, Proceedings of *The Fourth International Symposium on Measurement and Control in Robotics*, NASA, Houston, USA, Nov. 30–Dec. 3, 1994, Library of Congress #94–69310, 1994.

Tonfoni, G. (1996). *Information States, Communicative Patterns, Textual Forms.*

Yazdani, M. (1991). LINGERing On: Steps towards an 'intelligent' language tutoring environment. In Thompson, J. & Zähner, C. (eds.) Proceeding of *The ICALL Workshop*. CTI Centre for Modern Languages, University of Hull. Workshop held at UMIST.

Artificial Intelligence Review **10:** 209–234, 1996.

Integrating Vision, Motion and Language through Mind

NAOYUKI OKADA
Department of Artificial Intelligence, Kyushu Institute of Technology, Iizuka, 820 Japan
Email: okada@pluto.ai.kyutech.ac.jp

Abstract. This paper presents an integrated comprehension and generation system for vision, motion and language. First, a computer model of mind proposed previously is reviewed as the basis of the integration. It consists of nine domains according to the contents of mental activities and five levels along the process of concept formation.

Then, vision and motion are discussed based on the model. Real world objects are divided into four categories: substance, event, attribute and others. The first three are named as noun, verb and adjective, respectively. The comprehension process of the named objects and the generation process of the named motion are shown along the five levels. Furthermore, vision and motion are connected and controlled by planning.

Next, language is considered to "describe any data or processing in mind" in our model. From this are derived three functions: surveying any mental object, organizing high-level thought, and communicating with others. The realization of these functions is discussed from the point of generation.

Next, an integrated system for vision, motion, and language is implemented on workstations. The system, or an intellectual and emotional agent, simulates the protagonist or fox of an Aesop fable. Its mental and physical behavior is shown by graphic displays, a voice generator, and a music generator which expresses its emotional states.

In conclusion, this system could be expected to provide a good framework for integrated comprehension and generation systems from the technological point of view.

Key words: vision, motion, language, multimedia, integrated comprehension and generation, modeling mind, language association with mind, symbol grounding in perception or motion, intellect and emotion

1. Introduction

Integrated comprehension of language and vision has become a major interest recently. Although the technique for processing either language or vision has made great advances in each field, a new technique for their integration or organization is needed to make the current machine power come closer to the human power to process language or vision.

This paper reports the project AESOPWORLD conducted at Kyushu Institute of Technology. It attacks the integration of not only language and vision but also motion through mind, simulating the protagonist of an Aesop fable. Although the protagonist is a fox, we expect that it behaves like a boy in the lower grades of elementary school: he lives in some natural environment, has a desire or a goal, makes plans to achieve it, takes action to execute the plans, recognizes his surroundings, gets emotional, and utters those processes in natural language.

Activities such as desire, planning, cognition, emotion, motion, or utterance are all products of mental dynamics. To build integrated systems for these activities, a computer model of mind is needed as their basis from the technological point of view. Minsky proposed *frames* as a universal data structure that is available to various kinds of mental data [4]. He then proposed the Society of Mind that is organized by small processors called *agents* [5]. Both theories will serve to investigate a coherent system of mental activities. The Society of Mind made an analysis of mental activities by agents in a bottom-up manner. However, it didn't clearly present a global view of the structure of mind, and many problems remained open from the technological point of view when building a practical computational system.

We also proposed another model of mind in order to develop an integrated system of language, vision, and motion from the technological point of view [11]. It clarified mind both from the domains of mental activities and from the levels of concept formation.

Based on this model, AESOPWORLD attacks the four kinds of integration:

(1) Language association with mind
Needless to say, language is associated with mental data or processing. Most semantic theories until now avoided discussing this problem. For example, *situation semantics* treats various types of situations, which play the basic role of accounting for linguistic phenomena [1]. However, the process of interpreting such situations onto mental objects is unclear. AESOPWORLD attacks the problem of how to associate language with abstract symbols in mind.

(2) Symbol grounding in perception or motion
In computer vision, input analog signals of images are generally understood by abstract symbols in mind. In robotics, on the other hand, abstract symbols are grounded in concrete signals for physical motion. Artificial Intelligence research has often dealt with only abstract symbols, and missed the importance of their grounding in perception or motion. AESOPWORLD deals with the problem by the hierarchy of mind.

(3) Integration of multimedia
Not only language, vision and motion generated/accepted by the protagonist but animation and music showing his mental or physical states are processed in AESOPWORLD. Multimedia or hypermedia systems have become one of major interests in the fields such as human interface or intelligent agents. Most of them take computer-assisted approaches, and don't touch the meaning of each medium very much. AESOPWORLD tries to fully understand the meaning of each medium.

(4) Integration of intellect and emotion
The research work about emotion hasn't been so active as that about intellect in Artificial Intelligence. However, intellect and emotion are like both wheels of a cart, and one can't play its role without the other. In AESOPWORLD, emotion plays an important role of evaluating data and resolving ambiguities in various phases in mental activities.

AESOPWORLD is still ongoing, and this paper presents its rough idea, highlighting the integration of (1) and (2).

2. Model of Mind

A computer model of mind proposed previously [11] is reviewed briefly in this section. The unit of data or processing in mind is called *module* in our model. It roughly corresponds to Minsky's agent. Although each module has a simple function, they are recursively interrelated with one another, performing complicated activities.

They are classified into nine domains according to the contents of mental activities and into five levels along the processes of concept formation.

2.1. *Domains*

The nine domains are: (1) *sensor*, (2) *recognition-understanding*, (3) *planning-creation*, (4) *action-expression*, (5) *actuator*, (6) *desire-instinct*, (7) *emotion-character*, (8) *memory-learning*, and (9) *language*. The overall schema of those domains is shown in Figure 1.

Some of the domains are concerned with human intellect. An external data or stimulus is accepted by the domain of sensor, and its content is analyzed in the domain of recognition-understanding. As a result, plans to respond to the input are made in the domain of planning-creation, and then actions or expressions to execute the plans are designed in the domain of action-expression. Finally, control signals of hands or feet are processed in the domain of actuator to put the plan into motion.

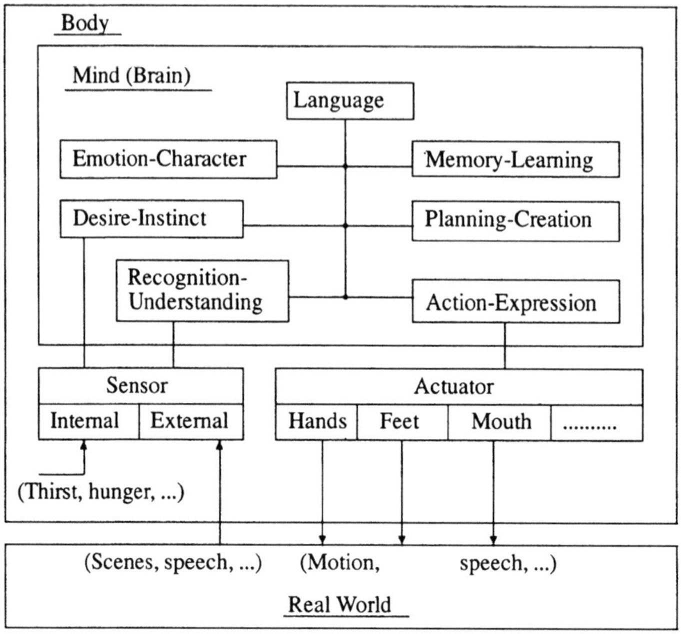

Figure 1. Domains of Mind.

On the other hand, some of the domains are concerned with human emotion or desire. The domain of sensor has another input channel, through which internal data such as "thirst" or "hunger" is accepted. Then, the domain of desire-instinct causes a desire or goal to arise. To achieve it, the domain of planning-creation makes plans which are executed in the domain of action-expression, and in turn in the domain of actuator. The domain of emotion-character evaluates given data and makes a subjective judgment, which often leads to some special action or expression.

The domain of memory-learning accepts processed data from all the domains and supplies necessary data to them. It contains a number of chunks of knowledge or emotion. Some of them may be first experience, while others may be learned. When a series of data or an episode is accepted in daily life, the learning process starts. A chunk of knowledge or emotion related with the episode cognition will be checked, modified, and reorganized.

What kind of role does the domain of language play in mind? Let us assume that its essential function is "to describe any data or processing in any domain." From this are derived three functions:

(1) To survey any data or processing in any domain,
(2) To organize high-level thoughts or inferences,
(3) To communicate with others.

The first is a prerequisite for language to describe everything in mind. The second comes from the following fact: An event is well described by a sentence, and a series of events are described by sentences, which are organized into paragraph, section, chapter, and larger units, successively. This mechanism might be an optimal method for "descriptions" which has been gradually created by human beings for years. The third is derived as a direct result of the description property and gives a basis for organizing the society in which human beings live.

Notice that the nine domains have no clear borderline. For example, desires and emotions are distributed continuously. Nevertheless, it is convenient to divide mind into those domains from the technological point of view.

2.2. *Levels*

Modeling by domains pays attention to the categories of various mental activities, and tries to make clear the relation among those categories. On the other hand, modeling by levels takes into consideration the symbol-grounding problem mentioned in the introduction. When input data such as natural scenes is given to the domain of sensor, it is first accepted as analog signals, and finally understood as abstract symbols. The hierarchy of mind tries to grasp the process as shown in Figure 2.

Level 1 Raw Data
This is the data that is not processed except for Analog-Digital conversion. It is represented by "codes" each of which is a meaningless, quantized unit. Digital images are typical examples.

Level 2 Cognitive Features
These are features extracted from raw data. The feature extraction in computer vision is done at this level. Many features are difficult to represent with "symbols" by which we mean a meaningful, symbolized unit. For example, we don't have any idea of how to describe complicated textures such as "lawn" or "mosaics" by symbols. *Connectionist* approaches may be a great help in computations at this level.

Level 3 Conceptual Features
These are symbolic data associated with cognitive features. Some of them can be compared to the *semantic markers* in semantic theories. Conceptual

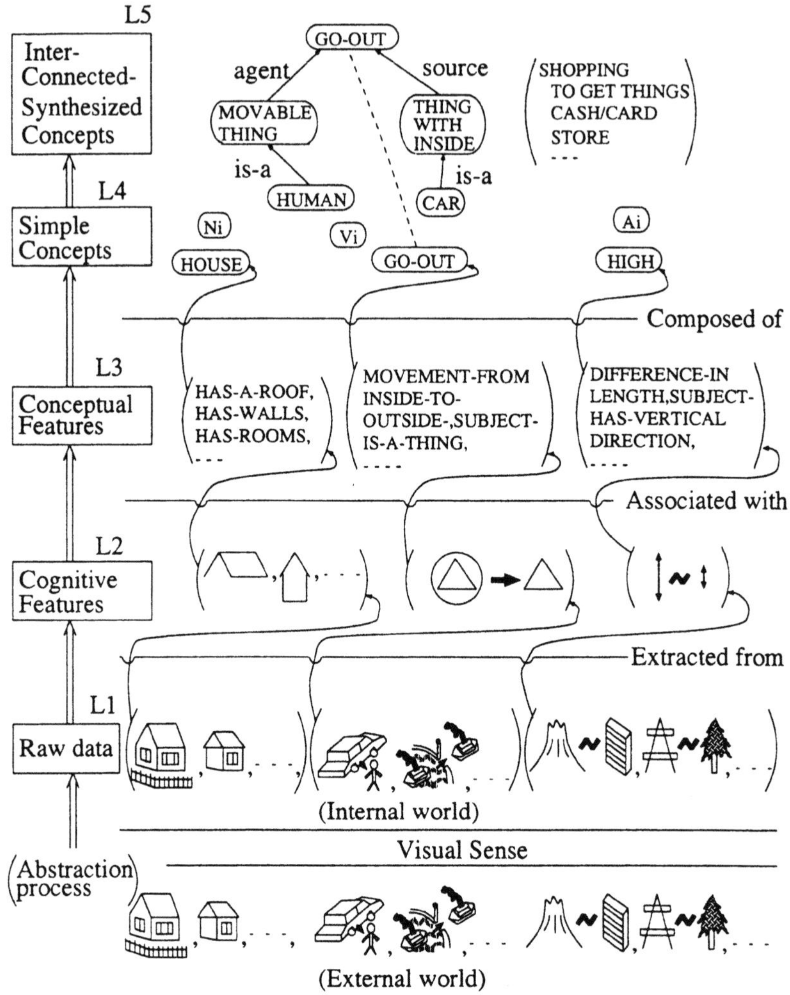

Figure 2. Levels of Mind.

features play a role of interfaces when a basic concept is formed through the five senses, or when a real world object is understood by natural language.

Level 4 Simple Concepts

These are conceptual data composed of conceptual features. Most of them are named by words. Concepts represented by verbs or adjectives have deep case frames. Simple concepts are concrete in the sense that they have direct referents in the real world.

Level 5 Interconnected-Synthesized Concepts
These concepts are obtained by interconnecting or synthesizing simple concepts. *Frame*, *script*, or *semantic networks* are examples of such interconnections. Some of them are named by words. They are abstract in the sense that they correspond indirectly to real world referents through simple concepts.

So far, we have discussed the hierarchy for modeling bottom-up processing. The hierarchy is also applied to top-down processing such as motion by planning. In this case, the raw data at level 1 is the signals to control the actuator, and the feature at level 2 is a "motion" feature which produces the control signals at level 1. Plans represented by high-level symbols are eventually transformed to a series of signals. Thus, our hierarchy shows not only the knowledge abstraction process in perception but the symbol-grounding process in motion.

2.3. *Chain activation*

Mind is composed of a great number of modules. They compose domains and levels mentioned in 2.1 and 2.2, respectively.

When a stimulus is given in some domain, it activates a module. Then, the modules directly related with it are activated. Next, the related modules activate their adjacent modules further, and thus activations of modules propagate inside and outside the domain. This dynamics is called *chain activation*, and an example is shown in 5.3.

There are two kinds of modules: *static* and *dynamic*. For example, the knowledge of substance such as "pond" or "grape" is represented by a static module which doesn't process anything by itself and plays just the role of data, while that of planning or motion is represented by dynamic one which processes something and often activates other static or dynamic modules.

3. Vision

Let us discuss the domain of recognition-understanding in Figure 1 in detail. It deals mainly with cognition of real world objects. There are innumerable objects to be recognized in the real world. From the linguistic point of view, however, the named objects or word referents are important.

3.1. *Categories of real world objects*

In general, real world objects can be divided into four big categories: substance, event, attribute, and others. Substance, event and attribute are represented by noun, verb and adjective, respectively. (Of course, a noun often

Table 1. Features of Simple Events/Concepts Represented by Verbs

No.	Feature	Example of verb
0.00	Emotional change	Fear
0.01	Sensual change	Feel
1.00	Movement	Fall
1.01	Change in direction	Turn
1.02	Change in shape	Bend
1.03	Change in quality	Rot
1.04	Change in quantity	Decrease
1.05	Optional change	Flash
1.06	Color change	Color
1.07	Thermal change	Heat
1.08	Change in force and energy	Fasten
1.09	Change in voice and sound	Sing
1.10	Appearance and disappearance	Appear
1.11	Starm, end and stop	Stop
1.12	Temporal change	Hasten
2.00	Continuation	Continue
2.01	Stat	Tower
3.00	Abstract	Base
4.00	Others	Eat

stands for objects other than substance.) We made conceptual analyses of those objects in detail [9, 12], and proposed an integrated system for vision and language [8, 10]. Table 1 shows features of *simple events* corresponding to level 3 of Figure 2. They are features of "concepts" as well as those of events.

3.2. *Understanding images*

The domain of recognition-understanding follows fundamentally the system developed previously [8, 10], but a more sophisticated architecture is designed. Figure 2 will give us a rough idea of the comprehension processes of real world substance, event and attribute, that is, HOUSE, GO-OUT, and HIGH, respectively. This domain consists of six big groups of modules: *object*(substance) *analyzer*, *structural analyzer*, *event analyzer*, *attribute ana-*

lyzer, interconnection analyzer, and *cognition manager*. Notice that each analyzer or manager isn't a single program, but a group of modules.

– Object analyzer
Some objects are simple in their shapes and functions and located at level 4 in Figure 2, and others are complicated and located at level 5. The object analyzer deals with the former, while the interconnection analyzer deals with the latter.

The object analysis follows conventional methods. That is, each object is described by properties or conceptual features which specifies it according to Table 1 in the case of events. Each conceptual feature represented by a symbol is associated with cognitive features which would be often procedural in the domain of sensor.

– Structural analyzer
This analyzer analyzes spatial relationships, or conceptual features, such as RIGHT or INSIDE among objects in a given image. Furthermore, it deals with temporal ones in input image sequences. For instance, let us take an example to the recognition of an event "X GOes OUT of Y" in a given image sequence. Then, the temporal feature "X INSIDE Y at time T0 and X OUTSIDE Y at time T1 where T0<T1" should be analyzed for the recognition.

– Event analyzer
Generally, a simple event is considered as a "change" from one state to another. For instance, "X INSIDE Y at T0" is one state, and "X OUTSIDE Y at T1" is another. The change is specified by a combination of several conceptual features. The event analyzer checks whether or not a simple event can be found among several objects in a given image sequence by checking the outputs of the object and the structural analyzers.

– Attribute analyzer
Generally, a simple attribute is considered as a "difference" between two objects, and a measure to detect the difference causes an attribute to be assigned to the objects [12]. Let us take an example to "O1(mountain) is HIGHer than O2(building)" as shown in Figure 2. The two objects O1 and O2 have the measure of HIGHer, that is, vertical length, and those values are compared with each other. The attribute analyzer deals with this kind of analysis.

– Interconnection analyzer
As mentioned in 2.2, interconnected-synthesized concepts are composed of simple concepts. This analyzer pays attention to the relation of interconnection or synthesis, and checks the outputs of the four analyzers mentioned above.

– Cognition manager
The cognition manager communicates mainly with both the *motion* and the *plan managers* mentioned in sections 4.2 and 5.2, respectively, and controls the analyzers mentioned above and other modules in the domains of recognition-understanding and sensor. There are two factors for control: direction and focus of analysis.

As for direction, the cognition manager orders the analyzers and other modules to make a top-down/bottom-up analysis of input images. For instance, it may choose a top-down analysis if an input image has to be associated with a memorized image in order to check whether or not the protagonist is on a scheduled point. On the other hand, it may choose a bottom-up one if an input image is given at a strange place.

As for focus, the cognition manager designates some part of an input image or scene to analyze. For instance, it designates a window enclosing some object in the image when he tries to move toward a target.

4. Motion

One of the main problems of the domain of action-expression is motion. Although human motion is diverse, the named motion is important from the linguistic point of view just as the named objects were so in vision.

4.1. *Human motion*

According to Table 1, human motion has the conceptual feature of *movement*, *change-in-direction* or *change-in-shape*. For example, motion "walk" has the conceptual features of movement and change-in-shape, and motion "bend" has those of change-in-shape and – direction. This kind of motion specified by Table 1 is called *u-motion* and analyzed below.

The human body has many joints and segments, and makes complicated, flexible motion. It is difficult to manipulate directly all the joints and segments, and to compute their motion at the same time. According to Jung and Badler [2, 3], it is possible to make the first order approximation of them with the following nine points and seven vectors:

– Points
Forehead-center, right/left-shoulder-center, pelvis-center, right/left-palm-center, right/left-foot-center, and body-ground site.

– Vectors
Forehead(view)-vector, torso-up-vector, pelvis-forward-vector, right/left-palm-up-vector, and right/left-foot-forward-vector.

The human posture can roughly be specified by these points and vectors.

U-motion is composed of conceptual features, each of which is in turn associated with several kinds of *motion features*. The motion feature can be represented by the points and the vectors. For example, "bend" has a rotation of the torso-up-vector about the pelvis-forward-axis by some angle at the pelvis-center and movement of the pelvis-center downward by some distance. They are represented as follows:

```
rotate(torso-up-vector, pelvis-forward-axis, angle),
movement(pelvis-center, downward, distance).
```

There are "dependencies" among motion features. For example, a rotation of the torso-up-vector in bending is accompanied by the movement of the forhead-center forward and the movement of both shoulder-centers downward. These dependencies are represented as follows:

```
rotate(torso-up-vector, pelvis-forward-axis, angle)
    ==>movement(forhead-center, forward, distance)
       and movement(both-shoulder-centers, forward,
       distance)
```

where `angle` implies downward.

Since we have had the representation of the motion feature and its dependency following Jung and Badler, the u-motion can be represented by a frame structure of conceptual features, and in turn of motion features and their dependencies. Notice that this structure follows Figure 2. The u-motion is located at level 4, the conceptual feature at level 3, the motion feature at level 2, and the control signals of the points and the vectors at level 1.

4.2. *Moving body*

The domain of action-expression contains the *motion manager*, the *motion planner* and the *motion executor*, each of which is composed of many static and dynamic modules related with one another.

– Motion manager
The motion manager mainly communicates with the plan manager shown in 5.2 and the cognition manager mentioned in 3.2, controlling other modules in the domains of action-expression and actuator.

The motion manager is informed of an execution of a plan by the plan manager. The plan is often composed of small subplans such as "go to point B from point A along path C," "find a grape trellis," "jump it," and "grasp grapes." The motion manager transfers them to the motion planner mentioned below one by one. In case of movement, which often occurs in AESOPWORLD, the domain of action-expression has two modes: *along* and *toward*. In the along mode, the protagonist moves along some base, while in the toward mode, he moves in the direction of some target. The motion manager makes decision of the mode, and selects an object as base or target together with the domain of recognition-understanding.

The motion manager has close communication with the cognition manager during a series of u-motion. In fact, the domain of action-expression needs the result of an execution of u-motion, because it has to make error correction in case of failure.

– Motion planner
The planning made by the domain of planning-creation is often vague and doesn't specify a detailed structure of motion. For example, "go to B from A along C" needs to specify the moving speed, the combination of u-motion, the landmarks or check points between A and B to confirm if one is along C, and so on.

Such a structure is usually described by a frame and stored in motion planning modules. The motion planner refers to them, and commands the motion executor to execute a series of u-motion.

– Motion executor
The motion executor executes each u-motion given by the motion planner, referring to the u-motion frame mentioned in 4.1 and sending signals to actuators.

5. Planning

Neither vision nor motion can play fully its role in mind if it stands alone. They need collaboration with each other. Mainly, planning at the domain of planning-creation connects and controls them.

5.1. *Planning type*

Planning is divided into four types in our model.

Type 0 No planning
When the domain of sensor accepts some special stimulus, the domains of action-expression and actuator immediately takes action reactively, and the domain of planning-creation doesn't perform any planning for it. For example, one quickly draws one's hand back when one touches a hot kettle.

Type 1 Simple planning
This is the plan that is immediately executed after simple checks of conditions. For example, one can immediately drink water if there is water around him/her.

Type 2 Habitual planning
This is the plan with which one is very familiar in one's everyday life. For example, one will have lunch at a habitual cafeteria near one's office at noon.

Type 3 General planning
Inference rules such as IF-THEN are used to make this plan. A new problem that one meets for the first time or a difficult problem that one can't solve by type 0 through 3 is solved by this type.

5.2. *Planning modules*

The domain of planning-creation consists of four major groups of modules:

– Reactive planner
The reactive planner manipulates the planning of type 0 and 1. In case of type 0, *demons* which watch special inputs are placed in the domain of recognition-understanding in advance. If one of them fires, an interruption occurs. The plan manager interrupts the current plan and motion, and drives the reactive response without planning.

An ordinary planning starts with a type-1 plan. The plan manager asks the domain of recognition-understanding to check conditions attached to it. If the conditions are met, then it is executed immediately. Otherwise, it ends in failure, and other plan is checked. When a type-1 plan ends in failure, the plan manager informs the domain of recognition-understanding of the names of objects – "water" in case of `psearch_for_and_drink_water` mentioned in 5.3 – related with the conditions, and demons are assigned to those objects in order to watch their appearance. If one of them is observed during motion, the plan manager compares the current plan being executed with the type-1 plan, and chooses the better one.

– Planner
The planner makes type-2 and -3 plans. Frame-structured *templates* (see 5.3) are used for type-2 or habitual plans. In general, those plans are iteratively expanded into subplans, and finally primitive plans which can be executed are obtained. There are several kinds of IF-THEN rules for type-3 plans in our system.

– Plan evaluator
Generally, a lot of ambiguities occur during planning. The plan evaluator evaluates them by five measures: *time, existence, possibility, danger*, and *preference.* It refers to the knowledge base in the domain of memory-learning which contains conceptual and temporary data, and evaluates a given plan as follows:

By time, it checks the needed time, mainly the time for movement along some path, to execute the plan. By existence, it investigates the objects related with the plan in memory. For example, a crock may be checked in case of `psearch_for_and_drink_water`. By possibility, it checks the realizability in the execution of the plan. For example, when one tries to jump to a grape trellis, one's ability in jumping is checked. By danger, it searches similar temporary, episodic data, inferring the danger of the current plan by a simple analogy. By preference, it chooses favorite objects.

– Plan manager
The plan manager controls the reactive planner, the planner, and the plan evaluator for change of plans, selection of strategies, or change of the evaluation weights:

- Change of plan
  The current plan executed is changed when (1) an interruption by type-0 or -1 plan occurs, (2) a new urgent plan is requested by the domain of desire-instinct, or (3) the current plan execution comes to a deadlock. In such a case, the plan manager halts the current plan execution, and deals with the problem.
- Selection of strategies
  When the reasoning of type 3 is done, a strategy such as depth-first, breadth-first or hill-climbing search is applied to it. The plan manager judges which one is the best in a given situation.
- Change of evaluation weights
  Weights of five measures for plan evaluation are flexible. For example,

existence and possibility may increase their weights whereas danger may decrease it in case of an urgent plan.

Furthermore, the plan manager controls both the cognition and the motion managers in the domains of recognition-understanding and action-expression, respectively. As was mentioned in sections 3.2 and 4.2, the plan manager transfers a plan both to the cognition and to the motion managers. The cognition manager makes a top-down control according to the plan. It sometimes returns a discovery to the plan manager when an object designated by type -0 or -1 plan comes into view. On the other hand, the motion manager commands the subplans to the motion planner one by one. Notice that both the cognition and the motion managers have also close communications with each other during the execution. When the execution comes to a deadlock, they appeal to the plan manager for the situation.

5.3. *Example of chain activations*

A detailed scenario was made according to the Aesop fable of "the Fox and the Grapes." Many modules are made along the scenario, and an example of the planning module is as follows:

```
planModule([psearch_for_and_drink_water,
  caseFrame(plan([agent,$self],[object,to_search_
            for_and_drink_water]),
            make([agent,$self], [object,Result])),
  goal([degree(Thirst),under(Threshold]),
  embodiment([
   type_1([if(exist_there(Water)),ppdrink(Water)]),
   type_2([
      [if(at_$home),ppdrink_$water1_in_$crock1],
      [if(in_$field),
          [[pgo_$home,ppdrink_$water1_in_$crock1],
           [pgo_$under_$bridge,ppdrink_$water5_of_
            $brook]]],
      [if(on_$mountain1),
          [pgo_to_$spring,ppdrink_$water9_of_
           $spring]]]),
    type_3(
      [isearch_for([vessel,contain(Water)],
       isearch_for([place,filled_with(Water)])])]).
```

where $ indicates an instance of a concept. The planning module has a frame structure: The slot of `caseFrame` will be described in 6.1. The slot of `goal` indicates that the goal of plan is to reduce the degree of thirst under the threshold. The slot of `embodiment` shows several subplans of type 1 through 3.

According to this example, a series of chain activations are shown below. It is expressed in English for convenience:

Initial Setting It is a little past noon on a day at the end of August. It is very fine and hot. The protagonist is down 300 meters to the south of an intersection in Aesop world where he lives. The degree of thirst is over the threshold, but other physiological states are normal.

Desire Process 1 Demon Thirst appeals to the *desire manager* for that the value of the memory is over the threshold, where Thirst watches a memory indicating the state of thirst, and the desire manager controls other modules in the domain of desire-instinct. The desire manager asks the plan manager to drive a planning module to relieve the thirst. The conditions are "within half an hour" and "by a safe way."

Planning Process 1 The plan manager accepts the desire immediately because there is no other request then. It orders `psearch_for_and_drink_water` to make precise plans. `Psearch_for_and_drink_water` looks up the subplans, where the plan of type 1 is available if his surroundings meet the condition. `Psearch_for_and_drink_water` asks both the cognition and the motion managers via the plan manager to check the condition, or the existence of something to drink around him.

Cognition and Motion Process 1 The cognition manager orders the check to the object analyzer in a top-down manner. During the check, the motion manager cooperates with the cognition manager to turn his body. Eventually, both managers fail in finding anything to drink.

Planning Process 2 `Psearch_for_and_drink_water` looks up the subplans again, where the two plans of type 2 are available because he is in the field. They are sent to the plan evaluator. It checks each plan, and returns the results that they are all inadequate because of lack of time. Next, it checks the plans of type 3. `Isearch_for` first infers a vessel. It retrieves the knowledge base of objects, and obtains, for instance, `[crock, $home]`. Then, it plans to go to the places where those objects can be found. But no place meets the two conditions. Another inference module `isearch_for` can't find a good place for water either. After all, `psearch_for_and_drink_water` returns the control to the plan manager. Finally, the plan manager returns to the desire manager the answer that any plan to satisfy the desire can't be found because the two conditions are too strict.

Desire Process 2 The desire manager has a talk with demon Thirst, and knows that the degree of thirst is much higher than the threshold. Then, the manager and the demon compromise with each other on the conditions. That is, the condition of "by a safe way" is weakened to "even a little dangerous way," and that of "within half an hour" is shortened a little. The deire manager asks the plan manager to drive `psearch_for_and_drink_water` once again.

- -

The plan manager finally makes complex plan C1 as follows: `pgo_to_$garden_of_mansion`, `psearch_for_pond`, and `ppdrink_water_of_pond`. The path to the mansion from the current point has obtained during the evaluation process, but means of how to search for a pond in the mansion is unknown, because he has never come into the mansion.

The C1 is handed to both the cognition and the motion managers for the preparation for the coming cognition and motion. Some of the objects checked during the planning process such as vessel, pond or fruit are also handed to the cognition manager as reference data.

Emotion Process 1 Demon Mortification, which is a complex emotion and has many sub-demons in several domains to extract features for its arousal, is aware of plan C1 running and starts to watch whether or not the cognition manager notifies the desire manager of the achievement of the desire.

Cognition and Motion Process 2 The cognition manager checks the walking mode(see 4.2) with the configuration of the animal trail that the protagonist is standing on. At the same time, the motion manager directs the motion planner to calculate the walking speed with the given path to the mansion and the given time. According to the mode and the speed checked, the domains of actuator and sensor start watching and walking, respectively. As he moves, the cognition manager becomes aware of that the view of the intersection is changing gradually compared with the original view.

- -

The protagonist reaches the mansion, and comes into it. He tries to search for a pond, but he can't find it. He decides to enter the main building of the mansion and to search for a crock. On the way to it, he happens to find a grape trellis at the corner of the garden. He tries to jump many times to get the grapes, but ends in failure. Demon Stubbornness, which is another complex emotion, makes him jump again and again, but demon Fatigue, which is another memory-watching demon, causes him to take a rest at last. Finally, Mortification makes him cry sour grapes.

6. Language

The domain of language in Figure 1 is discussed in detail in this chapter. The essential function of language was defined as describing any data or processing in mind in 2.1. The function is discussed from the point of generation, which has two big phases: generation of deep structures from mental dynamics and that of surface structures from deep ones. We focus our attention on the former.

6.1. *Proposition and mood*

To generate a sentence, two kinds of linguistic information are needed: *propositional* and *modal*. The propositional information can be represented by a deep case frame. What is essentially important is how non-linguistic mental activities can be translated into deep case frames.

Let us pay attention to the dynamic module mentioned in 2.3. Two kinds of information will be available to describe their activations, that is, behavior and its result. In case of the planning module `psearch_for_and_drink_water`, the followings may be a description of its activation:

> Behavior - - - `plan([agent,$self],[object,to_search_for_and_drink_water])`
> Result - - - `make([agent,$self],[object,Result])`

where Behavior describes that `$self`, that is, the protagonist plans to `search_for_and_drink_water`, and Result describes that he makes plan `Result`. After the planning, plan `pgo_to_$mansion`, `psearch_for_pond`, and `pdrink_water` may be substituted for `Result`.

It is assumed that each dynamic module, which has a frame structure, contains the slot of the *deep case frame*, and that it is filled with these two kinds of information, or predicates. Furthermore, when a dynamic module is activated, static modules such as substance or location are also activated together with it. They play the roles of case elements of the deep case frame.

The situation surrounding the activation of a dynamic module provides mood for the proposition. For instance, if the desire manager generates a desire, "desire" mood is attached to the proposition, while if a plan is selected from several alternatives by the plan evaluator, "decision" mood to the proposition.

6.2. *Generating deep structures*

The overall schema of the domain of language is shown in Figure 3. The part of Deep Structure: Generation consists of five big groups of modules:

– Proposition&Mood analyzer
When a dynamic module is activated in a domain, this analyzer watches the activation to extract case frames together with case elements filling them. Furthermore, it attaches mood to the propositional content according to the

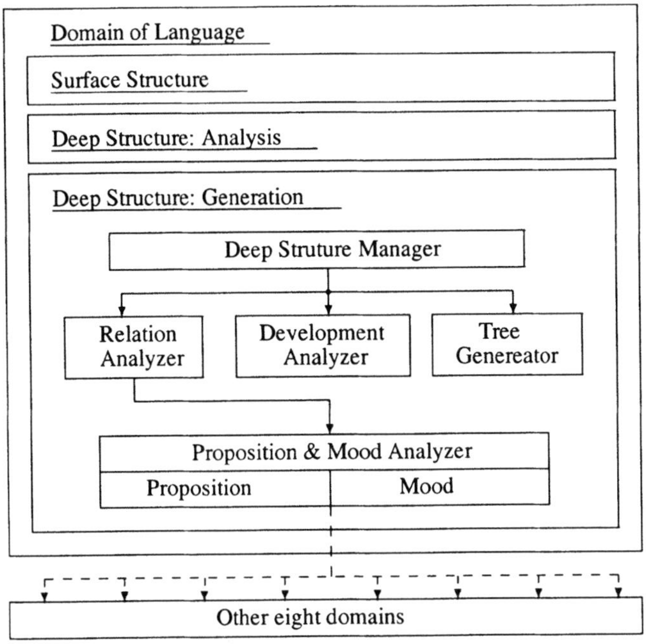

Figure 3. Major Groups of Modules in the Domain of Language.

situation in which the module is activated. The pair of a proposition and its mood is called *P&M-pair*.

Notice that the proposition&mood analyzer doesn't pay attention to the "codes" at the lowest level in Figure 2. For example, a digital image is composed of many digits each of of which carries some information. But the analyzer doesn't go into the level.

– Relation analyzer
Modules are related with one another in various ways. Some relations are physical *cause-effect*, and others are mental *stimulus-response*. Some are *spatial*, and others are *temporal*. Some are *upper-lower*, and others are *brother*. The relation analyzer checks these kinds of relations among P&M-pairs, making a subtree of P&M-pairs gradually.

– Development analyzer
The development analyzer deals with transition of chain activations. For example, if the domain of desire-instinct requests some planning and the domain of planning-creation ends in failure, the result may be sent back

to the domain of desire-instinct. Then, the domain of desire-instinct thinks something for a while, and asks the domain of planning-creation to try again with other planning. Such a transition mainly occurs from one domain to another. Thus, the development analyzer identifies a subtree of P&M-pairs as a chain activation with a coherent content, and arranges subtrees in sequence or in a temporal order.

Notice that the information analyzed here serves to make a paragraph in surface structures.

– Tree generator

The tree generator connects subtrees to a tree in the temporal order. What is important here is to prune the tree. Generally, many modules are activated in a series of chain activations, and so the tree becomes very big. Consulting the relation analyzer, the tree generator prunes the tree according to the criteria for summarization proposed previously [14]. Thus, an obtained tree shows a summarized story of all the activations of modules with a hierarchical structure and a temporal relationship.

– Deep structure manager

The deep structure manager mainly controls the relation analyzer, the development analyzer, and the tree generator, but it also controls the sequential structure of language. In general, chain activations occur in parallel in different domains. For example, modules of cognition and motion cooperate with each other when the protagonist walks, and two chain activations occur in the domain of recognition-understanding and the domain of action-expression. On the other hand, a single chain activation occurs when he makes plans under deep considerations. Therefore, we assume that a single chain activation occurs in deep considerations whereas parallel ones occur in routine work. Parallel chain activations are tied up in a bundle, and put in the subtrees of the relation analyzer mentioned above. Thus, parallel chain activations are arranged as a subtree in the whole tree generated by the tree generator.

Thus, the essential function of language, that is, the descriptive function was realized by the slot of the case frame of dynamic modules and by extraction of the predicates. The function of surveying any data or processing was realized by the proposition and mood analyzer, that of organizing high level thought by the relation analyzer, the development analyzer, and the tree generator, and that of communicating with others by generated sentences.

7. Implementation

An integrated system or agent based on the computer model in Figure 1 and the methods in chapter 3 through 6 is being implemented on SUN Workstations with voice and music generators. Most modules are developed along "the Fox and the Grapes" as mentioned in 5.3.

7.1. *Behavior of the system*

The nine domains of Figure 1 are being developed in parallel. Each domain has several versions. After some improvement, they are connected to one other, and a total simulation is repeated. Figure 4 indicates a screenshot of such a simulation.

The mental and the physical states of the protagonist are shown in several windows of the graphic displays. The accepted image sequence or changing view is shown in a window when he moves on. His current position is displayed on a map in another window. His physiological states in the domain of sensor also appear in another window, and changes as he moves. When a physiological state changes to red, a desire arises. At present, the animation of his motion is under development [7].

In planning, the planning module in the domain of planning-creation flashes on the screen. The generated deep structures or sentences appear in a window. At the same time, the speech of the protagonist is generated by the voice generator.

The emotional state such as gladness, anger or fear is checked by a feature-extraction method in pattern understanding, and the result is converted into music by the music generator developed in our laboratory [6]. The music is played for the background of the screen.

To make a simulation mentioned above, a support system as external world was also developed. For example, it supplies changing views for the domain of sensor, and changes his current position on the map when the protagonist moves on.

7.2. *Generated story*

A Japanese language story was generated as part of of the chain activation described in 5.3. Its meaning may roughly be expressed in English as follows:

```
It's very hot today. I'm on the animal trail
down 300m to the intersection.
   I'm very thirsty. I'd like to relieve my
thirst in a safe way in a hurry.
```

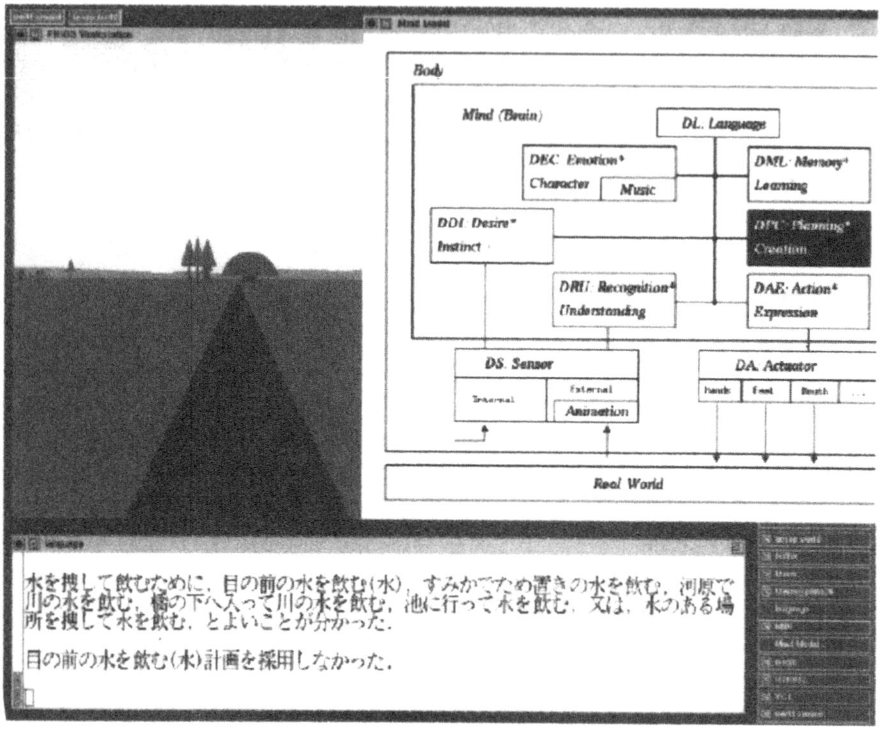

The left-upper window shows what the protagonist sees now. The image changes as he moves. The right-upper window shows the states of his mind, that is, the nine domains. A module in the domain of planning-creation is activated now. The lower window indicates what he thinks now. His mental activities, or the chain activations, are represented in Japanese sentences. At the same time, Japanese speech is generated from those sentences. Furthermore, his mental states of emotions are automatically transformed into music, which is played for the background of the screen.

Figure 4. A Screenshot of the System Behavior.

I'll search for and drink water. If there is water around me, I'd like to drink it. There is no water. I'm on the field. I'll go home. My home is far. I give up going home. I'll go under the bridge. It's far. I give up going there. I study other ways. - - - - -

I'll search for a place with water. I remember ponds. I'll find one of them. I remember the B pond. It is in the Aesopworld. A

```
hunter's lodge is close to it. He will probably
be in it. He is dangerous. It is dangerous to go
to the B pond. I give up going there.
   I'll eat watery foods. I'll search for and
eat fruits. I'll eat strawberries. They grow in
spring. It's summer now. It isn't a good season
to eat them. I give up eating them.
   - - - - -
```

8. Discussions

Residual problems

Several problems have remained unsolved: sensor, actuator, learning, language analysis and so on. In particular, learning is important, because it supports the adequacy of our theory of language. That is, the case frame slot of dynamic modules should be filled with the predicates by learning processes. The system constructed previously [10] will serve the development of an algorithm which describes non-linguistic events in the external world by natural language predicates. Furthermore, we have already developed a feature-extraction method for emotion arousal in the internal world. This will serve partially the automatic assignment of predicates to the deep case slots.

Another problem is to extend the system to two characters. Then, they can have conversations with each other. Dialog processing needs a new technique for constructing the other's model in one's mind. We are actively attacking the problem right now.

Generalization

AESOPWORLD is a typical case study, and manipulates only a special domain, that is, the world of Aesop fables. It looks too ad hoc to bring about successful fruits to the study of Artificial Intelligence. But, notice that its main purpose is to make clear the various mental activities in "a coherent way." No one can manipulate the whole mental phenomena at the same time with the current level of techniques, and so a meaningful specification is important.

We think that the more basic a system is, the more meaningful it is in the development of such an integrated system. From this point of view, our protagonist makes basic plans or inferences, basic cognition of familiar scenes, or basic motion following everyday experiences and common sense. Furthermore, our computer model of mind is nothing specific to the domain of fables, and the architecture of planning, cognition, motion, language can be applied in principle to other systems. Thus, AESOPWORLD could contribute to make the power of current Artificial Intelligence come closer to that of human beings from the technological point of view.

Fusion with psychological fruit

AESOPWORLD aims at the integration of the main fields, for example, natural language understanding, image understanding, or intelligent robots in Artificial Intelligence research. They are deeply involved in the essential concepts of human intellect or emotion: e.g. perception, cognition, desire, emotion, creation, inference, expression, memory, learning, or language. At the moment, however, we don't take the approach to make them clear studying human mechanisms and testing by computers, but the approach to realize them by computers and to provide useful devices or systems for human society. From this point of view, it can be considered that as far as a realization or implementation of such a concept is useful for development of some device or system, it is meaningful even if it doesn't a direct reflection of a human mechanism. In fact, some of table-look-up or parsing algorithms developed in natural language processing so far can't be said to reflect human mechanisms. Nevertheless, they are useful from the point of computer engineering.

However, we will not ignore valuable fruit obtained by psychology or other related areas. We believe that the human mind is the highest of all in its quality to process intellect and emotion. The long history of psychology gives us much information for clarification of the concepts mentioned above. For example, Plutchik [15] proposed a multifactor-analytic theory of emotion, and showed four pairs of *primary emotions*: joy-sadness, acceptance-disgust, surprise-expectancy, and fear-anger. There will be various kinds of estimation about it from the point of psychology. However, the theory is convenient as a whole for our computer architecture, because it shows us what kind of primary emotions we should pay attention to, and matches our feature extraction algorithm to detect emotion arousal in mind.

We think that our computer model of mind and the system following it should be fused with the fruit of psychology or related areas at the next stage of the research.

9. Conclusion

Integrated comprehension and generation of vision, motion and language at the level of the lower-grades of elementary school have been discussed. First, a mental model with the nine domains and the five levels were reviewed as the basis of the integrated system. *Modules* were introduced as the unit of data or processing in mind, and the mental and physical activities were grasped as *chain activations* of them.

Next, the features of real world objects were classified, and the method for understanding *simple objects*, *events* and *attributes* were shown along the concept formation hierarchy. Next, human motion with the feature of *movement*, *change-in-shape*, and *change-in-direction* was discussed. *U-motion* was well generated by the combination of *motion features* developed by Jung and Badler. Vision and motion were connected and controlled by the four types of planning.

Language was regarded as *describing any data or processing in mind.* Every dynamic module with a frame structure has a slot of a *deep case frame*, in which two kinds of predicates are embedded.

Finally, implementation showed that the system worked well as was expected.

Thus, the integration of vision, motion and language, in particular,

(1) Language association with mental objects, and
(2) Symbol grounding in perception or motion

was realized in AESOPWORLD. In conclusion, our AESOPWORLD could be expected to provide a good framework for integration of intellectual and emotional processing from the technological point of view.

Acknowledgements

AESOPWORLD owes many thanks to many people. In particular, we would like to thank the leading coworkers, Jun-ichi Nakamura and Tsukasa Noma. Discussions with them were very helpful.

References

1. Barwise, J. and J. Perry. 1981. Situation and attitudes. Journal of philosophy, Vol. 78, No. 11, pp. 668–691.
2. Jung, Moon-Ryu. and N. Badler. 1992. Posture planning for agent animation, Extended Abst. 1st Int'l Conf. AI Planning and Systems, College Park, Maryland.
3. Jung, Moon-Ryu. 1992. Human like agents with posture planning capability, PhD thesis, Computer and Information Science, University of Pennsylvania, Philadelphia.
4. Minsky, M. 1975. A Framework for representing knowledge. In The psychology of computer vision. Edited by P. Winston. McGraw-Hill, p. 282.
5. Minsky, M. 1985. The Society of mind. Simon and Schuster, p. 339.
6. Nakamura, J. et al. 1993. Automatic back-ground-music generation based on actor's emotion and motion. Proc. Pacific Graphics '93, pp. 147–161.
7. Noma, T., K. Kai, J. Nakamura, and N. Okada. 1992. Translating from natural language story to computer animation, Proc. SPICIS '92, pp. 475–480.

8. Okada, N. 1979. SUPP:Understanding moving picture patters based on linguistic knowledge, Proc. IJCAI, pp. 690–693.
9. Okada, N. 1980. Conceptual taxonomy of Japanese verbs for understanding natural language and picture patterns, Proc. COLING '80, pp. 123–135.
10. Okada, N. 1983. Understanding moving picture patterns by natural language. In Computer science and technology. Edited by T. Kitagawa. Ohm∗North-Holland, p. 314.
11. Okada, N. 1987. Representation of knowledge and emotion – an engineering approach to modelling mind. Kyushu Symp. Inf. Process. pp. 47–65. (In Japanese.)
12. Okada, N. 1991. Modeling of attribute concepts and their classification for machine thesaurus. In The advances in information modelling and knowledge bases. Edited by H. Jaakola, H. Kangassalo and S. Ohsuga. IOS Press.
13. Okada, N. and T. Endo. 1992. Story generation based on the dynamics of the mind. Computational Intelligence, Vol. 8, No. 1, pp. 123–159.
14. Okada, N. and J. Namera. 1991. AESOPWORLD – Structural representation and summarization of stories based on thinking and behavior processes. JSAI,SIG-KBS-8805(2/2), pp. 61–69. (In Japanese.)
15. Plutchik, R. 1960. The multifactor-analytic theory of emotion, Journal of psychology, Vol. 50, pp. 153–171.

Artificial Intelligence Review **10**: 235–252, 1996.

Automatic Reconstruction of Vasculature

PAUL MC KEVITT

Department of Computer Science, Regent Court, University of Sheffield, 211 Portobello Street, GB- S1 4DP, Sheffield, England, U.K., E.U.; E-mail: p.mckevitt@dcs.sheffield.ac.uk

and

PETER HALL

Department of Computer Science, P.O. Box 600, Victoria University Wellington, Wellington, New Zealand; E-mail: peter@comp.vuw.ac.nz

Abstract. Two of the most difficult problems in Artificial Intelligence are processing visual scenes and processing natural languages. There has been a large amount of research in each of these fields but little on their integration. This is surprising given the potential importance of integrated systems, not only for understanding human cognition but also for the range of practical applications that will be enabled. We review previous work and provide an overview of our own work. We focus upon the medical application of reconstructing complicated cerebral blood vessel structures and associated pathologies from images and medical reports. This gives our work a clear and significant practical aim. We show how the ostensibly disparate technologies can be married using a single knowledge representation. Previous attempts at reconstruction have used images alone and no satisfactory solution exists. We believe that the synergy provided by integrating vision and natural language processing provides an information-rich environment that will enable progress toward an efficient and robust solution. Such an integration will have not only have important practical uses but also implications for Artificial Intelligence, Cognitive science, Philosophy, and Psychology.

Key words: angiogram, artificial intelligence, natural language processing, text processing, vasculature, vision processing.

1. INTRODUCTION

Humans are able to combine the processing of vision and language, apparently with ease. For instance, humans can use words to describe a picture and can reproduce a picture from a language description. Moreover, humans can exhibit this kind of behaviour over a very wide range of input pictures and language descriptions. Even more impressive is the fact that humans can look at images and describe not just the picture itself but a set of emotions evoked by it. Although there are theories of how we process vision and language there are few theories about how such processing is integrated. There have been large debates in Philosophy and Psychology with respect to the degree with which people store knowledge as propositions or pictures (see Pylyshyn 1973; Kosslyn and Pomerantz 1977).

There has been much research in Artificial Intelligence (AI) on the processing of natural language like English and on the processing of visual scenes (see Ballard and Brown 1982; Partridge 1991). However, there has been little work on linking natural language processing (NLP) and vision processing (VP). There are at least two advantages of linking the processing of natural languages to the processing of visual scenes. First, investigations into the nature of human cognition may benefit. Such investigations are being conducted in the fields of Psychology, Cognitive Science, and Philosophy. Computer implementations of integrated VP and NLP can she light on how people do it. Second, there are advantages for real-world applications. The combinations of two powerful technologies promises new applications that include: automatic production of text from images; automatic production of images from text; and the automatic interpretation of images with text. Research into any of these must be regarded as AI, but other disciplines may benefit. For example, the first of these application areas would benefit the discipline of *scientific visualization* and its applications, the second would benefit *computer graphics* and its applications, the third would benefit AI itself, specifically in *machine learning* and *information acquisition*. The theoretical and practical advantages of linking natural language and vision processing have also been described in Wahlster (1988).

We believe that the way forward for developing general theories of language and vision processing is to focus on specific applications such as the medical domain. We are building a system that processes x-ray projections (*angiograms*) and their associated medical reports. The angiograms are separated by an angle of about ninety degrees making them *biplane angiograms*. The medical reports are prepared by expert radiologists as they examine the angiograms and describe the appearance of the vasculature in them. A typical pair of angiograms are shown in Figure 1, and an associated medical report in Figure 2. Each of these input datum relate to blood vessel structures (*vasculature*) and arteriovenous malformations (AVMs) within the human body. AVMs are congenital abnormalities of the vasculature. These AVMs are dangerous because if they hemorrhage the results can be fatal. The clinical reasons for acquiring angiograms are fully explained in Hall *et al.* (1995b).

Our goal is to reconstruct vasculature and AVMs in three-dimensional space given biplane angiograms and associated medical reports. Previously this problem has been addressed using images alone and work has concentrated on reconstructing *coronary vasculature* around the heart. The *cerebral vasculature* comprises many vessels which are smaller than the coronary vessels; and there are wide variations in the branching structure between individuals. So reconstruction of cerebral vasculature is much harder than of coronary vasculature. Our work differs in two important ways: (1) it provides a unique representation of a *collection of vasculature* and, (2) it uses information acquired from medical texts in addition to images. We believe that our approach provides an information-rich environment that will enable reconstruction of vasculature in the brain in an efficient and robust manner.

FRONT

SIDE

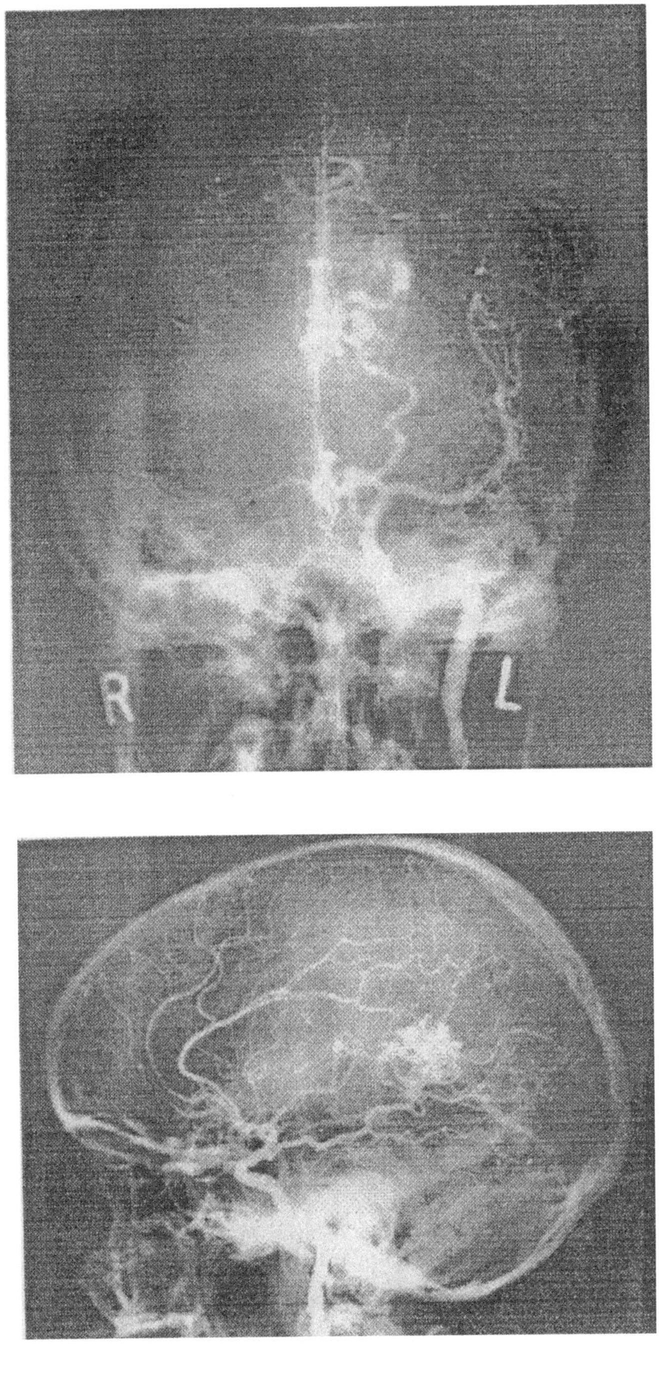

Fig. 1. An example angiogram pair.

RIGHT AND LEFT INTERNAL AND EXTERNAL CAROTID ANGIOGRAPHY, RIGHT VERTEBRAL ANGIOGRAPHY.

On the (L) side there is an arterio-venous malformation with small tortuous vessels in a nidus of a dia. of about 2cms, situated close to the midline in the forceps major, supplied mainly by two posterior branches of the occipital division of the widened (L) posterior cerebral artery, which in turn is supplied both from the carotid syphon via a wide posterior communicating artery, and also from the basilar atery. The upper part of the lesion is also to some extent supplied from two dilated small arterial branches of the posterior pericallosal artery on the (L) side. The main drainage is via the medial atrial vein to the vein of Galen and the straight sinus. Otherwise normal, free communication across all parts of the circle of Willis with the possible exception of the (R) posterior medial portion, the (R) posterior cerebral artery filling directly from the (R) carotid syphon and not at all from the basilar artery.

Fig. 2. An example medical report.

In this paper we first give the background necessary to understand our problem and discuss previous work on medical image and report analysis, and the integration of NLP and VP (see section 2). Next, we present our contribution. The knowledge representation which is a representation of a collection of vasculature is described in section 3.1. We then show how this knowledge is used by the VP module in section 3.2 and the NLP module in section 3.3. We outline an architecture that integrates the knowledge representation with both the VP and NLP modules in section 3.4. In that section we also discuss the implications and benefits of integration. We conclude in section 4.

2. BACKGROUND

Reconstruction of vasculature and AVMs given x-ray angiograms is impossible unless some information prior to the angiograms is used. This can be seen when it is realised that reconstruction from angiograms may be likened to recovering a matrix from its row sums and column sums; the problem is *under-determined.* Traditional techniques that were developed in the computer vision literature deal with images that are separated by an angle of just a few degrees (for example, see Marr 1982; Mayhew and Frisby 1981) and cannot be used here. Prior information is required so that the ostensibly disparate images can be matched. We begin by describing existing systems for reconstruction of vasculature from angiograms, systems that process medical reports, and systems that integrate NLP and VP.

2.1. *Reconstruction of vasculature from angiograms*

There are many problems associated with reconstructing vasculature and AVMs from x-ray angiograms (see Hall 1993a). Previously we have considered the problem of reconstructing AVMs from angiograms (see Hall *et al.* 1993). Here, we confine our discussion to reconstructing vasculature. A full review of systems is available in Hall (1993b) and now we describe a representative subset of systems.

Stansfield (1986) describes an early system that recognises individual vessels within angiograms. Her system, called ANGY, is composed of three major parts: a low-level image processing model for segmenting images; a mid-level module that combines segments into large-scale cohesive units; and a high-level module that recognises these large-scale units and labels them according to standard clinical terminology. Suetens *et al.* (1987) follow an almost identical line as do Rake and Smith (1987) though the latter authors use a blackboard architecture. Delaere *et al.* (1990) not only label features in angiograms with clinical names but use a Boolean expression to specify those sets of labels that are self consistent. Some control over variance in vascular topology is gained this way. Garreau *et al.* (1991) use a three-dimensional model that contains qualitative rather than quantitative descriptions. A Prolog program provides rules that drive reconstruction.

The common characteristic of most of these attempts is that they tend to be very domain specific. They describe angiograms of the coronary vasculature from specific views. In short, they use rules to describe angiograms. Rules seem ill-suited for reconstruction of the cerebral vasculature. This is principally because the wide variation of branching patterns observed in cerebral vasculature between individuals makes it a complex structure not easily described by rules. Garreau *et al.* (1991) provide an exception in that their model is three dimensional. However, their model does not appear to make anatomy explicit.

Our representation differs because (1) it explicitly represents physical vasculature in three-dimensions and is therefore less domain specific, and (2) is an adaptive representation that can learn. Not all vascular branching patterns are documented, and it is unclear that they can be, so an adaptive model is essential. In short, our model of a collection of vasculature is an information repository that is designed to handle the level of complexity manifested by the cerebral vasculature. So far as we are aware our representation is unique.

2.2. *Medical report processing*

Schröder (1992a, 1992b, 1992c) has built a natural language system called METEXA (MEdical TEXt Analysis) that can process radiological reports that are spoken. METEXA is used for analysis of such reports. Another goal of the project is to conduct continuous speech recognition. METEXA centres on a solution to speech analysis by the use of domain-specific knowledge and contains a lexicon of about 1000 forms that specify the syntax and semantics of words. METEXA has 100 grammar rules and semantic analysis is conducted by constructing a conceptual graph (see Sowa 1984). Knowledge about the domain is encoded in canonical graphs of anatomical objects, pathological alterations, radiological terms, and other more general concepts. The knowledge-base contains about 400 concept types. A rule-base is used to answer questions about radiological reports. Plan (see Wilensky 1983) and script (see Schank and Abelson 1977) knowledge structures are used to generate expectations about the next incoming utterance. These structures contain knowledge about typical contents of radiological reports.

With respect to domain knowledge there is a lattice of concept types and relations are defined between them. Concept types important for radiological applications are ANAT (anatomical), PATHO ALT (pathological), and ATTRIBUT (anatomical, pathological and radiological attributes). The definitions of valid connections or relations between concept types and relations are provided by canonical graphs (see sowa 1984, p. 91). The definitions express restrictions and some relations used are shown in Table I below.

Table I. METEXA concepts and their relationships.

concept type	relation type	concept type
[ANAT]	PATHO	[PATHO ALT]
[ANAT]	SIDE	[SIDE]
[ANAT]	LOC	[ANATLOC]
[ANAT]	AATTR	[AATTRIBUTE]

Schröder (1992c) points out that the language style found in radiological reports shows characteristics of being a sublanguage. It is also important that such sublanguages have a restricted and simplified structure compared to full natural languages. Reports are written in *telegraphic* style where standard phrases are used and where verbs may be omitted. The semantics or meaning of utterances is more important than their structure or syntax. Utterances often consist of constituents without syntactic glue. Specialised domain knowledge is important for understanding and producing such clinical reports. Certain anatomical locations and their characteristics are expected to occur in order to remove ambiguity of meaning. Although Schröder has considered the possibility of applying NLP to medical reports there has been no proposal to link this work to the processing of visual data.

Other work on NLP of clinical reports includes the Linguistic String Project (see Sager *et al.* 1987), a system for acquiring medical facts from radiological reports (see Ranum 1988), knowledge-based processing of radiological reports (see Baud *et al.* 1991), and a dialogue system for querying and updating medical databases (see Mery *et al.* 1987). Scherrer *et al.* (1989) present work on knowledge acquisition and a compilation of other work is found in Kingsland (1989). Again, none of this work is linked to any vision processing. In contrast, we apply NLP to medical reports to assist our VP module in locating AVMs and vascular reconstruction.

2.3. *Integrated language and vision processing*

A number of natural language systems for the description of image sequences have been developed (see Herzog and Retz-Schmidt 1990; Neumann and Novak 1986). These systems verbalise the behaviour of human agents in image sequences about football and describe the spatio-temporal properties of the behaviour observed. Retz-Schmidt (1991) and Retz-Schmidt and Tetzlaff (1991) describe an approach that yields plan hypotheses about intentional entities from spatio-temporal information about agents. The results can be verbalised in natural language. The system called REPLATI-II takes observations from image sequences as input. Moving objects from two-dimensional image sequences have been extracted by a vision system (see Herzog *et al.* 1989) and spatio-temporal entities (spatial relations and events) have been recognised by an event-recognition system. A focussing process selects interesting agents to be concentrated on during a plan-recognition process. Plan recognition provides a basis for intention recognition and plan-failure analysis. Each recognised intentional entity is described in natural language. A system called SOCCER (see André *et al.* 1988; Herzog *et al.* 1989) verbalised real-world image sequences of soccer games in natural language and REPLAI-II extends the range of capabilities of SOCCER. Here, NLP is used more for annotation through text generation whereas we are interested in analysis.

Maaß *et al.* (1993) describe a system, called VITRE GUIDE, that generates mutlimodal route descriptions for computer assisted vehicle navigation. Information is presented in natural language, maps and perspective views. Three classes of spatial relations are described for natural language references: (1) topological relations (e.g. "in,", "near"), (2) directional relations (e.g. "left," "right") and (3) path relations (e.g. "along," "past"). The output for all presentation modes relies on one common three-dimensional model of the domain. Again, VITRA emphasises annotation through generation of text, rather than analysis, and the vision module considers interrogation of a database of digitized road and city maps rather than vision analysis.

3. VASCULAR RECONSTRUCTION

There have been efforts devoted to reconstructing vasculature from angiograms, analysis of medical texts, and the integration of vision and language processing. This section describes our contribution to all three areas. Because our representation of a collection of individual vasculature is central to our approach we begin with that. We then describe VP and NLP processing separately, and finally bring all of these together with the description of a single architecture.

3.1. *Knowledge representation*

Our model of a collection of vasculature is the *knowledge representation* (KR) used by all other modules in our overall system. We have diverted from all previous representations of vasculature by providing a KR that models many vasculature, that models the physical anatomy of individual vasculature, that is capable of adaptive modification, and that can be used for many purposes. Indeed, we have succeeded in using our KR to simulate the complete angiographic procedure which involves animating blood flow through the vasculature (see Hall 1994a, 1994b, 1994c). Our KR partitions the vasculature into three parts: topological (branching structure), geometric (such as shapes of vessels), statistical (such as variances in shape or the frequency at which a given vessel appears). Our KR was influenced by *ModelVisual* which is a program for visualisation developed by Kunii and Shinagawa (1991). Hall and McGregor (1993) give a full description of our KR. An overview is given here.

3.1.1. *Topology*

In our model the topology of any given individual vasculature is represented by a labelled graph:

$$G_i = (V_i, E_i),$$

where V_i is a set of vertices and E_i is a set of edges. The vertices correspond to vascular points that are branches (furcations) and vessel ends. The edges are vessel segments that connect these points. A vessel, as defined in clinical texts (see Salamon and Huang 1976) corresponds to a path through our total graph. The vertices and edges are labelled with geometric and statistical information as discussed below.

A collection, L, of such graphs, each representing a distinct individual, constitutes the supposed initial state of the knowledge base and we write:

$$L = \{G_i\}.$$

The individual graphs are 'added' together to generate a *proto-graph*:

$$G^+ = \cup\, G_i\ (\cup\, V_i, \cup\, E_i) = (V^+, E^+),$$

where $\cup$ runs over all G_i, and in which the individual graphs appear as subgraphs. Notice that union distributes over the individual sets that comprise the graph. This is a valid step provided that the symbols are all drawn from the same alphabet, say $\mathcal{P}$ for the vertices and $\mathcal{P}^2$ for the edges. We note two things: (1) the union can be performed incrementally which is the basis of the adaptive modelling and (2) to generate such an alphabet between any pair of graphs is equivalent to solving a maximal common sub-graph (MCS) problem where the alphabet symbols are correspondences between nodes. In the general case the problem is NP- complete which makes the MCS problem intractable and our method untenable. Read and Corneil (1977) give an excellent discussion on such problems. We note that solving the MCS problem is made feasible because the graphs are richly labelled so we are dealing with a special rather than the general case.

The proto-graph is insufficient as a KR because there is no way to distinguish between its subgraphs that are elements of L and sub-graphs that are not. We wish to make this distinction because we cannot be sure that an arbitrary sub-graph of the proto-graph represents a valid vasculature. To overcome this problem we might label the nodes and arcs of the proto-graph with references that identify which graphs they came from and in many cases there will be more than one such graph. Although these labels are a sufficient representation we choose instead to use a matrix in which columns are labels of the proto-graph and the rows are valid sub-graphs (elements of L) of the proto-graph. Let's consider an example.

Consider the vasculature depicted in Figure 3, which shows both geometric and topological aspects. The following sub-structures can identified

$$G_1 = (\{a, b, c, d, e, g\}, (ab, bc, bd, ce, dg\})$$
$$G_2 = (\{f, i, j, m, o\}, (fi, fj, fm, mo\})$$
$$G_3 = (\{h, k, l, n, p\}, \{hk, hl, hn, np\})$$

To form the proto-graph for these three graphs we construct:

$$\begin{aligned} G^+ &= G_2 \cup G_2 \cup G_3 \\ &= (\{a, b, c, d, e, f, g, h, i, j, k, l, m, n, o, p\}, \\ &\quad \{ab, bc, bd, ce, dg, fi, fj, fm, hk, hl, hn, mo, np\}) \end{aligned}$$

and a matrix as shown below in Table II.

Table II. Matrix representation of the example.

G^+	a	b	c	d	e	f	g	h	i	j	k	l	m	n	o	p	ab	bc	bd	ce	dg	fi	fj	fm	hk	hl	hn	mo	np
G_1	1	1	1	1	1	0	1	0	0	0	0	0	0	0	[illegible]	191	[illegible]	[illegible]	1	1	1	0	0	0	0	0	0	0	0
G_2	0	0	0	0	0	1	0	0	1	1	0	0	1	0	1	0	0	0	0	0	0	1	1	1	0	0	0	1	0
G_3	0	0	0	0	0	0	0	1	0	0	1	1	0	1	0	1	0	0	0	0	0	0	0	0	1	1	1	0	1

Note that columns of the matrix are equivalent to the labels on the nodes and arcs of the protograph. We can use this matrix to generate a Boolean valued expression by reading rows:

$$\begin{aligned} &B\,(G^+, G) = \\ &(ab \wedge bc \wedge bd \wedge ce \wedge dg \wedge \overline{fi} \wedge \overline{fj} \wedge \overline{fm} \wedge \overline{hk} \wedge \overline{hl} \wedge \overline{hn} \wedge \overline{mo} \wedge \overline{np}) \vee \\ &(\overline{ab} \wedge \overline{bc} \wedge \overline{bd} \wedge \overline{ce} \wedge \overline{dg} \wedge fi \wedge fj \wedge fm \wedge \overline{hk} \wedge \overline{hl} \wedge \overline{hn} \wedge mo \wedge \overline{np}) \vee \\ &(\overline{ab} \wedge \overline{bc} \wedge \overline{bd} \wedge \overline{ce} \wedge \overline{dg} \wedge \overline{fi} \wedge \overline{fj} \wedge \overline{fm} \wedge hk \wedge hl \wedge hn \wedge \overline{mo} \wedge np) \end{aligned}$$

which can be reduced to:

$$\begin{aligned} B(G^+, G) = ((ab \wedge bc \wedge bd \wedge ce \wedge dg) \\ \neq (fi \wedge fj \wedge fm \wedge mo) \neq (hk \wedge hl \wedge hn \wedge np)) \end{aligned}$$

where $\neq$ is the exclusive OR (XOR) proposition. We call $B(G^+,G)$ the *discrimination proposition* because it discriminates between valid and invalid sub-graphs of the proto-graph. Notice that if we wish to add a new graph to the KR then we need to update both the proto-graph and the discrimination proposition. This addition may be regarded as form of *machine learning*.

This example serves to illustrate the essential features of our KR. We have carefully defined the meaning of the matrix and derived the discrimination

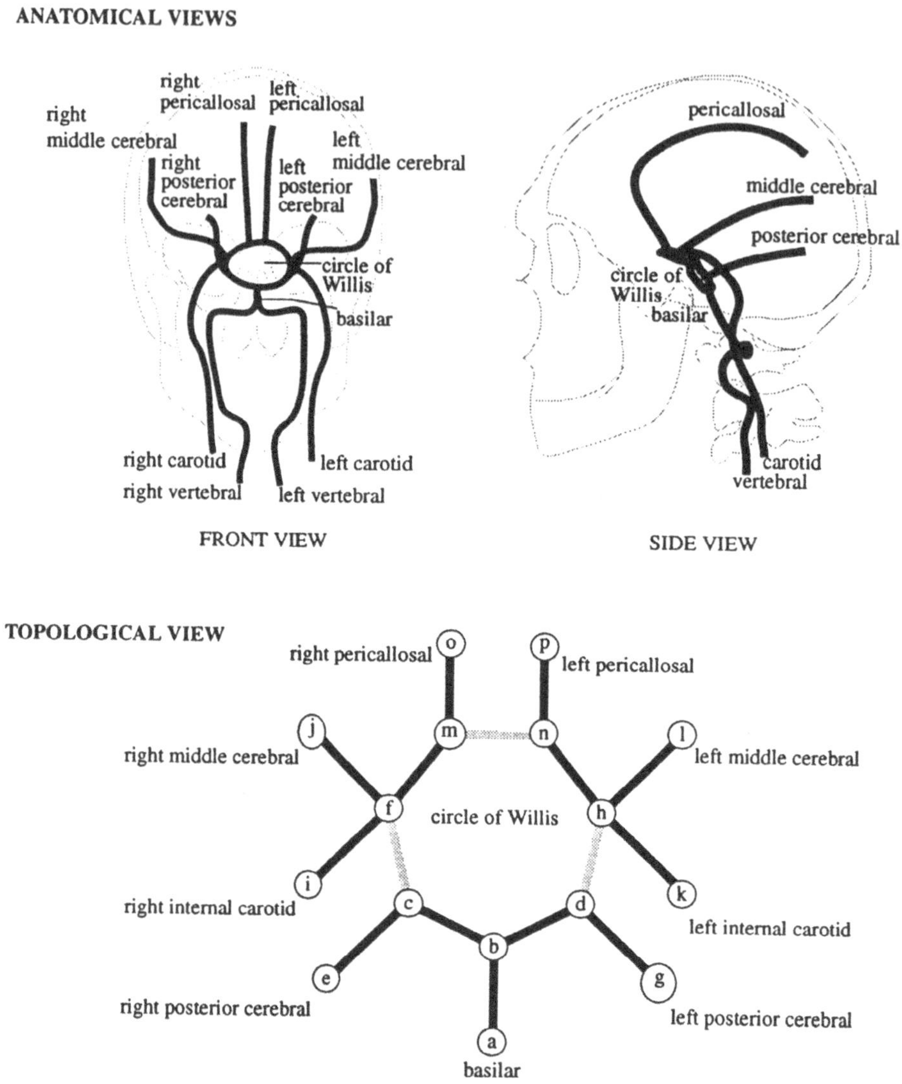

Fig. 3. A proto-typical cerebral vasculature showing the circle of Willis.

proposition from it (see Hall and McGregor 1993). We have also constructed the discrimination proposition by considering the need to recover valid sub-graphs as an injection from the proto-graph to the set all possible sub-graphs.

3.1.2. *Geometry and statistics*

Geometrical information is held in labels associated with graph features. These labels may be retrieved from the feature symbols. Labels are used to fix the three-dimensional shape of the vasculature. We define the *geometric model*:

$$F(G) = (F_V(V), F_E(E))$$

where F_V and F_E are bijective functions. The set $F_V(V)$ contains geometric descriptions of furcations and $F_E(E)$ are geometric descriptions of vessel fragments. Typically, elements of both these sets comprise generalised cylinders (see Ballard and Brown 1982). Hall (1994a, 1994b, 1994c) gives a full account of geometry.

Statistical information is also held in feature labels and we define the *statistical model:*

$$S(G) = (S_V(V), S_E(E))$$

where S_V and S_E are bijective functions. Statistical information is used to allow the shapes of vessels and furcations to vary and may also count the frequency with which a particular geometric element is observed to occur in a given population.

3.2. *The vision module*

The VP module uses the KR to enable it to predict what vessels will appear in an angiogram and to recognise them should they appear. Because the KR is three-dimensional this prediction and recognition can occur from any viewpoint. In short, reconstruction is driven on a *hypothesise and test* basis. In particular, vascular reconstruction can be considered as an attempt to prove that some arbitrary graph, H, is a valid sub-graph of the proto-graph. Hence, reconstruction can be regarded as graph matching. The description we give here is expanded upon in Hall *et al.* (1995a).

We use a search algorithm for the match. Nodes in the search space are propositions that a particular vessel fragments in the KR corresponds to particular vessel fragments that have been segmented from the angiograms from different points of view. For example,

$$\mathrm{CORR}(\mathrm{AB}, ab, a'b')$$

is a proposition that vessel AB in the KR corresponds to vessel *ab* in one angiogram and *a'b'* in another. The value of this correspondence is taken to be the minimum of the individual correspondences. This is determined by geometrically matching the projected model vessel, AB, to the relevant vessel in the angiogram. We note that this match requires the vessel being matched to be oriented in space so that a plausible projection occurs. We assume that there is some heuristic available that enables a root node to be decided, otherwise we will appeal to the expert user to determine the correspondence. Given this initial correspondence a 'root' vessel can be oriented; and this gives an initial orientation to the whole KR.

The expansion of the search is controlled by the KR. The KR is consulted so that an hypothesis of which vessels should appear next in the angiograms can be generated. Vessels that are predicted to appear simultaneously are combined into a single proposition headed by AND. For example, AND(CORR(BC, *bc*, *b'c'*), CORR(BD, *bd*, *b'd'*) would indicate that vessels BC and BD in the model must simultaneously correspond to vessels bc and *b'c'*, and bd and *b'd'* respectively, in an angiogram pair. Such constructions are used where the model furcates. Where the model offers a choice between possibilities that were component to the proto-graph we use NAND rather than XOR because this admits the possibility of no component of the KR being present in the angiograms.

As the search space expands the raw correspondences are pushed to the leaves of the search space leaving propositioned operators at the branches. At each step in the expansion vessels in the KR are locally re-oriented so that the vessels that are predicted to appear have a high chance of matching a counter-part in the angiogram. The hypothesis can then be tested against the real angiograms by geometric matching, as explained above.

At any stage in the search the tree can be parsed to reveal which components of the KR currently best account for the angiograms. Those components that fail to meet a threshold can be disregarded in future expansions and this prunes the search space. The expansion stops whenever the KR or the angiograms are exhausted of data. In the ideal case this exhaustion occurs in both at the same time. The final reconstructed vasculatures are determined by a simple parse of the search tree.

3.3. *The natural language module*

The NLP module is concerned with reconstructing the vasculature and AVMs from text. This module does this by mapping natural language text into a meaning representation which can be used to extract a labelled graph from the knowledge base. We propose a computational model for translating medical reports into a meaning representation. The model is similar in spirit to that incorporated in the OSCON (Operating System CONsultant) system that answers English questions about computer operating systems (see Mc Kevitt 1986, 1991a, 1991b, 1992; and Mc Kevitt and Wilks 1987; and Mc Kevitt *et al.* 1992a, 1992b, 1992c, 1992d).

The NLP module will generate hypotheses about the component of vasculature under scrutiny independent of the VP module. Central to the NLP module is the meaning representation that is a formal description of the medical reports. The format of the meaning representation reflects the format of the medical report representing all of the immediate features mentioned.

We note that there are a number of standard phrases that the NLP module can search for in a medical report. First, there are standard phrases referring to specific objects such as AVMs or particular vessels. Second, there are references to attributes of these objects that describe their shape or size. Third, there are typically specifications of the spatial or topological relationships between objects. Finally, there are references to whether treatment is recommended or not. We propose the meaning representation template shown below. There is one root object:

```
[[Object(1) Attributes]
    [Object(2) Attributes]
    [Spatial/TopologicalRelationship]
    .
    .
    [Object(N) Attributes]
    [Spatial/TopologicalRelationship]
    [treatment]]
```

and many sibling objects:

```
[[Object(I) Attributes]
    [Object(J) Attributes]
    [Spatial/TopologicalRelationship]
    .
    .
    [Object(M) Attributes]
    [Spatial/TopologicalRelationship]]
```

This meaning representation is intended to be recursive in nature. We have constructed a set of rules that will map the medical text into this meaning representation.

The terms in the meaning representation will be matched to the KR in order to build a graph reconstruction from the medical report. This matching process will require a search that is analogous to that described for the vision module. The principle difference is the way in which individual matches are performed. In the vision module matches between vasculature are determined on a geometrical basis but here such matches are determined by comparison of text. We note also that the NLP module can facilitate learning of medical terminology.

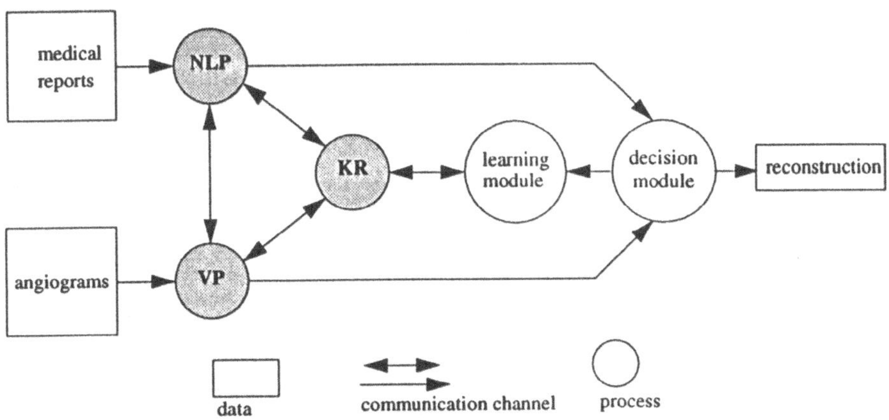

Fig. 4. The integrated system architecture.

3.4. *An integrating architecture*

The architecture of the integrated vision and language system is shown in Figure 4.

So far the KR, VP, and NLP modules have all been outlined. We now briefly discuss the operation of the decision module and the purpose of the communication channels.

Suppose the VP and NLP modules each worked independently to produce a set of reconstructions. Each of these reconstructions should be regarded as an hypothesis. We can discover where the modules agree by intersection of hypotheses. More generally we can consider Table III below.

Table III. Decision table for integrated language and vision.

$(G_{lang} \cap G_{vis})$	(G_{lang} / G_{vis})	(G_{vis} / G_{lang})	Row interpretation
∅	∅	∅	no reconstruction
∅	∅	match	vision only
∅	match	∅	language only
∅	match	match	no agreement
match	∅	∅	full agreement
match	∅	match	vision dominant
match	match	∅	language dominant
match	match	match	inconclusive

where G_{vis} and G_{lang} are the hypotheses from the VP and NLP modules respectively, ∅ is the empty set, and "match" denotes a non-empty set. Thus we see that the benefit of combining NLP and VP is that they disambiguate one another. Of the possibilities shown above the most useful has the interpretation "full agreement". In this case and when $(G_{lang} \cap G_{vis})$ is a singleton set we have an optimal result because then there is a unique solution. We argue that if the NLP and VP are allowed to communicate directly then this analysis will not be altered. This is because we have added no new information into the overall system so that no further ambiguity resolution is possible. Rather, the system will become more efficient.

4. CONCLUSION

We have described an architecture under which the power of NLP and VP are harnessed, via a single KR, for the purpose on reconstructing vasculature. Our contributions to this application are (1) a KR that is flexible and robust, (2) a novel reconstruction algorithm that is intended to yield more than one plausible result and (3) the proposal that medical reports can be used to assist reconstruction.

Future work involves closely addressing the issues of geometric matching and of learning geometrical shapes, implementing the natural language processor, and interfacing it to the visual processor.

Integrated models of vision and language processing will increase the speed and effectiveness of practical applications. More importantly, each processing module will help resolve ambiguities raised in the other. It is concluded that such investigations will not only aid in the development of practical systems but may shed light on the way in which humans integrate language and vision.

ACKNOWLEDGEMENTS

We would like to acknowledge: Ulf Bergvall of the Department of Radiology at the Royal Hallamshire Hospital; Lee Walton of the Department of Medical Physics at the Weston Park Hospital; Jim McGregor at the Department of Computer Science at the University of Sheffield; and Peter Andreae at Victoria University of Wellington for their comments on this work.

REFERENCES

André, E., Herzog, G. & Rist, T. (1988). On the Simultaneous Interpretation of Real-world Image Sequences and their Natural Language Descriptions: The System SOCCER. In Proceedings of *The 8th European Conference on Artificial Intelligence*, 449–454, Munich, Germany.

Ballard, D. H. & Brown, C. M. (1982). *Computer Vision*. Prentice-Hall, Englewood Cliffs, NJ, U.S.A.

Baud, R. H., Rassinoux, A.-M. & Scherrer, J.-R. (1991). Knowledge Representation of Discharge Summaries. In Proceedings of *The Third Conference on Artificial Intelligence in Medicine (AIME 91)*, 173–182, Maastricht, June.

Delaere, D., Smets, C., Suetens, P. & Marchal, G. (1990). A Knowledge-based System for the Angiographic Reconstruction of Blood Vessels from Two Angiographic Projections. In Proceedings of *The North Sea Conference on Biomedical Engineering*, Nov. 1990.

Garreau, M., Coatrieux, J. L., Collerec, R. & Chardenon, C. (1991). A Knowledge Based Approach for Reconstruction and Labelling of Vascular Networks from Biplane Angiographic Projections. *IEEE Transactions on Medical Imaging* **10**(2): 122–131.

Hall, P. M. (1993a). *Problems in Reconstructing Vasculature and Lesions from Angiograms*. Technical Report. CS-93-05, Department of Computer Science, University of Sheffield, GB-S1 4DP, Sheffield, England, U.K., EU.

Hall, P. M. (1993b). *A Review of Procedures for Reconstruction of the Vasculature from Angiograms*. Technical Report CS-93-06, Department of Computer Science, University of Sheffield, GB-S1 4DP, Sheffield, England, U.K., EU.

Hall, P. M. (1994a). *Simulating and Animating Flow Through a Network of Tubes*. Technical Report CS-TR-94-13. Department of Computer Science, Victoria University of Wellington, Wellington, New Zealand. Or, via ftp.comp.vuw.ac.nz/doc/vuw-publications/CS-TR-94-13, or http://www.comp.vuw.ac.nz/Publications/CS-TR-94-13.

Hall, P. M. (1994b). *Simulating Angiography*. Technical Report CS-TR-94-15. Department of Computer Science, Victoria University of Wellington, Wellington, New Zealand. Or, via ftp.comp.vuw.ac.nz/doc/vuw-publications/CS-TR-94-15, or http://www.comp.vuw.ac.nz/Publications/CS-TR-94-15.

Hall, P. M. (1994c). *Simulating Angiography, a User Manual*. Technical Report CS-TR-94-17. Department of Computer Science, Victoria University of Wellington, Wellington, New Zealand.

Or, via ftp.comp.vuw.ac.nz/doc/vuw-publications/CS-TR-94-17, or http://www.comp.vuw.ac.nz/Publications/CS-TR-94-17. Source code available from: ftp.comp.vuw.ac.nz/pub/graphics/peter/xras-1.0.tar.gz.

Hall, P. M., Brady, J., Watt, A. H., Walton, L. & Bergvall, U. (1993). Segmenting and Reconstruction of Vascular Lesions from Biplane Angiograms. In Proceedngs of *DICTA 1993*, Sydney, Macquarie University, 802–809.

Hall, P. M. & McGregor, J. J. (1993). A Graph Based Model of a Collection of Physical Vasculature. In Proceedngs of *DICTA '93, Sydney, Macquarie University*, 414–421.

Hall, P. M., Andreae, P. & Ngan, M. (1995a). Reconstruction of Blood Vessel Networks from a Few Perspective Projections. *Artificial Neural Networks and Expert Systems '95*, Dunedin, New Zealand.

Hall, P. M., Feltham, R. & Fitzjohn, T. (1995b). Automated analysis of x-ray angiograms. *New Zealand Computer Society Conference*, 1995, Wellington, New Zealand. Also in Technical Report CS-TR-94-14, Department of Computer Science, Victoria University of Wellington, Wellington, New Zealand. Or, via ftp.comp.vuw.ac.nz/doc/vuw-publications/CS-TR-94-14, or http://www.comp.vuw.ac.nz/Publications/CS-TR-94-14.

Herzog, G., Sung, C.-K., André, E., Enkelmann, W., Nagel, H.-H. & Wahlster, W. (1989). Incremental Natural Language Description of Dynamic Imagery. In Freksa, C. & Brauer, W. (eds.), *Wissenbasierte Systeme. 3. Internationaler GI-Kongress*, 153–162. Springer-Verlag: Berlin.

Herzog, G. & Retz-Schmidt, G. (1990). Das System SOCCER: Simultane Interpretation und naturalichsprachliche Beschreibung zeitveranderlicher Szenen. In Perl, J. (ed.), *Sport und Informatik*, 95–119. Hofmann: Schorndorf.

Kingsland, L. C. (ed.) (1989). The 13th Annual Symposium on Computer Applications in Medical Care, *IEEE Computer Society Press*, November.

Kosslyn, S. M. & Pomerantz J. R. (1977). Imagery, Propositions and the Form of Internal Representations. *Cognitive Psychology* **9**: 52–76.

Kunii, T. L. & Shinagawa Y. (1991). New Concepts and techniques to Integrate Diverse Application Areas. In Patrikalakis, N. M. (ed.), *Scientific Visualization of Physical Phenomena, Proc. Computer Graphics International*, 3–24. Springer-Verlag: Tokyo.

Marr, D. (1982). *Vision*. Freeman: San Francisco.

Mayhew, J. E. W. & Frisby, J. P. (1981). Physcophysical and Computational Studies Towards a Theory of Human Stereopsis. *Artificial Intelligence* **17**: 349–385.

Maaß, W., Wizinski, P. & Herzog, G. (1993). *VITRA GUIDE: Multimodal Route Descriptions for Computer Assisted Vehicle Navigation*. Bereich Nr. 93, Universitat des Saarlandes, FB 14 Informatik IV, Im Stadtwald 15, D-6600, Saarbrücken 11, Germany, EU, February.

Mc Kevitt, P. (1986). *Building Embedded Representations of Queries about UNIX*. Memorandum In Computer and Cognitive Science, MCCS-86-72, Computing Research Laboratory, Dept. 3CRL, Box 30001, New Mexico State University, Las Cruces, NM 88003-0001, U.S.A.

Mc Kevitt, P. (1990). Acquiring User Models for Natural Language Dialogue Systems through Wizard-of-Oz Techniques. In Proceedings of *The Second International Workshop on User Modeling*, University of Hawaii at Manoa, Honolulu, Hawaii, U.S.A., March.

Mc Kevitt, P. (1991a). Principles and Practice in an Operating System Consultant. In Partridge, Derek (ed.), *Artificial Intelligence and Software Engineering, Vol. 1 Chapter on 'AI Mechanisms and Techniques in Practical Software'*, Ablex Publishing Corporation: New York.

Mc Kevitt, P. (1991b). *Analysing Coherence of Intention in Natural-language Dialogue*. Ph.D. Thesis, Department of Computer Science, University of Exeter, Exeter, GB- EX4 4PT, England, EU, September.

Mc Kevitt, P. (ed.) (1992). Natural Language Processing. *Artificial Intelligence Review* **6**(4): 327–332, Dec. Kluwer-Academic Publishers: Dordrecht, The Netherlands.

Mc Kevitt, P. & Wilks, Y. (1987). Transfer Semantics in an Operating System Consultant: The Formalization of Actions Involving Object Transfer. In Proceedings of *The Tenth International Joint Conference on Artificial Intelligence (IJCAI-87)* **1**: 569–575, Milan, Italy, EU, August.

Mc Kevitt, P., Partridge, D. & Wilks, Y. (1992a). *Analysing Coherence of Intention in Natural Language Dialogue*. Technical Report 227. Department of Computer Science, University of Exeter, GB- EX4 4PT, Exeter, England, EU.

Mc Kevitt, P., Partridge, D. & Wilks, Y. (1992b). *Why Machines should Analyse Intention in Natural Language Dialogue*. Technical Report 233. Department of Computer Science, University of Exeter, GB- EX4 4PT, Exeter, England, EU.

Mc Kevitt, P., Partridge, D. & Wilks, Y. (1992c). *Experimenting with Intention in Natural Language Dialogue*. Technical Report 234. Department of Computer Science, University of Exeter, GB-EX4 4PT, Exeter, England, EU.

Mc Kevitt, P., Partridge, D. & Wilks, Y. (1992d). Approaches to Natural Language Discourse Processing. *Artificial Intelligence Review* **6**(4): 333–364, Dec. Kluwer-Academic Publishers: Dordrecht, The Netherlands.

Mery, C., Normier, B. & Ogonowski, A. (1987). INTERMED: A Medical Language Interface. In Proceedings of *The Third Conference on Artificial Intelligence in Medicine (AIME 87)*, 3–8. Springer-Verlag: Berlin.

Neumann, B. & Novak, H.-J. (1986). *NAOS: Ein System zur naturalichsprachlichen Beschreibung zeitveranderlicher Szenen*. Informatik. Forschung und Entwicklung **1**(1): 83–92.

Partridge, D. (1991). *A New Guide to Artificial Intelligence*. Ablex Publishing Corporation: Norwood, New Jersey.

Pylyshyn, Z. (1993). What the Mind's Eye Tells the Mind's Brain: A Critique of Mental Imagery. *Psychological Bulletin* **80**: 1–24.

Rake, S. T. & Smith, L. D. R. (1987). The interpretation of x-ray Angiograms using a Blackboard Control Architecture. In Proceedings of *Computer Assisted Radiology 1987*, 681–685.

Ranum, D. L. (1988). Knowledge Based Understanding of Radiology Text. In Greenes, R. A. (ed.), *The 12th Annual Symposium on Computer Applications in Medical Care*, IEEE Computer Society Press, November.

Read, R. C. & Corneil, D. G. (1977). The Graph Isomorphism Disease. *J. Graph Theory* **1**: 339–363.

Retz-Schmidt, G. (1991). Recognizing Intentions, Interactions and Causes of Plan Failures. *User Modelling and User-Adapted Interaction* **1**: 173–202.

Retz-Schmidt, G. & Tetzlaff, M. (1991). *Methods for the Intentional Description of Image Sequences*. Bereich Nr. 80, Universitat des Saarlandes, FB 14 Informatik IV, Im Stadtwald 15, D-6600, Saarbrucken 11, Germany, EU, August.

Sager, N., Friedman, C. & Lyman, M. S. (1987). *Medical Language Processing: Computer Management of Narrative Data*. Addison-Wesley: Reading, MA.

Salamon, G. & Huang, Y. P. (1976). *A Radiological Anatomy of the Brain*. Springer-Verlag: Berlin.

Schank, R. C. & Abelson, R. P. (1977). *Scripts, Plans, Goals and Understanding: An Inquiry into Human Knowledge Structures*. Lawrence Erlbaum Associates: Hillsdale, NJ.

Scherrer, J. R., Cote, R. A. & Mandil, S. D. (1989). (eds.) *Computerized Natural Language Processing for Knowledge Representation*. North-Holland: Amsterdam.

Schröder, M. (1992a). Knowledge-based Processing of Medical Language: A Language Engineering Approach. In Ohlbach, Hans-Jurgen (ed.), Preprints of the Proceedings of *The German Conference on Artificial Intelligence (GWAI-92)*, 190–199, Technical Report MP-1-92-232, Max-Planck-Institut fur Informatik, July.

Schröder, M. (1992b). Supporting Speech Processing by Expectations: A Conceptual Model of Radiological Reports to Guide the Selection of Word Hypotheses. In Gunther Gorz (ed.), *KONVENS 92-1 Konferenz, Verarbeitung naturlicher Spracher*, 119–128, Informatik aktuell, Nurnberg, October. Springer-Verlag: Berlin.

Schröder, M. (1992c). Knowledge based Analysis of Radiology Reports using Conceptual Graphs. In Pfeiffer, Heather (ed.), Proceedings of *The Seventh Annual Workshop on Conceptual Graphs*, 213–222. New Mexico State University (NMSU), Las Cruces, New Mexico, U.S.A., July.

Sowa, J.F. (1984). *Conceptual Structures: Information Processing in Mind and Machine*. Wesley: Addison.

Stansfield, S.A. (1986): ANGY: A Rule Base Expert System for Automatic segmentation of Coronary Vessels from Digital Subtracted Angiograms. *IEEE Transactions on Pattern Analysis and Machine Intelligence* **8**(2): 188–199.

Suetens, P., van Cleynenbreugel, J., Fierens, F., Smets, C., Oosterlink, A. & Wilms, G. (1987). An Expert System for Blood Vessel Segmentation on Subtraction Angiogram. *SPIE 767 Medical Imaging*, 454–459.

Wahlster, W. (1988). *One Word Says More than a Thousand Pictures.* On the Automatic Verbalization of the Results of Image Sequence Analysis. Bereich Nr. 25, Universitat des Saarlandes, FB 14 Informatik IV, Im Stadtwald 15, D-6600, Saarbrucken 11, Germany, EU, February.

Wilensky, R. (1983). *Planning and Understanding*. Addison-Wesley: Reading, MA.

Artificial Intelligence Review 10: 253–273, 1996.

Visualization of Rhythm, Time and Metre

NEIL P. McANGUS TODD[1] and GUY J. BROWN[2]

[1] *Department of Music, University of Sheffield, Sheffield S10 2TN, U.K. (Current address: Department of Psychology, University of Manchester, Manchester M13 9PL, U.K.; E-mail: todd@hera.psy.man.ac.uk);* [2] *Department of Computer Science, University of Sheffield, Sheffield S10 STN, U.K.; E-mail: g.brown@dcs.shef.ac.uk*

Abstract. Developments in the theory of auditory processing of rhythmic signals have enabled the construction of a robust algorithm for recovery of rhythmic grouping structure. This algorithm appears to be effective for both speech and music signals. The theory upon which the algorithm was based was inspired by the theory of edge detection in vision. The output of the algorithm can be visualised in the form of a "rhythmogram", examples of which are shown for a variety of speech signals. The relationship between rhythm, time perception and metre is discussed in the light of a recent "auditory-motor" theory of beat induction.

Key words: rhythm, time perception, metre, beat induction, temporal grouping, prosody

INTRODUCTION

Prosody plays a vital role in speech comprehension since it can assist in the segmentation of utterances into phrases and syllables, and in resolving syntactic or semantic ambiguities. A computational model for the recovery of prosodic structure from a speech signal would therefore be of great value for the goals of comprehension and synthesis. Such a model, in the form of a multi-scale analysis, has recently been developed (Todd 1994; Todd and Brown 1994). This model was inspired by the theory of edge detection in low-level vision (Marr 1982). The basic idea, in the case of vision, is that following retinal transduction the optical signal is blurred over a range of spatial scales by a number Gaussian low-pass filters. Edges are detected by looking for zero-crossings in the second derivative of the Gaussian which has a characteristic "Mexican hat" shape. Information from each of these spatial channels can be combined to form a higher representation.

In the case of hearing it is possible to do a similar computation on a simulation of the auditory nerve response. The essential difference is that the low-pass filtering is done in time rather than space. The result of such a computation can be represented in a number of ways. One way is to plot the output of each low-pass filter to form an "energy flux surface" in a three dimensional (energy, time, time-constant) space. Another way is to plot zero-crossing points of the derivatives of the low-pass response. This can be done either in the energy/time plane or the time-constant/time plane. Such a representation, referred to as a "rhythmogram", in case of the time-constant/time projection, resembles the trees used in the phonological analysis of prosody (Liberman and Prince 1977; Selkirk 1984). In this paper we describe this algorithm and its relationship to a more general "auditory-motor" theory of rhythm and metre.

I. RHYTHM AND METRE IN MUSIC AND SPEECH

It is generally agreed that rhythm in music can be described by two hierarchical structures – *grouping*, the organisation of events into well-defined sections, phrases, motifs, etc. and *metre*, a regularly repeating pattern of strong and weak beats. It is no accident that some theories of rhythm in speech (Geigerich 1985; Selkirk 1984) similarly require two complementary components (although there are some differences in the way they are defined), since they are based on the premise that speech rhythm is analogous to musical rhythm. According to Selkirk (1984) a phonological representation is formed by a *prosodic constituent structure*, which refers to the grouping of linguistic units such as the syllable into higher level units including the foot and phonological phrase, and a *metrical grid*, which represents a "hierarchy of temporal periodicities". (In practise though, metrical grids in speech are measures of relative stress, rather than periodicity.)

Whilst both grouping and metre are important for the description of rhythm, computational models of rhythm perception in the case of music have concentrated, almost exclusively, on the metrical component (Longuet-Higgins and Steedman 1971; Longuet-Higgins and Lee 1982, 1984; Lee 1991; Povel and Essens 1985; Desain 1992; Rosenthal 1992; Large 1994; Parncutt 1994). A further characteristic of all these models is that they start with a very abstract, symbolic representation of the musical signal, which has been already segmented into discrete events. One danger of this approach is to fall into the trap of believing that rhythmic beats are isochronous.

Another, more empirical approach has been to measure the subtle variations in timing during rhythmic performance. For example Sloboda (1983) has shown that musicians communicate metre by making tones falling on intended strong beats, longer, louder and more legato. Further, it is well known in performance analysis (Seashore 1938; Shaffer 1981; Todd 1985, 1989, 1992; Clarke 1988; Repp 1990, 1992) that expressive performance involves large modulations of tempo and that the modulations themselves carry important information about structure. Most metrical models simply cannot deal with such large tempo variations (but see Todd (1995) for further discussion of expressive timing and dance music).

In some ways this division, between abstract models of metre induction and empirical analysis of music performance, parallels the historical division of speech science into phonology on the one hand, and phonetics on the other (Cutler and Ladd 1983). The phonological approach has been concerned with the place of prosody in linguistic structure and defines as prosodic "any phenomena that involve phonological organisation above the segment" (Cutler and Ladd 1983). The phonetic approach defines prosody in more physical terms, as "those phenomena that involve the acoustic parameters of pitch, duration and intensity".

It has been realised for some time though, that a proper understanding of speech prosody requires an integration of the phonological and phonetic views (Kingston and Beckman 1990). Similarly in music research, attempts are being made to bring together the abstract and the more psychoacoustic approaches (Leman 1994). The model of rhythm perception advocated here falls into this category (Todd 1994a; Todd and Lee 1994).

II. A MULTI-SCALE MODEL OF RHYTHM PERCEPTION

As discussed above the inspiration for the model was the work of David Marr and co-workers in the theory of low-level vision. Before describing the model then, the theory of vision is briefly reviewed.

II.1. *Review of The Theory of Low-Level Vision*

In the theory of vision as proposed by Marr the first stage in the detection of edges involves blurring the image I by convolution with a Gaussian low-pass filter g. A 2-D Gaussian function is given by

$$(1) \qquad g(r, \sigma) = \frac{1}{\sigma\sqrt{2\pi}} \exp[-r^2/2\sigma^2],$$

where r is *radius* and σ is a *space-constant.* Since it is not possible to capture all information about intensity changes in a single convolution operation this blurring or smoothing process is carried out over a range of scales. In other words the image is convolved with a number of Gaussian functions with a range of space-constants $\{\sigma_k | k = 0 \ldots N - 1\}$.

The next stage in edge detection involves differentiating the smoothed versions of the image and looking for either peaks in the first derivative or zero-crossings of the second derivative which in the 2-D case is given by the Laplacian operator ∇^2. Since this is a linear operation it can be taken inside the convolution so that effectively the image is convolved with

$$(2) \qquad \nabla^2 g(r) = \frac{-1}{\pi\sigma^4}\left(1 - \frac{r^2}{2\sigma^2}\right) \exp[-r^2/2\sigma^2],$$

which has a characteristic "Mexican hat" shape.

A symbolic description of the image, which Marr refers to as the *primal sketch,* could then be parsed from sets of zero-crossings from different channels over a range of scales. The actual rules for combining different channels are quite complicated. However, the basic principle is that if different channels agree on the spatial position of a zero-crossing segment then they can be combined to form a description of a single phenomenon. This principle is referred to as the *spatial coincidence* assumption.

II.2. *A Temporal Analog to Low-Level Vision*

The simplest way of applying the visual analogy is to substitute *time t* for radius and *time-constant* τ for space-constant to obtain a function $g(t, \tau)$ which has the properties of a Gaussian low-pass impulse response. Then substitute *signal power* $|x(t)|^2$ for image intensity. In this way a smoothed or "windowed" measure of the *power density* $S(t)$ may be obtained by convolution of the impulse function with the signal energy, i.e.

$$(3) \qquad S_g(t) = g(t, \tau) * |x(t)|^2 = \int_0^\infty g(t', \tau)\, |x(t - t')|^2 \, dt'.$$

Like the visual case it is not possible to capture all information about energy changes in a single channel. This smoothing operation is therefore carried out over a range of time-constants $\{\tau_k | k = 0 \ldots N - 1\}$ and thus we obtain a measure of the *power density spectrum* $S_g(t, \tau_k)$. Finally, to complete the analogy, the direct temporal analogue of the ∇^2 operator used for edge detection (Marr 1982), i.e. d^2/dt^2, can be used involving the condition

$$(4) \qquad \frac{d^2}{dt^2} S_g(t, \tau_k) = 0 \quad \text{and} \quad \frac{d}{dt} S_g(t, \tau_k) > 0.$$

The product of such an analysis, if carried out over a suitable range of time-constants, is a single hierarchical structure whose terminal elements are the onsets of individual events. As the time-constants are gradually increased, more and more detail is smoothed out so that eventually the sequence will be "reduced" to a single event.

There are two fundamental reasons why the simple analogue of visual processing cannot be a good model of auditory processing. The first is that the auditory system is causal. It is not possible to physically realise the Gaussian ideal as a causal system. The second reason is that the peripheral auditory system first carries out a frequency analysis via the basilar membrane followed by transduction by hair-cells which are subject to adaptation. A realistic model of rhythm perception must therefore take into account the effect of this transformation on any incoming signal (Figure 1).

II.3. *A Multi-Scale Auditory Model*

In the first stage of the proposed model, the transfer function of the outer and middle ears is approximated by a simple high-pass filter. The frequency selective properties of the basilar membrane are modelled by a bank of gammatone filters (Patterson *et al.* 1988) spaced according to the ERB-rate scale of Glasberg and Moore (1990). Each of the cochlear channels are then processed by the Meddis (1986) inner hair-cell model which gives the auditory nerve firing probability (Brown 1992; Brown and Cooke 1994).

In the second stage, the auditory nerve response is pooled across frequency and passed to a multi-scale Gaussian low-pass filter system. The Gaussian filters were based on an analogue polynomial approximation to the Gaussian ideal

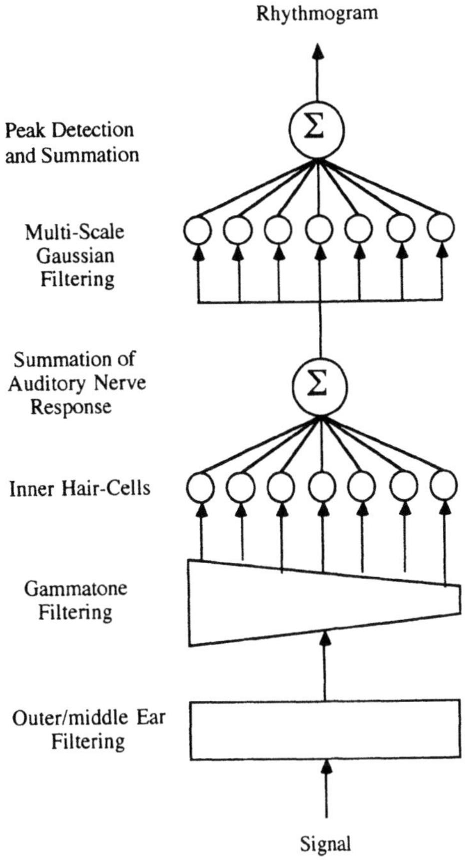

Fig. 1. The "rhythmogram" algorithm.

(Dishal 1957). These were then discretized by using a bilinear transformation to form an efficient digital IIR form. It turns out that these polynomial approximations are quite close to the gamma distribution

$$(5) \qquad g(\tau;\, t,\, n) = \frac{t^{n-1}}{(n-1)\tau^n} \exp[-t/\tau],$$

where n is the order of approximation. Thus, for example, when $n = 1$ the impulse response is just that of a 1st order low-pass filter or leaky integrator. Figure 2 shows the response of a bank of 8th order Gaussian approximation filters to a 50 ms pulse.

The last stage of the model involves looking for peaks in the low-pass response, or zero-crossings of the 1st derivative of the low-pass response (Figure 3) (equation (5)), i.e.

$$(6) \qquad \frac{\mathrm{d}}{\mathrm{d}t} S_g(t;\, \tau_k,\, n) = 0 \quad \text{and} \quad \frac{\mathrm{d}^2}{\mathrm{d}t^2} S_g(t;\, \tau_k,\, n) < 0.$$

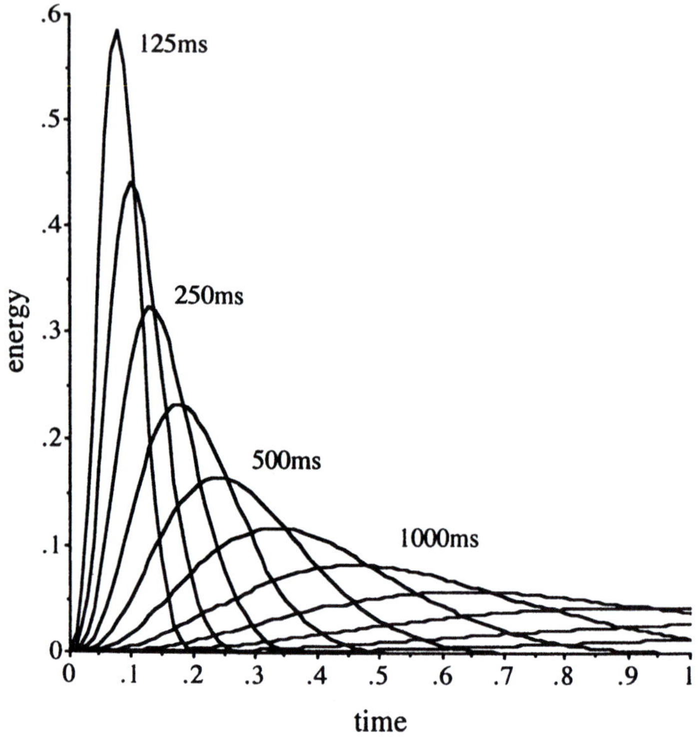

Fig. 2. The response of a Gaussain filter-bank to a 50 ms unit pulse. Each filter is an 8th order Taylor series approximation. The time-constants range from 125 to 400 ms. The sampling rate is 100 Hz.

When these points are plotted in a time-constant/time graph they give rise to a representation referred to as a rhythmogram, examples of which are shown in the next section.

It should be noted also that the rhythmograms obtained give a picture of the temporal grouping of identified segments. The actual boundaries between segments are obtained by looking for troughs, rather than peaks, in the sound energy flux. That is when

$$(7) \qquad \frac{d}{dt} S_g(t, \tau_k, n) = 0 \quad \text{and} \quad \frac{d^2}{dt^2} S_g(t, \tau_k, n) > 0,$$

over a range of time-constants $\{\tau_k | k = 0 \ldots N-1\}$. However, since the boundary structures have a one-one relationship with the temporal grouping structures they are omitted here (but see Todd (1994a) for examples).

One way of interpreting this mechanism is as a form of sensory memory. From this point of view the low-pass responses may be seen as representing the overall distribution of neural activity as one ascends the central auditory system. Thus, according to this view, very close to the periphery, after an input burst, the overall

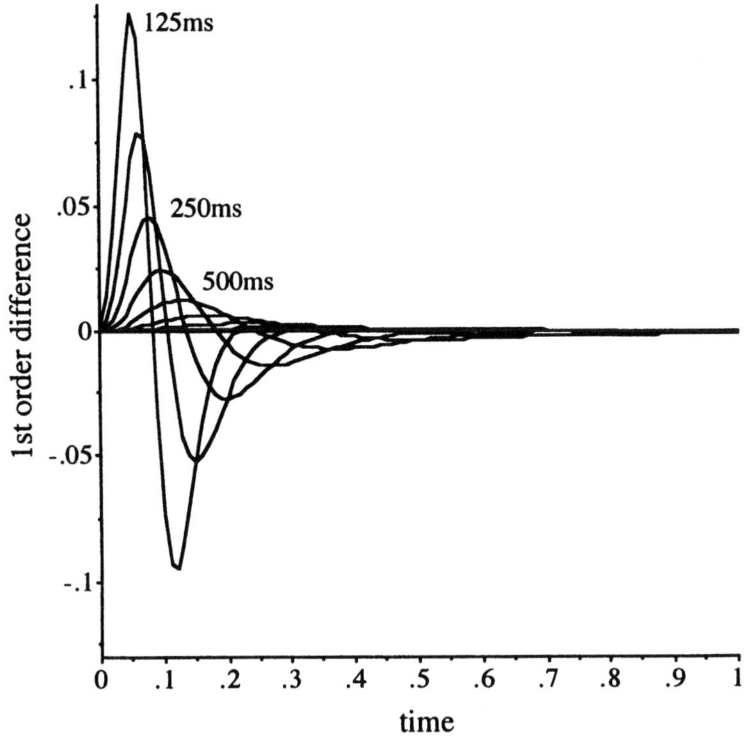

Fig. 3. The first derivative response of a Gaussain filter-bank as in Figure 2.

activity is very sharply defined in time. As activity spreads into the system though, the distribution becomes more diffuse. The increasing time-constant in this picture then, corresponds to the "distance" from the periphery at which a "snap-shot" is taken of the distribution of overall activity (Todd 1994b). In other words, the behaviour becomes more low-pass the further one ascends the system.

III. RHYTHMOGRAM ANALYSIS OF PROSODIC STRUCTURE

In order to demonstrate the behaviour of the mutiscale mechanism in this section we look at a number of example analyses. The analyses are classified as large scale and small scale according to the time scale of interest. In the case of the large scale the smallest phonological constituent we are interested in is the phrase. For the small scale the smallest constituent is the syllable or phoneme.

III.1. *Structure of Individual Words*

Since the work of Liberman and Prince (1977) it has become standard practise in metrical phonology to represent they rhythmic structure of an utterance in the form of a tree. In most cases these metrical trees are strictly binary so that the relationship between a strong and a weak syllable may be either SW or WS (Figure 4 left). We refer to this representation as the binary tree (BT) approach. Lerdahl and Jackendoff (1983) have suggested an alternative representation refered to as a time-span reduction (TSR) (Figure 4 right). Although this was developed primarily to describe musical structure, Lerdahl and Jackendoff have suggested that it may also be useful for speech rhythm. In this section we show three examples of rhythmograms compared in each case to the Liberman and Prince and Lerdahl and Jackendoff representations.

According to the standard theory a core syllable (Sy) can be structured hierarchically into an onset (On) and a rhyme (Rh). The rhyme of a syllable further divides into the syllable peak (Pe) or nucleus and a coda (Co). The standard phonological approach represents this as in Figure 5a left (Giegerich 1985) whilst the time-span equivalent is shown in Figure 5a right.

Figure 5c shows a rhythmogram for the word "clamp". This has clearly segmented the onset, peak and coda. However, the rhythmogram looks more like the time-span reduction, but with one main essential difference. The outer stop consonants /k/ and /p/ have a greater prominence than /l/ and /m/ – a clear contradiction of the sonority principle.

This next example (Figure 6) looks at the tri-syllabic word "pa-me-la". The stress clearly falls on the first syllable. In this example the rhythmogram shows a striking resemblance to the time-span reduction. There is a very clear syllabification and the stressed syllable has been clearly identified.

The next level of phonological organisation above the syllable is the foot (Ft). The third example (Figure 7) is the word "re-con-ci-li-a-tion" which contains three feet according to conventional analysis. Each foot has two syllables the first of which is stressed.

Again we may see strong similarities between the rhythmogram and the time-span reduction but with two main differences. First, the particular speaker has divided the word into two feet of four and two syllables, rather than three feet of two syllables. Thus the two most prominent syllables are "re" and "a".

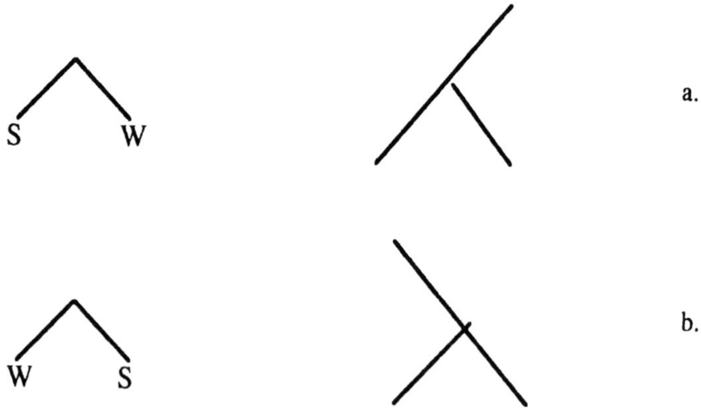

Fig. 4. Strong-weak vs weak-strong stress relationships. Liberman and Prince's representation (left) vs Lerdahl and Jackendoff's equivalent time-span representation (right).

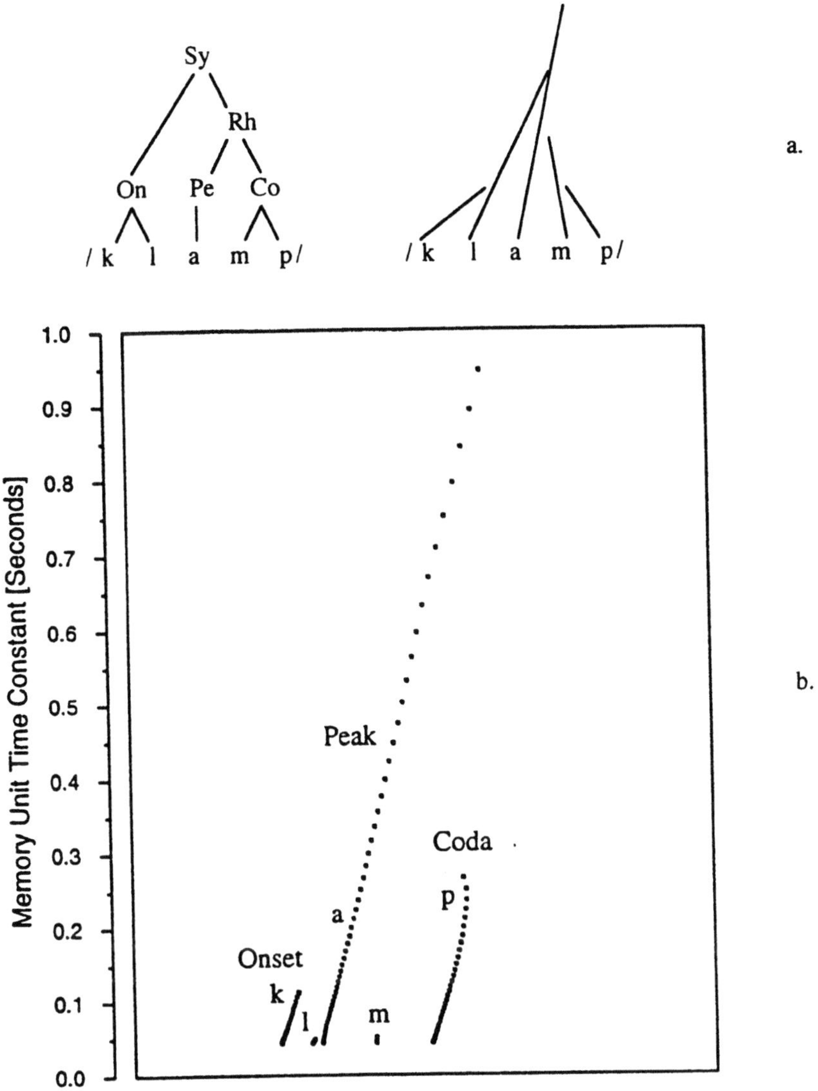

Fig. 5. (a) Conventional vs Lerdahl and Jackendoff representation of a syllable. (b) Rhythmogram of monosyllabic word "clamp".

Second, there are a number of individual phoneme segments which have the same, if not more prominence than some of the weak syllables, the last nasal /n/ is a clear example.

III.2. *Structure of Complete Utterances*

The case of large scale phonology although in principle the same as small scale, in practise, because of the large time-scale, it is convenient to compute the

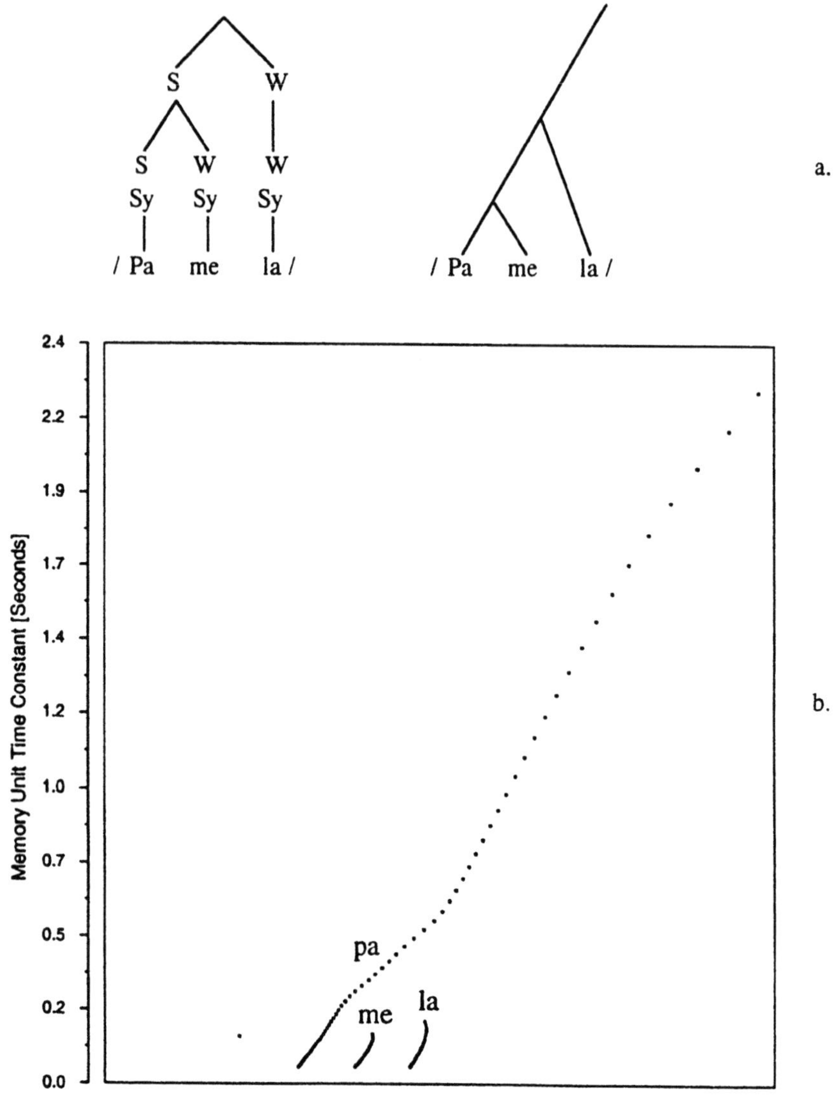

Fig. 6. (a) BT vs TSR for the tri-syllabic word "pamela". (b) Rhythmogram of word "pamela".

rhythmograms from the total energy rather than the nerve simulation. The input to the system is an analog signal $x(t)$ which is full-wave rectified $|x(t)|$ then integrated with a user-selectable cut-off frequency. Since rhythmic phenomena typically have a range of frequencies from 10–0.01 Hz this cut-off is also usually low, about 50 Hz. The output of the analog front-end is then sampled, forming the input to a digital filter-bank. Since the frequency content of the input signal is low we can sample at a low rate, typically about 100 Hz, thus saving massively on computation time and storage space.

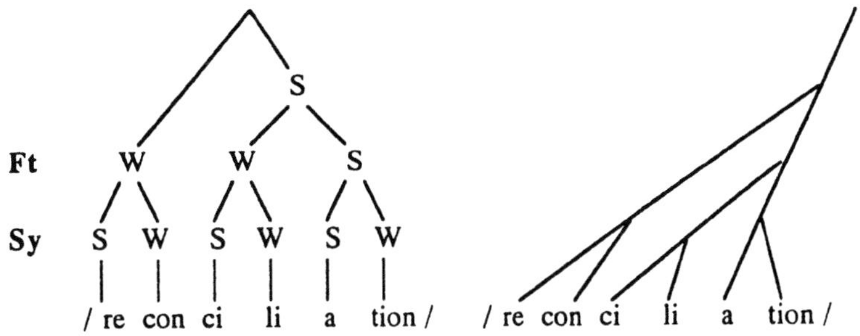

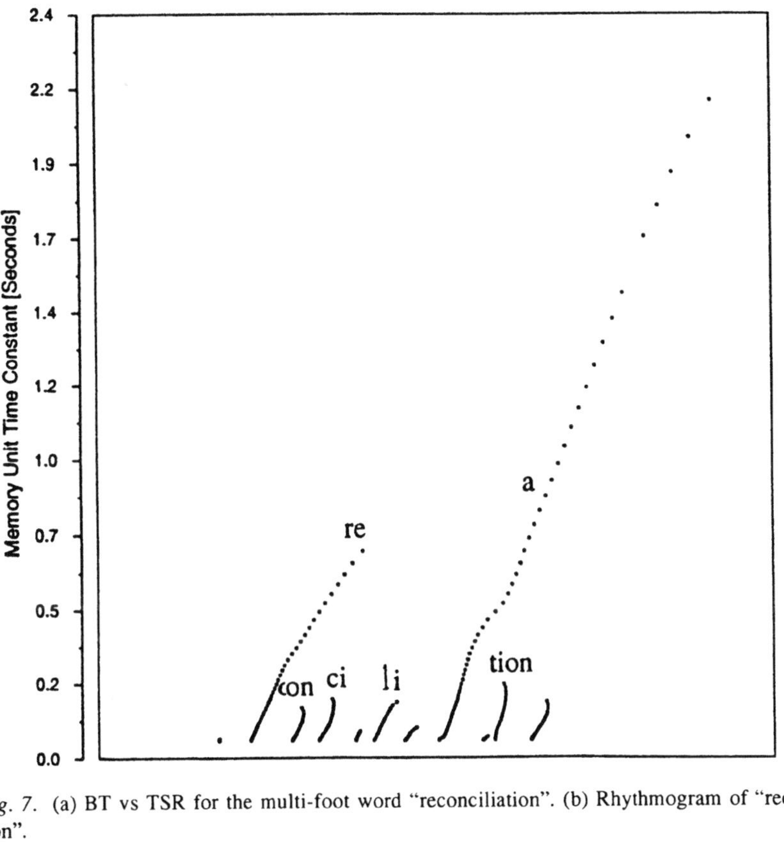

Fig. 7. (a) BT vs TSR for the multi-foot word "reconciliation". (b) Rhythmogram of "reconciliation".

In this section two examples are shown of large time-scale prosody. The first example is a recital of a poem by Thomas Hardy by a male professional actor, the second is a performance the Chopin Prelude Op. 28 No. 7 by a concert pianist.

Hardy Poem "To the Moon"

The poem (Hardy 1923) can be analysed to consist of four iambic anisometric stanzas of seven lines (Figure 8) which are denoted by V_1, V_2, V_3 and V_4. Each

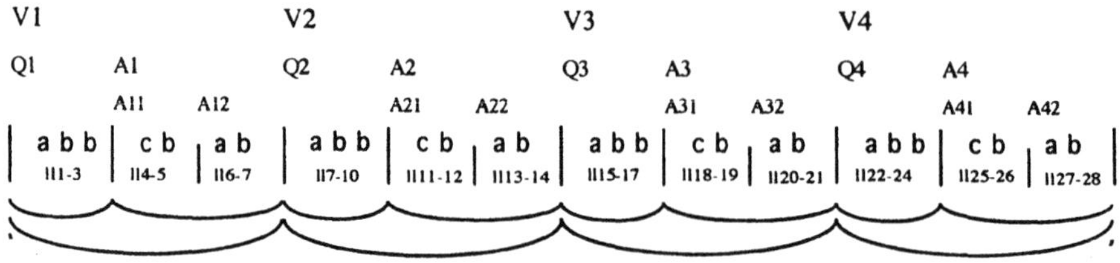

Fig. 8. A conventional metrical analysis of the Hardy Poem "To the Moon".

stanza is neatly sub-divided into a question and answer part which take three and four lines respectively, (Q ? A). There are two rhyme patterns per stanza, a and b, which occur in lines with an irregular number of stressed syllables or feet (denoted by superscript). The answer section seems also to divide naturally into two parts (A_1, A_2) with the b^2 forming a cadence. The rhymes are distributed as $Q \rightarrow (a^3, b^2, b^3)?$, $A_1 \rightarrow (c^4\ b^2)$, $A_2 \rightarrow (a^4, b^2)$. This subdivision is further strengthened by the fact that there is no syntactic break at the end of c^4.

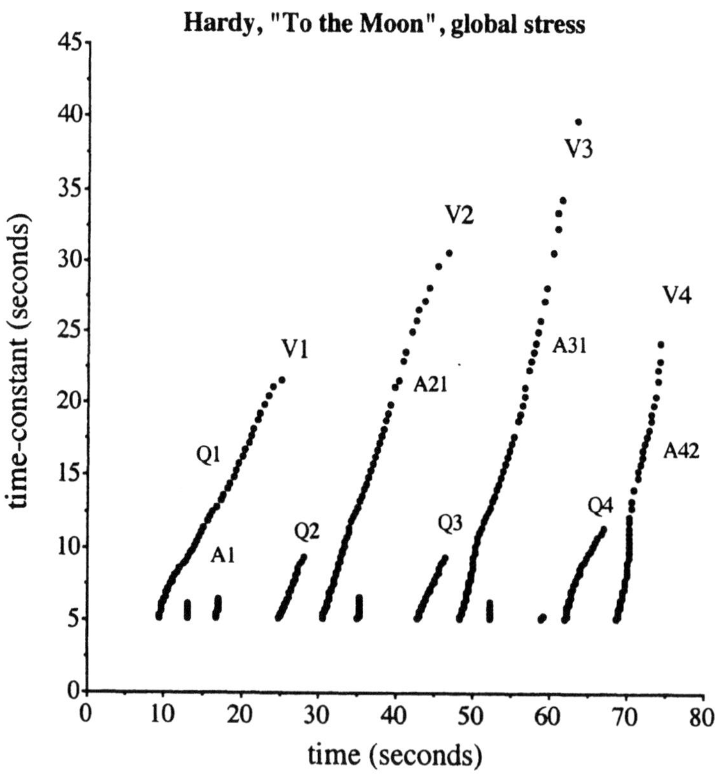

Fig. 9. Rhythmogram showing the high level prosodic structure from a performance of the Hardy Poem "To the Moon".

The rhythmogram has clearly resolved the global prosody of the poem. The rhythmogram also suggests a clear pattern of relative importance between the *Q* and *A* sections.

Chopin Prelude Op. 28

Figure 10 shows a conventional analysis of the Prelude Op. 28, No. 7. At the highest level it consists of two 8-bar sections A_1 and A_2. Each of the sections contain four 2-bar phrases p_1, p_2, p_3, p_4. In the first section there is one harmonic change per phrase consisting of V-I-V-I. Whilst the second section parallels the first p_1*, p_2*, p_3*, p_4*, the harmonic rhythm is doubled in the inner two phrases, p_2* and p_3*, to allow insertion of a "tonicization" of the supertonic so that the harmony consists of V-I (V/ii-ii) V-I (see Lerdahl and Jackendoff 1983).

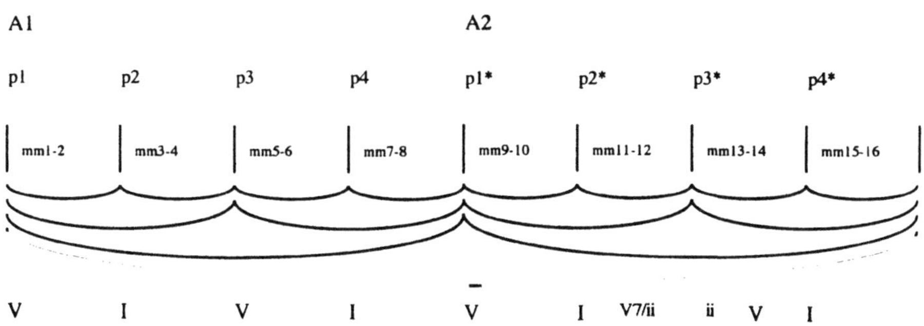

Fig. 10. A conventional musical analysis of the Chopin Prelude Op. 28 No. 7.

Figure 11 shows the rhythmogram structure obtained from a sample of a performance by a concert pianist. It can be seen that this structure neatly picks out the phrasal grouping structure. Further, the rhythmogram reflects the hierarchical organisation of the phrases in the Prelude and gives a measure of the relative importance of the phrases within the structure. According to this analysis the climax of the whole piece is the F-sharp dominant seventh chord (V7 of ii) in section A_2 phrase p_2*.

IV. RHYTHM AND METRE

Although it is beyond the scope of this paper to properly cover the issue of metre, for the purpose of being able to see the previous work in relation to the complete theory of rhythm, we discuss the basic outline of the theory.

IV.1. *An Auditory-Motor Theory*

Elsewhere an auditory-motor model (Todd and Lee 1994) has been proposed which has the following architecture (see Figure 12): (1) An *Auditory System*, which consists of (a) peripheral processing and (b) central processing in the form of band-pass and low-pass AM processes (including the multi-scale model

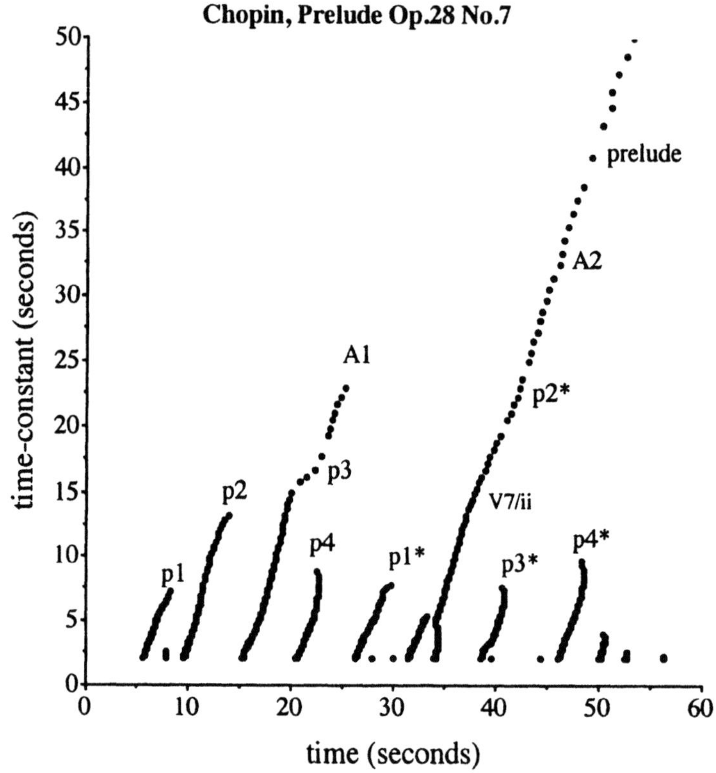

Fig. 11. Rhythmogram showing the hierarchical phrase structure from a performance of the Chopin Prelude Op. 28 No. 7.

above); (2) A *Motor System*, which consists of (a) sensory-motor filters representing the global dynamics of the motor system, (b) a central-pattern generator which is centrally programmed and (c) an output system; (3) An *Interpretation and Control System*, which both combines information from the various auditory processes and programs the central pattern generator.

IV.2. *Auditory Processes*

It has now been realised that the multi-scale process described above can be seen as a component of a more general theory. The basic idea of the more general theory is that following transduction a number of populations of cells responsive to amplitude modulation (AM) at different levels of the auditory system extract information from temporal patterns in the auditory nerve response. A similar scheme has been proposed for auditory segregation (Yost and Sheft 1993). Neurophysiology suggests perhaps three or four levels, including the cochlear nucleus, inferior colliculus, thalamus and cortex – the cut-off frequency becoming lower the higher one ascends the system (Popper and Fay 1992). A priori, the uncertainty principle dictates that two types of AM processes must

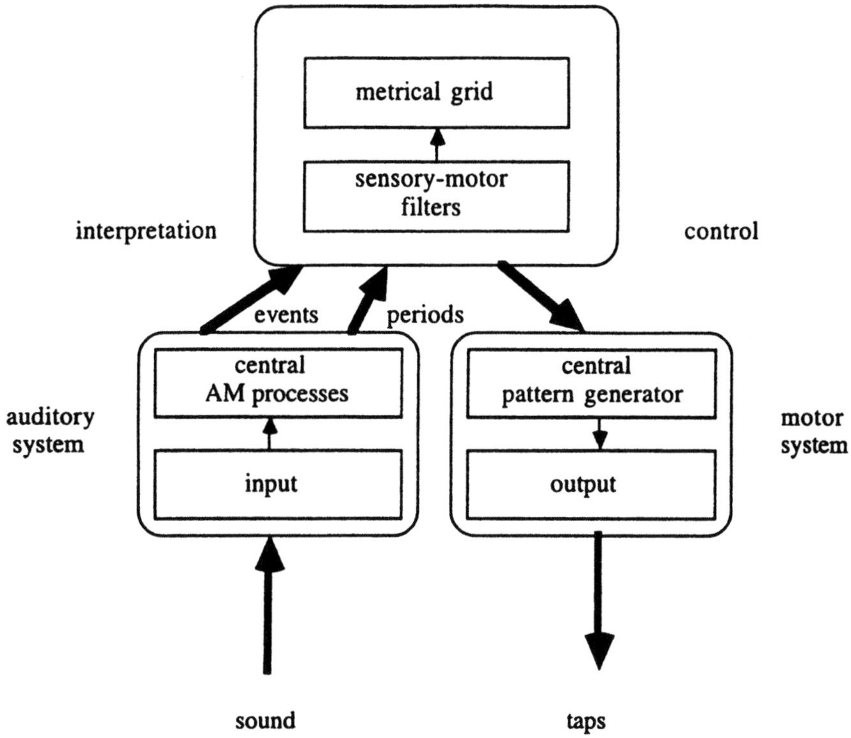

Fig. 12. An auditory-motor model of rhythm and metre.

exist, i.e. low-pass and band-pass, since it is not possible to simultaneously localise an event in time and obtain information on event periodicity. Given such a division, it is possible to classify the various psychophysical processes accordingly. Thus, on the one hand, phenomena such as temporal grouping (Todd 1994a) of multiple events or temporal integration (Todd 1994b) for single events can be viewed as the product of a low-pass process, whereas, on the other hand, phenomena such as periodicity pitch or tempo sensitivity can be seen as the product of a band-pass type process. Despite the apparent diversity of these phenomena, the general computational theory describing the behaviour of the underlying AM process may be seen in three stages for each case: (1) the nerve response is decomposed by an array of low/band-pass filters; (2) the decomposition is coded in terms of zero-crossings and has three dimensions (firing rate, AM frequency, time) so that three sorts of information are available – (a) phase (AM frequency, time), (b) amplitude (firing rate, time) and (c) spectrum (firing rate, AM frequency); (3) the zero-crossings are accumulated in a sensory memory which has a decay time-constant.

The multi-scale mechanism proposed earlier is just one example of a central low-pass AM process. This process provides information on onsets, loudness and grouping. However, it turns out that in order assign a metrical description to a rhythmic pattern it is necessary to compute the periodicity content of the rhythm by means of a population of cells, assumed to be at the level of the auditory cortex, which behave as a bank of band-pass filters of AM. Similarly to the low-pass process the pooled nerve response is processed by a bank of band-pass filters of AM spaced at 24 per octave with a range 0.5 to 20 Hz. The impulse response of the filters are those of damped simple harmonic motion, i.e. exponentially decaying cosines, with a Q of about 3 so that the decay is quite rapid. The output of each filter is represented by only peak responses, i.e. it is assumed that at the neurophysiological level the response of a band-pass unit is in the form of a series of spike trains. The peak responses across the filter-bank are stored in a buffer which simulates a "sensory memory". Since the Q of the band-pass units is quite small the sensory memory also decays quite rapidly. Figure 13 shows the overall responses for a single time interval of 600 ms.

Time Perception

In addition to the neurophysiological evidence further support is given to this component of the theory since it able to account for tempo sensitivity (Drake and Botte 1993). Figure 14 shows the predicted sensitivity for single time intervals. According to this model the auditory system is maximally sensitive to intervals of between 300 and 600 ms because the fundamental period and its harmonics are maximally represented in a population of cortical units which

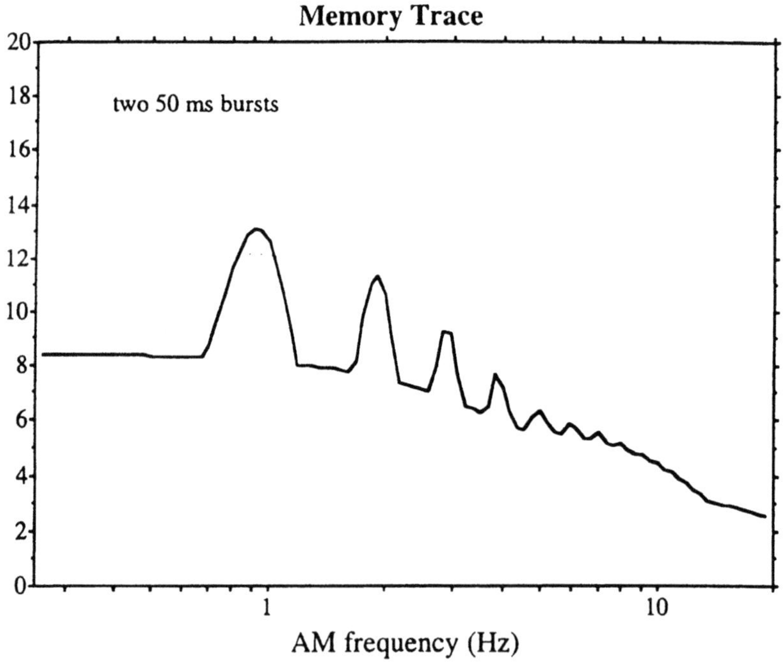

Fig. 13. The spectrum induced in the band-pass of AM process by a pair of 50 ms tone bursts with IOI 600 ms. Thus, a single (empty) time interval is represented in the form of a harmonic series.

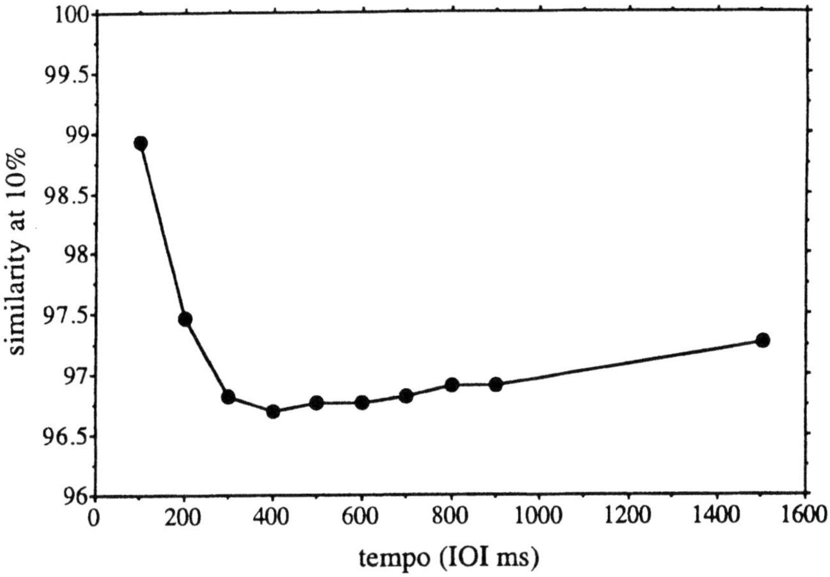

Fig. 14. The predicted tempo sensitivity curve for single intervals by the band-pass of AM process. Similarity is computed from the correlation coefficient between spectra induced by intervals which differ by 10%, e.g. 100 ms IOI and 110 ms IOI.

functionally behave as a bank of band-pass filters of AM whose range is approximately 0.5 to 20 Hz. For fundamental periods shorter than about 300 ms the harmonics become attenuated and for fundamental periods longer than about 1000 ms the fundamental becomes attenuated. Sensitivity increases with increasing interval number because the cortical units take time to build a resonance. However, sensitivity as a function of interval number reaches an asymptote quite quickly because the cortical units have a finite and small Q.

IV.3. *Motor Processes: Phase-locking a "Foot-tapper"*

After a short time for any fixed rhythm the auditory system will have produced both phasic (i.e. low-pass) and periodicity (i.e. band-pass) AM images. This enables an interpretation and control system to construct a motor programme for a foot-tapper which may be synchronised with stressed elements in the image. The basic procedure then, for metrical induction in the model, is the following: (1) set the tactus period equal to the strongest resonance in the band-pass sensory memory which is closest to the natural frequency of motor output; (2) lock the tactus phase to the most stressed event in the low-pass sensory memory within the time-span of the tactus period.

The natural frequency of the motor output system is represented in the form of a bio-mechanical filter which models the dynamics of the system during locomotion or foot tapping. It turns out that the sensitivity of the auditory system to tempo is coincident with the natural frequency of the motor system – perhaps a product of the coevolution of the auditory and motor systems.

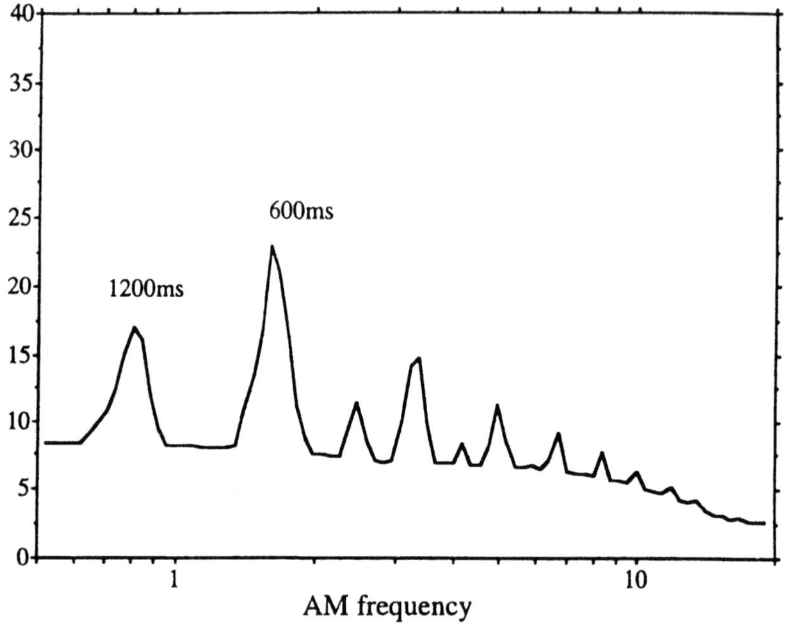

Fig. 15. The spectrum induced in the band-pass of AM process by an isochronous sequence of 50 ms tone bursts with a binary stressed/unstressed pattern.

As an example, the response of the model to a binary stressed-unstressed pattern is shown in Figures 15 and 16. Research is currently being undertaken to investigate the behaviour of the model to metrical verse recital.

V. CONCLUSION

We have demonstrated, albeit for a small set of data, that the multi-scale mechanism provides a method for the visualisation of rhythm in the form of a "rhythmogram" at all levels of rhythmic structure, from individual phonemes to the structure of a complete poem. A number of important issues have been raised.

(1) Rhythmogram structures are not as simple as BTs. Are these differences purely to do with the individual variation of the speakers, or do they suggest a more fundamental difference, between an acoustically based representation on the one hand, and a more abstract schema based representation on the other?

(2) Whilst there are often striking differences with the BTs, the rhythmograms often show equally striking similarities with TSRs. This seems to suggest that Lerdahl and Jackendoff's approach is closer to the perceptual reality than the idealised structures of conventional metrical phonology. This view is strengthened by the fundamental similarity of large-scale musical and stanzaic grouping structure.

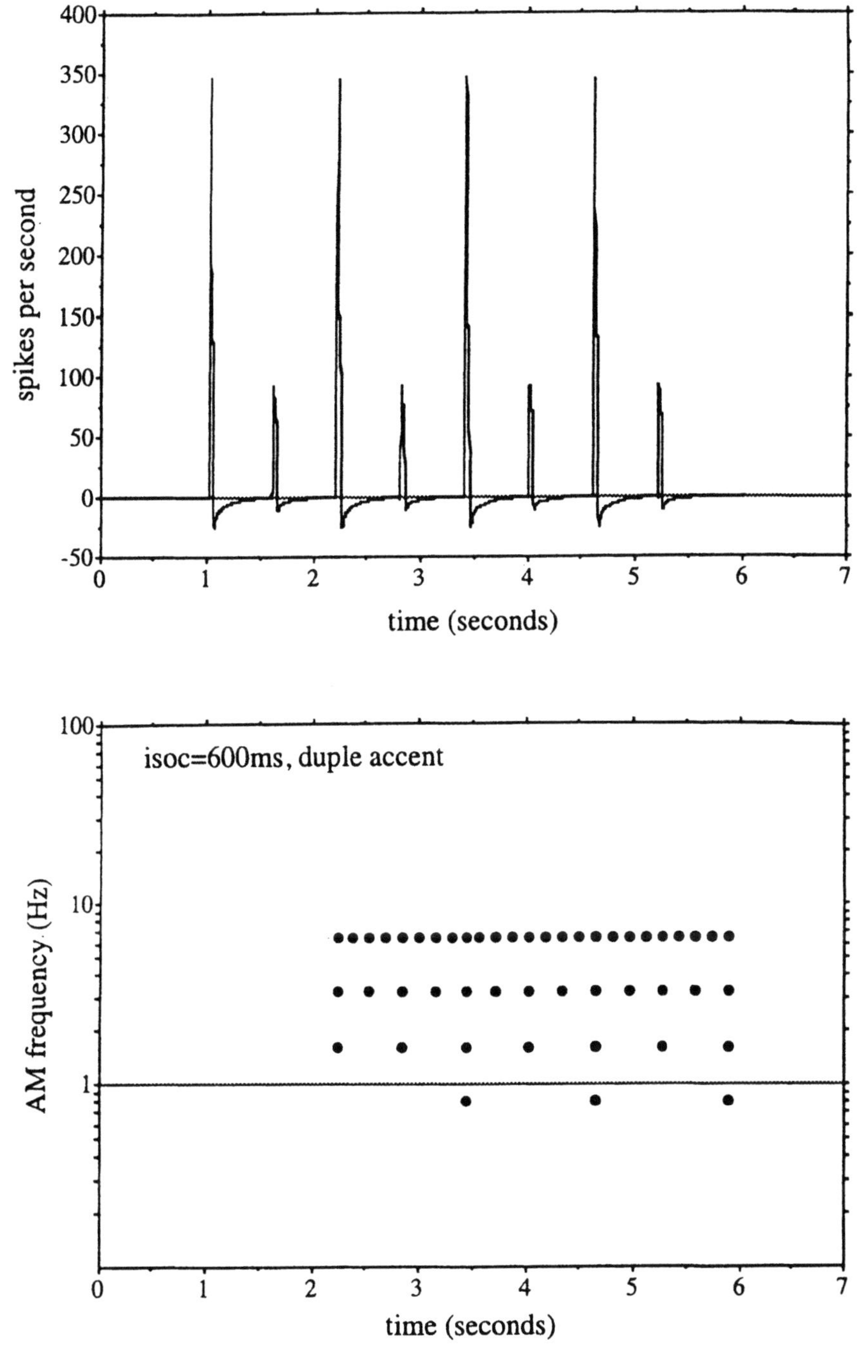

Fig. 16. Hair-cell input (top) vs the metrical-grid output (bottom) of the model for a binary stressed/unstressed pattern.

(3) A fundamental difference though with either BTs or TSRs is that the edges which make up the rhythmogram have a right slope – a consequence of the causality of the Gaussian filters – unlike the TSR which may have left and right sloping.
(4) There are many occasions when onset or coda consonant phonemes may have greater prominence in structure than an unstressed vowel, which is counter to the sonority principle. Does this suggest that the sonority theory may have to be revised? Or again, does this suggest that the acoustic level is an inappropriate level for the comparison with phonological principles.

It is too early yet to be able to say if such visualisations will be of benefit for the assistance of comprehension. However, given their high degree of similarity to conventional analyses the use of rhythmograms is surely an area worthy of further research. Finally, given that the starting point was the analogy to edge detection in vision, the success of the rhythmogram algorithm lends further support to the view that the approach advocated by Marr is entirely appropriate for perceptual computation in general.

ACKNOWLEDGEMENT

Research supported by MRC grant G9018013.

REFERENCES

Brown, G. J. (1992). *Computational Auditory Scene Analysis: A Representational Approach.* Ph.D. Thesis, University of Sheffield.
Brown, G. J. & Cooke, M. (1994). Perceptual Grouping of Musical Sounds: A Computational Model. *J. New Music Research.*
Clarke, E. (1988). Generative Principles in Musical Performance. In Sloboda, J. (ed.) *Generative Processes in Music: The Psychology of Performance, Improvisation and Composition.* Oxford: Claredon Press.
Cutler, A. & Ladd, D. R. (1983). *Prosody: Models and Measurement.* Springer-Verlag: Berlin.
Desain, P. (1992). A (De) Composable Theory of Rhythm Perception. *Music Perception* **9**: 439–454.
Dishal, M. (1959). Gaussian Response Filter Design. *Electrical Communications* **36**(1): 3–26.
Drake, C. & Botte, M. (1993). Tempo Sensitivity in Auditory Sequences: Evidence for a Multiple-Look Model. *Perception and Psychophysics* **54**(3): 277–286.
Geigerich, H. J. (1985). *Metrical Phonology and Phonological Structure.* Cambridge University Press: Cambridge.
Glasberg, B. & Moore, B. (1990). Derivation of Auditory Filter Shapes from Notched-Noise Data. *Hearing Research* **47**: 103–138.
Hardy, T. (1923). *Collected Poems of Thomas Hardy.* Vol. I. London: Macmillan.
Kingston, J. & Beckman, M. E. (1990). *Papers in Laboratory Phonology: Between the Grammar and Physics of Speech.* CUP: Cambridge.
Large, E. (1994). The Resonant Dynamics of Beat Tracking and Meter Perception. Proceedings of *The International Computer Music Conference.* Denmark: Aarhaus.
Lee, C. S. (1991). Perception of Metrical Structure: Experimental Evidence and a Model. In Howell, P., West, R. & Cross, I. (eds.) *Representing Musical Structure,* 59–127. London: Academic Press.
Leman, M. (1994). Introduction to Auditory Models in Music Research. *J. New Music Research* **23**(1): 5–9.

Lerdahl, F. & Jackendoff, R. (1983). *A Generative Theory of Tonal Music*. MIT Press: Cambridge, MA.
Liberman, M. & Prince, A. (1977). On Stress and Linguistic Rhythm. *Linguistic Inquiry* **8**(2): 249–336.
Longuet-Higgins, H. C. (1976). The Perception of Melodies. *Nature* **263**: 646–653.
Longuet-Higgins, H. C. & Lee, C. S. (1982). Perception of Musical Rhythms. *Perception* **11**: 115–128.
Longuet-Higgins, H. C. & Lee, C. S. (1984). The Rhythmic Interpretation of Monophonic Music. *Music Perception* **1**(4): 424–441.
Longuet-Higgins, H. C. & Steedman, M. J. (1971, 1987). On Interpreting Bach. In Longuet-Higgins, H. C. (ed.) *Mental Processes: Studies in Cognitive Science*, 82–104. MIT Press: Cambridge, MA.
Marr, D. (1982). *Vision*. Freeman: New York.
Meddis, R. (1988). Simulation of Auditory-Neural Transduction: Further Studies. *J. Acoust. Soc. Am* **83**(3): 1056–1063.
Parncutt, R. (1994). A Model of Beat Induction Accounting for Perceptual Ambiguity by Continuously Variable Parameters. Proceedings of *The International Computer Music Conference*. Denmark: Aarhaus.
Patterson, R, D. & Holdsworth, J. (1992). A Functional Model of Neural Activity Patterns and Auditory Images. In Ainsworth, W. A. (ed.) *Advances in Speech, Hearing and Language Processing*. Vol. 3. JAI Press: London.
Popper, A. N. & Fay, R. R. (1992). *The Mammalian Anditory Pathway: Neurophysiology*. Springer-Verlag: NY.
Povel, D. J. & Essens, P. (1985). Perception of Temporal Patterns. *Music Perception* **2**(4): 411–440.
Repp, B. (1990). Patterns of Expressive Timing in Performances of a Beethoven Minuet by Nineteen Famous Painists. *Journal of the Acoustical Society of America* **88**(2): 622–641.
Repp, B. (1992). Probing the Cognitive Representation of Musical Time: Structural Constraints on the Perception of Timing Perturbations. *Cognition* **44**: 241–281.
Rosenthal, D. (1992). *Machine Rhythm: Computer Emulation of Human Rhythm Perception*. MIT Media Lab. Ph.D Thesis.
Seashore, C. (1938). *The Psychology of Music*. McGraw-Hill: New York.
Selkirk, E. (1984). *Phonology and Syntax: The Relation between Sound and Structure*. MIT Press: Cambridge, MA.
Shaffer, H. (1981). Performances of Chopin, Bach and Bartok: Studies in Motor Programming. *Cognitive Psychology* **13**: 326–376.
Sloboda, J. (1983). The Communication of Musical Meter. *Quarterly Journal Of Experimental Psychology* **35**: 377–396.
Todd, N. P. (1985). A Model of Expressive Timing in Tonal Music. *Music Perception* **3**: 33–58.
Todd, N. P. McAngus (1989). Towards a Cognitive Theory of Expression: The Performance and Perception of Rubato. *Contemporary Music Review* **4**: 405–416.
Todd, N. P. McAngus (1992). The Dynamics of Dynamics: A Model of Musical Expression. *J. Acoust. Soc. Am* **91**(6): 3540–3550.
Todd, N. P. McAngus (1994a). The Auditory "primal sketch": A Multi-Scale Model of Rhythm Grouping. *J. New Music Research* **23**(1): 25–70.
Todd, N. P. McAngus (1994b). A New Theory of Temporal Integration. *British Journal of Audiology*.
Todd, N. P. McAngus (1995). The Kinematics of Musical Expression. *J. Acoust. Soc. Am* **97**(3), 1940–1950.
Todd, N. P. McAngus & Brown, G. (1994). A Multi-Scale Auditory Model of Prosodic Perception. Proceedings of *The International Conference on Spoken Language Processing*. Yokoyama, Japan.
Todd, N. P. McAngus & Lee, C. S. (1994). An Auditory-Motor Model of Beat Induction. Proceedings of *The International Computer Music Conference*. Denmark: Aarhaus.
Yost, W. A. & Sheft, S. (1993). Auditory Perception. In Yost, W., Popper, A. & Fay R. (eds.) *Human Psychophysics*, 193–236. Springer-Verlag: NY.

Artificial Intelligence Review **10**: 275–298, 1996.

The Sensitive Interface*

PAUL MC KEVITT

Department of Computer Science, Regent Court, 211 Portobello Street, University of Sheffield, GB- S1 4DP, Sheffield, England, EU;
E-mail: p.mckevitt@dcs.shef.ac.uk

and

JOHN G. GAMMACK

Department of Computing and Information Systems, High Street, University of Paisley, GB- PA1 2BE, Paisley, Scotland, EU;
E-mail: gamm-ci0@paisley.ac.uk

Abstract. One of the most important problems in human-computer interaction is that of maximising communication between the user and the computer. We claim that optimum communication will be facilitated when the computer can analyse and respond to the intentions of the computer user. We propose a philosophy for computer interface design in which the computer analyses the intentions of users through verbal and nonverbal media. With respect to verbal media we describe a computer program called Operating System CONsultant (OSCON) which can analyse users' intentions from English in the domain of computer operating systems. With respect to non-verbal media we argue that computers will be better able to analyse people's intentions when recognising the media of facial expression, touch, and sound. Some results and implications from a recent experiment on cross-cultural emotions in faces are discussed. We describe the IDIOMS (Intelligent Decision-making In On-line Management Systems) project which implements a design philosophy for capturing users' concepts and intentions. We argue that this approach will ensure the computers will become more understanding of their users and this will result in a more sensitive human-computer interface.

Key words: anthropocentrism, emotion, face recognition, human-centredness, human-computer interaction (HCI), IDIOMS, interfaces, natural-language processing, OSCON.

1. INTRODUCTION

One of the most important problems in developing computer technology is to ensure that human-computer communication is maximised at the interface. The best interface will result in optimum communication between a computer and its user. We believe that one of the most important factors in good communication is the development of interfaces which maximise the analysis (recognition and representation) of users' intentions. The best interface will be one which operates a large number of media for communication with its user. We will be mainly concerned here with communication media in the form of language and facial expressions.

In many situations the whole interpretation of an utterance is qualified by the accompanying facial expression, or prosodic information such as the tone of originator. Notwithstanding sophisticated video-conferencing this is generally lost in computer-mediated situations and in reclaiming this information it is surely preferable to base the semantics of intelligent models on universally shared understandings rather than imposing the values of a dominant culture. Particularly for international communication it is important that the representations of intention or affective state through expression are culture free and unambiguous. Whilst video-conferencing technology can be expected to supplant simulated faces in certain groupware applications, until this technology is stabilised and cheaply available conveying affective content will remain problematic. Furthermore, there is likely to remain a general requirement for conveying affective information in effective cooperative working and in electronic communication.

Here, we consider the expression of emotional state in terms of both language and vision and address the cross-cultural stability of the latter. We note the effectiveness of faces as a concise representation for complex or hard-to-describe information. We propose that if the affective context of a message can be represented stably in a small set of icons this information can be attached to computer mediated messages to enhance their interpretation in general situations requiring collaboration. Given an ongoing requirement for conveying affective information through iconic representations we consider contexts where the use of iconic information has properties which can enhance the use of verbally mediated language. In fact, people have been using icons of faces for years in order to add emotional content to their electronic mail (E-mail) messages. A list of such icons is given in Appendix A. These ASCII icons are schematic and indicate the acknowledged intent of the sender. Whilst the ASCII character set has limited expressiveness, in future, drawings from a standard set or photographic images may well accompany written messages which better express the sender's emotional intent. These may be useful in aiding interpretation.

We suggest that, if not definitive, our icon set shown in Appendix B is at least representative as that in A and we would claim that for particular applications some appropriate set can be identified. Linking the ergonomics of the interface with culture is seen as a long term goal of the work presented here (see Wang 1993). Although being able to communicate such information can be expected ultimately to help in groupworking applications there are many problems to be resolved. Here, it is of more interest to examine how such information can be mapped by an Artificial Intelligence (AI) regulating the interface.

Leaving aside questions of social desirability, if technology is to empower all sections of society in environments such as the SuperInformationHighway, access must be made available through interfaces which disadvantaged users, such as the physically disabled or the computer or otherwise illiterate, can easily use. This, at least in part, involves increasing the sensitivity and adaptability of the interface to human characteristics. In addition, for facilitating international working an over-reliance on a single dominant language is likely to lead to impoverished interaction and cultural misunderstandings. If instead, intelligence can be applied to recognising the user's intent and to incorporating that within message processing, work in machine translation will result in more effective interactions. Effective translation however involves more than simple substitutions and mappings. A deep semantic understanding is implicated, which requires the integration of information from various sources, both verbal and nonverbal. It is to the development of such a model that the present work points.

We divide human characteristics of intention display into two types: *verbal* and *nonverbal*. First, we describe linguistic characteristics or the requirement for seeing beyond utterances to the intentions of a human communicator. We describe some ways in which this can be practically achieved. We then discuss human nonverbal communicative characteristics such as facial expression exhibiting emotion which could be accommodated by interfaces in the future. We describe a study examining the perception of iconically-represented emotional expressions in two groups (British and Chinese subjects) and look at the similarities across the two cultures. Next, a particular philosophy for interface design is described. This philosophy, *anthropocentrism* or *human-centredness*, stresses situatedness and accommodates flexible initiative in computer use. Finally, a particular interface implementation in the domain of credit control illustrates some of these principles. It is our goal here to indicate some directions for human-computer interaction which lead to the truly sensitive interface.

2. BACKGROUND

People frequently have the perception that computers are stupid, insensitive or unresponsive. This causes alienation, resistance and apathy. A major reason for this can be attributed to the fact that the computer lacks emotional capability, particularly the lack of ability to understand where the human is "coming from". As communication between people and machines is mediated through the interface it may be instructive to examine some points of difference between human-human interfaces and human-computer interfaces as a guide to directions for improvement. The first is that whereas machines are literal, humans seek meaning. Asking a creative person to read from a page of newsprint is illuminating. Often they will paraphrase the text, missing or substituting words, and this is often unconscious. Contrast the pedantry of the average computer. Analogously, when someone speaks to you it is intelligent to perceive the intention behind the utterance, and respond to that, not merely to the words. We can go on to look at methods for detecting intentions in language and in vision.

2.1. *Intentions in language*

There are a number of theories of natural-language discourse processing and various computational models of these theories exist. Theories concentrate on the themes of semantics, structure, and intention. A common principle of all approaches is that they provide a model of the coherence of discourse. Semantic theories argue that the coherence of a discourse is a feature of its meaning and that if you model the meaning the coherence falls out of that. For example, there are theories regarding the coherence of semantics in discourse such as those proposed by Fass (1988), Schank (1972, 1973, 1975), Schank and Abelson (1977), and Wilks (1973, 1975a, 1975b, 1975c).

Structure-based theories argue that a discourse can be modelled in terms of structural units which can be recognised and marked out in the discourse. These theories have given names like *topic* and *focus* to such units. Examples of such theories are proposed in Alshawi (1987), Dale (1988, 1989), Grosz (1983), Grosz *et al.* (1983), Grosz and Sidner (1986), Sidner (1983, 1985), and Webber (1978).

Classically, *openness* within systems refers to those systems which interchange material, energy or (particularly) information with their environment (von Bertalanffy 1950). For the intelligent understanding of the communication environment contextual operators must be brought to bear on the logical formulations of the base language. Collen *et al.* (1994) examine the general concept of openness within such systems concentrating particularly on its logical aspect. According to their analysis, information exchange lies at the first level of a hierarchy where metalevel logical computational reflection has been analysed and formalised and the context operators are passive. This level of the logical hierarchy presumes objectivised, observer-independent and static worlds which are unrealistic for natural language applications. Instead, Collen *et al.*, noting the introduction of reflexive systems in formal logic and computer science (see Maes and Nardi 1987), propose a hierarchy culminating in reflexive openness characterised by active and evolving processes which include the observer as part of the system. Such a system can design, adapt and utilise communication strategies for interaction with other systems, of which it may construct a model, along with the relevant contextual consideration of both systems.

Collen *et al.* indicate applications in robotics, and in the study of language, where "the ability to produce statements is contrasted with the ability to represent and process meaning" (p. 70). This leads to a reformulation of the semantic retrieval problem in AI as changing from "the grammar generating the text" to "the text (social usage) generating the grammar" in which the human being is theoretically central to this process. Such work has implications for structure-based approaches to intention analysis.

Finally, other theories model the coherence of discourse from the point of view of intention, or the goals, plans and beliefs of the participants in the discourse. These approaches argue that people's intentions underlie their use of language and that by modelling these intentions one can model language. Examples of such approaches are given in Allen (1983), Appelt (1981, 1985), Carberry (1989), Cohen *et al.* (1982), Hinkelman and Allen (1989), Hobbs (1979), Litman and Allen (1984), Schank and Abelson (1977), and Wilensky (1983). The approaches do not argue that intentions in people's brains can be seen but that people's intentions can be recognised and inferred from the utterances they use. Although intentions can't be seen, they can be detected electrographically (see Libet

1985), a fact used in the development of thought-based interfaces (see Normile and Barnes-Svarney 1993). Ideas here emerge from claims made by philosophers of language such as Austin (1962) and Searle (1969). Such philosophers argue that the motivation for people to use language is to achieve their intentions.

Structure-based theories by themselves are inadequate for capturing intended meaning since they rely on well-formed sentences. Yet the psycholinguistic literature enumerates many instances of effective understanding of intended meaning when the utterance is not well-formed or even inconsistent. When a common understanding is shared the words are less relevant, and equally when other (paralinguistic) clues countermand a verbal message perceived intention governs the interpretation. It has long been recognised in the social sciences that a substantial amount of communicative information can be inferred.

2.2. *Intentions in faces*

As an area of Psychology, *face recognition* is of immense theoretical and practical interest. Long before formal studies were conducted folk theories relating facial expression to emotional states were established. The Chinese raised face reading to an art form, known as *siang mien*, a skill which still survives, and is recorded in both popular and scholarly books describing observable correspondences which betray character and temperament[1] (see Tao 1989). Also, of popular note is that the Ministry of International Trade and industry (MITI) in Japan have promoted computerised secretaries that recognise their bosses' voices and have six different facial expressions. The cyborgs specifically do jobs like taking messages and making the day go more sweetly so the boss doesn't get bored (see Computer Weekly 1995 (1/6/95)). Darwin (1872) was also interested in the relation of emotional state to facial expression and although his account suggested inborn human universals anthropologists and others have noted cultural differences which can radically modify the interpretation of expressions (see Eibl-Eibesfeldt 1972). For this reason it is important to establish widely understood expressions of emotional content.

Ekman (1993) summarises cross-cultural work on facial expression and emotion and raises numerous questions for further research. Citing evidence for universality in facial expressions he notes that there is no strong evidence for cross-cultural disagreement on the interpretation of *fear, anger, disgust, sadness* or *enjoyment* expressions.

In the world of computer mediated communication where communicators are distanced from one another some simulacrum of the sender's intentions provides helpful interpretive context. Such a situation would recognise that conveying *universally understood* information is not possible using only words and a restoration of lost context is required. Representing facial expressions may give fairly unambiguous culture-free clues to emotional state but respecting those aspects of expression which are culture-specific is also required.

Since pictorial forms allow for the interrelationship among parts to be grasped along with the simultaneous perception of multifarious aspects there is an increase in efficiency of information transmission which in Japan has resulted in learning several times more efficient than learning in verbal form (see Maruyama 1986). Maruyama suggests that encoding complex information in pictorial form allows business people to process recorded messages more rapidly and with reference to the combination of character parts in Classical Chinese describes a general scheme for keyboard input of *pictemes* which are basic components of picture coded information systems. Keyboard interfaces based on simplifying classical idiographic characters have met popular resistance in China and Japan and developing picture-coded representations is seen as an important extension to the often isolating and (currently) communicationally impoverished world of networked organisations.

Within AI, vision-based face recognition by computer is also undergoing a revival after 20 years (see Brunelli and Poggio 1993; Pentland 1993) and this has applications in security, criminology and other areas. The algorithms involved traditionally tend to view face recognition as part of visual processing and consider the face purely as a geometric image to be distinguished from others. However, the features used in the model described by Brunelli and Poggio (1993) which achieved perfect recognition on their test set are interesting. Taking anthropometric standards as initial measures, and then refining them mathematically, 35 facial features are extracted. Of these, 4 concern the eyebrows' thickness and position and 11 concern the arch of the left eyebrow. Thus almost half of the distinguishing features concern the eyebrows. The eyebrows are one of the most expressive parts of the face and this has implications for differentiating among emotions as Ekman (1993) has suggested.

By basing vision processing work on humanly meaningful features there is a potential for linkage to an integrated model constructed in terms of human semantics. Every division of the human nervous system has some physical structure related to emotion with the limbic system (the emotional core of the nervous system) regulating the information being communicated along various channels (see Cytowic 1992). Effective visual scene interpretation must likewise relate to a semantic context and for Human Computer Interaction in particular one constructed along humanly meaningful lines.

The image analysis techniques developed in vision processing systems have direct implications for user interface design. The literature suggests that difficult or long tasks are characterised by increased grimacing and other cues to indicate stress (see Delvolvé and Queinnec 1983). Sheehy *et al.* (1987) examine nonverbal behaviour at the computer interface using an image analysis approach to categorise detected gestures and looking behaviours along with frowns, grimaces and other facial expressions. Detecting and acting upon this information can avoid failures and suggest remedial action. In addition to facilitating the social interpretation of visually transmitted information one implication of linking face recognition with interface design lies in the intelligent processing of information within specialised human-computer interaction. With cameras built into faster machines, and by using intelligent automated image classification, the possibilities of conveying richly differentiated information to a machine are realistic.

Research at the Science University of Tokyo has resulted in a program which can distinguish among human expression such as *anger*, *surprise* and *fear*. Already *seeing chips* have been developed which can be programmed to recognise faces and respond appropriately (see Davidson 1993). Dolls with such seeing chips behind their eyes can recognise their owners and respond to their expressions. Naoko Tosa at Musashino Art University has already developed, *Neuro Baby*, a 3-D digital child which simulates emotional patterns based on those of humans (see Graves 1993). Neuro Baby responds to inflections in human voice input, and if ignored will pass the time by whistling, and when addressed directly will respond with a cheerful *Hi*. Intelligent applications can then be programmed to respond appropriately and this line of work is liable to lead towards more sensitive interfaces in future computer based information systems.

Having summarised some work on the analysis of intentions in both language and vision we now go on to look at some work we have done in each of these areas.

3. ANALYSIS OF INTENTIONS IN LANGUAGE

In any research on natural language processing the variety of domains one can investigate is enormous. We have chosen the domain of natural language consultancy as it a common application for natural language dialogue technology. We also limit the domain to that of computer operating systems to narrow down the enormous set of possible natural language utterances. We use the domain of computer operating systems, as it is a domain of natural-language consultancy which is well-defined, and has been used before by a number of researchers investigating theories in natural-language processing. A Unix Consultant (UC) (see Chin 1988; Wilensky *et al.* 1984, 1986, 1988), implemented in Lisp, acts as a natural-language consultant on the UNIX operating system. Another natural-language consultant, implemented in Lisp, called the Sinix Consultant (SC) (see Hecking *et al.* 1988; and Kemke 1986, 1987) has been developed for the Sinix[2] operating system. Both of these systems are similar in scope and intent to the OSCON system.

The OSCON (Operating System CONsultant) program is a natural-language dialogue interface which answers English queries about computer operating systems (see Mc Kevitt 1986, 1988, 1991a, 1991b; Mc Kevitt and Wilks 1987; and Mc Kevitt *et al.* 1992a, 1992b, 1992c, 1992d). OSCON enables a user to enter written English queries and then answers them in English. The program is written in Quintus Prolog and runs on a Sun-4 computer in real-time. OSCON can answer queries for over 30 commands from each of the UNIX[3] and MS-DOS[4] operating systems and handles four basic query types. OSCON can also answer queries about options on UNIX commands and complex queries about command compositions. The system is intended to be used by varying types of users with different levels of expertise. The architecture of OSCON is modular, so that it is easily updated, and can be easily mapped over to other domains.

The OSCON program currently answers four basic query types, queries about options, and command composition queries, for both the UNIX and MS-DOS

Operating Systems. The fact that queries are of a given type aids in understanding and generating answers to them. Understanding queries is a combination of both filtering the query type and then understanding the query.

The architecture of the OSCON system consists of six distinct basic modules and two extension modules. There are at least two arguments for modularising any system: (1) it is much easier to update the system at any point, and (2) it is easier to map the system over to another domain. The six basic modules in OSCON are as follows: (1) ParseCon: natural-language syntactic grammar parser which detects query-type,[5] (2) MeanCon: a natural-language semantic grammar (see Brown *et al.* 1975; and Burton 1976) which determines query meaning, (3) KnowCon: a knowledge representation, containing information on natural-language verbs, for understanding, (4) DataCon: a knowledge representation for containing information about operating system commands, (5) SolveCon: a solver for resolving query representations against knowledge base representations, and (6) GenCon: a natural-language generator for generating answers in English. These six modules are satisfactory if user queries are treated independently or in a context-free manner. However, the following two extension modules are necessary for dialogue-modelling and user-modelling: (1) DialCon: a dialogue modelling component which uses an *intention matrix* to represent intention sequences in a dialogue, and (2) UCon: a user-modeller which computes levels of user-satisfaction from the intention matrix and provides information for context-sensitive and user-sensitive natural language generation. A diagram of OSCON's architecture is shown in Figure 1.

We have described a system which can determine user intentions in natural-language dialogue and in turn use that to determine the level of user satisfaction. Now, we shall move on to describe alternative nonverbal means of modelling intention in human-computer interaction.

4. NONVERBAL MEANS OF ANALYSING INTENTION

There are many more dimensions to communication than merely the verbal or linguistic. There is a whole realm of semiotics which the computer in its current form does not begin to touch and for users who prefer to operate through channels other than the superficially verbal the computer is frustrating in its insensitivity. It is not our intention to get into a sophomoric debate about whether computers can have emotions, rather to consider what might be realistic in enabling them to have a more sensitive response.

First, is sensitivity to the expression of the user. Humans can usually tell from nonverbal cues if someone is tense, angry or impatient. This gives clues to formulate a response that is neither long winded nor patronising but considered and calming. This would be particularly useful in help or consultant systems. There is both an existing science and an ancient lore of how to read faces to detect such characteristics (see Tao 1989).

Other cues to the mood of the user may be indicated by touch. For example, a user who is in a bad mood might indicate this by over-vigorous keypresses

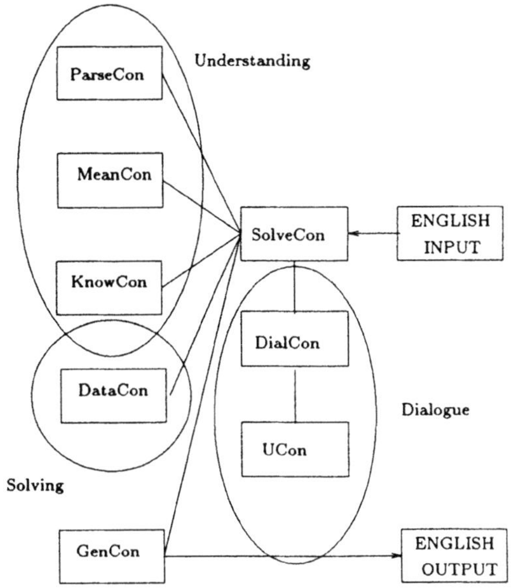

Fig. 1. Architecture of the Operating System CONsultant (OSCON) system.

or bashing the mouse and this could be detected. Sensors can readily detect this sort of symptom and use it in forming a user model. Another cue which indicates user-intention is *sound.* User satisfaction levels such as irritation, hesitancy, and other personal characteristics can potentially be detected through voice interfaces.

Although perhaps fanciful, there is a serious point behind these ideas which has a definite message for design: typewritten interaction is a very superficial level of communication and limits the experience of interaction for many users. Although work in natural language processing is beginning to address intentions which underlie utterances, this is only one dimension of communication available to humans, and if computers are to be really user friendly they have to become a lot more sensitive to their users' needs. Some skeptical and empirical studies might indicate an agreed codified basis for recognising expression information and we have begun some cross-cultural work in this direction.

In an initial study, Wang and Gammack (1995) set out to investigate how context-free representations of facial expressions would be perceived in two distinct cultures. A group of Chinese and a group of British subjects were shown 70 iconic drawings of different facial expressions and their patterns of labelling and association were examined (see Appendix B). Assuming that each expression outwardly betrayed a characteristically intended emotional state Wang and Gammack examined the cross-cultural agreement in the identification of this. For the major theoretical categories of emotion, such as *happiness*, *sadness* and *fear*, there was good cross-cultural agreement in line with previous studies. Since the faces were drawn simply it would seem that a few facial characteristics may be enough to form a basic model of someone's emotional state, or the quality of intention, and pattern recognisers already exist which discriminate faces effectively using humanly meaningful (rather than purely statistical) parameters (see Brunelli and Poggio 1993). Similar findings for voice tones and other paralinguistic information imply that incorporating nonverbal information into user models can allow intelligent responses to be formulated: a critical requirement in a world where household appliances and gadgets will increasingly include intelligent processors.

Other work on the nonverbally mediated computer recognition of intention is described by Radin (1993) and has many potential outcomes in human machine interaction applications. Radin's study confirmed previous work showing that an artificial neural network can learn to associate machine generated random data with the mental intentions of specific individuals who are not physically connected to the machine. Humans forming a conscious intention somehow affect the interaction with a random number generator to produce non-chance, person-specific patterns. Such findings have implications for intention based interfaces such as robots operating remotely in environments with impaired conventional communication facilities, or to controlling the wheelchairs of quadriplegics.

Thought or intention based interfaces are also being researched in various countries, summarised by Normile and Barnes-Svarney (1993). Researchers in New York are training users to emit brain signals which control cursor movement, and in Illinois, typewritten output is being produced by people spelling out words in their minds. In Japan, research concerns the mental formation of syllables before actually being voiced, and researchers can determine accurately when subjects prevocally form a particular syllable. Such work relies on the brain producing varying electrical signals just prior to action: such signals can then be detected and matched with specific actions.

Having now looked at the analysis of intentions from both a language and vision point of view we can now go on to provide our general philosophy of interface design.

5. A PHILOSOPHY OF INTERFACE DESIGN

We argue that one key to effective usability lies in system interfaces designed to allow the maximum responsiveness to the user's intentions, however expressed. The human centred philosophy (see Gill 1991) of users as designers fits well with such requirements, taking advantage of the symbolic relationship between human and machine in information systems. In this the strengths of the computer in numbercrunching and memory aspects complement the situated awareness and contextual judgment of the human. For effective communication between human and machine there must be some provisions for a shared appreciation of the context of action and the assumptions which the user brings to the interaction. Work on user modelling (see Kobsa and Wahlster 1988) and the research of Suchman (1987) on "communicating" with photocopiers indicates some directions for this work. *Spreadsheets*, probably the most useful and versatile applications in organisational life, owe this status largely to their making minimal assumptions about the user and thus not constraining the interaction.

Some of these principles were adopted in the design of the interface to the IDIOMS[6] (Intelligent Decision-making In On-line Management Systems) management information system (see Gammack *et al.* 1989, 1991, 1992) which is summarised below. In this project a major aim was to allow any decision support system generated within the development environment to embody the assumptions, meaningful semantic categories, contextual concerns and temporal exigencies of the situated user or application developer. In effect, this provided a qualitative and semantic processing environment analogous to the quantitative manipulations of spreadsheets.

We believe that a good interface design will take advantage of the strengths of both the computer and the human. These may be roughly characterised as:

(1) the computer having a huge memory and powerful numbercrunching ability
(2) the human having an ability to judge the appropriateness of rule-based advice in a given context

The contextual awareness and subjectivity in (2) is extremely difficult (if not impossible) to model in advance of the context of use but for many information systems it is not an issue which can be ignored. It can be facilitated by the analysis of intention as mentioned already.

We have applied this philosophy in the design of a *human-centred* interface to a decision support system accessing a massive corporate database. The system discovers implicit patterns in the database and reports the variables which best predict some attribute of interest. This, in effect, is a database classifier which generates a decision model. The design allows both *objective* description of information in the data to be reported for inspection and evaluation and the *subjective* judgments and contextual considerations of the human to be communicated to the decision-making software.

Effective management decision making is a combination of lessons from past experience and judgement of the current situation. How can these be combined in a human-computer system? Our solution is to divide the labour of decision making along the lines of these complementary strengths. The human-computer interaction becomes an issue of detailing how this design goal can be achieved.

In an example domain of *credit control* the likely outcome of granting a loan application can be determined by examining the historical database to find the best predictors (see Fogarty *et al.* 1992). This information, once extracted from the database can be represented to the user, who can then use it immediately for inference, can fine tune it in various ways, or can actively introduce new influences into the decision model. The next section describes an example interface which facilitates this along with some of the criteria considered in choosing the design.

5.1. *Designing the interface*

In keeping with current trends we developed a graphical user interface (GUI) using XView and keeping in mind the standard *look and feel* which makes transfer of training relatively painless. We also retained the developer's interface as a *set up* option which is text and cursor based. This allows transfer to environments which do not yet support windows, and gives relatively unsophisticated computer users a more guided dialogue. There is some evidence that certain classes of user prefer text-based interfaces and greater guidance in the interaction (see Fowler and Murray 1987) and so a choice is provided. However, the GUI is more interesting and forms the basis of our discussion.

The next issue concerns the amount of user involvement with the system. The interface to a piece of application software does not exist in isolation: it is there to facilitate the use of the software and to help the user gain power and freedom in its use without obstructing the user's intentions. The amount of control exercised over the software in our design is left to the user's discretion: minimally, the user may simply run the unprocessed (*objective*) output from the database classifier, or, at the opposite extreme, override it completely by building his/her own (*subjective*) model. Something in between is more typical and of course different decision models can be experimentally compared. Rather than have a fixed level of involvement, such as usually found with expert system interactions, our design aim was to allow the system to be used compatibly with the user's own volition and to adapt to represent his/her intentions.

Econometric modellers and business decision analysts routinely adjust the outputs of decision support models to take account of current circumstances and their own experience. These post hoc adjustments offer little scope for finely principled decision making. For a true interaction there should be some to-ing and fro-ing where the best decision is negotiated. This is likely to be a function of both empirical data and subjective opinion. We now illustrate this general problem by way of an example which brings out the features of interfaced design which we alluded to earlier.

5.2. *Credit scoring for loan applications*

The IDIOMS project is one which uses techniques from AI to detect patterns in large databases and to convey this information in a humanly understandable manner. Although supporting rule-based descriptions of expertise, IDIOMS represents a break from traditional expert system developments in several important regards. First, it uses a more flexible representation of knowledge, allowing the same knowledge base to conclude on numerous goal variables, and has straightforward extensibility and maintainability. Second, it allows the user to take the initiative and alter the thresholds and criteria for decision making. This *human centred design* coupled with an adaptive machine learning component allows many of the traditional problems of expert systems development to be overcome, such as knowledge acquisition, insensitivity to context and inevitable obsolescence, while retaining the desirable features of heuristic processing, natural-language like communication, and reasoning transparency. The underlying hardware, a powerful parallel processing engine, allows fast management access to information without interfering with routine processing jobs and empowers complex decision making.

The IDIOMS project has been applied to the domain of credit control. A typical problem for a bank manager or insurance underwriter involves looking at the entries on a loan application form and deciding whether it is a good or a bad risk. This is a complex function of predictors such as salary or outgoings, but may also be affected by indications such as phone ownership and length of time at an address. The bank manager has a certain amount of experience with particular cases, the insurance underwriter rarely receives direct feedback, and in both cases a database has a massive history of example forms and their outcomes. Figure 2 shows the sorts of criteria in the database which can influence a decision to grant a loan. An arc shows a dependency of some sort between a pair of attributes.

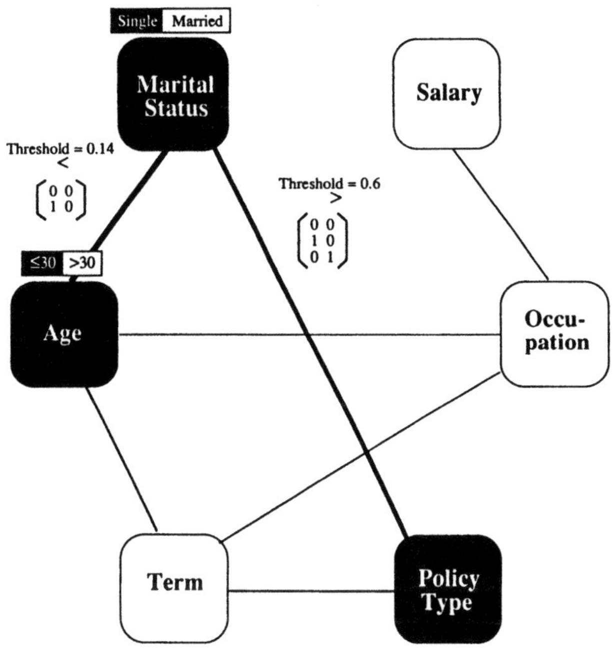

Fig. 2. Example criteria for granting loans.

The manager, however, may wish to add some relevant information to that available from the database as Figure 3 illustrates. In this case although the applicant's salary is high and other indications are good the manager knows that the applicant is likely to be made redundant soon and that this may affect the outcome. A mechanism for introducing this into the decision making is provided as a menu option and new classes can be subjectively built into the model.

Conversely, existing classes can be ignored: if a globetrotting millionaire of independent means applied for a loan categories such as *time at address* and *salary* might be considered irrelevant. Figure 4 shows the sorts of adjustment that the user can make. The classifications of a category are provided by optimising the

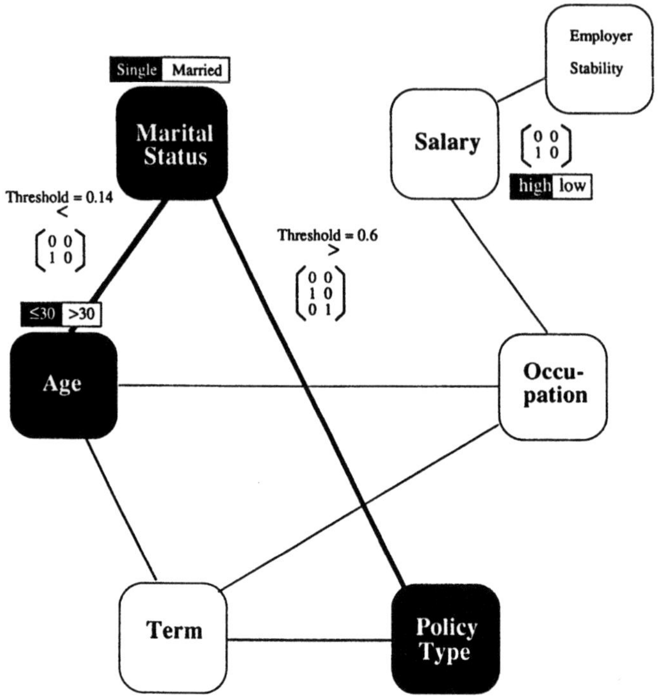

Fig. 3. Addition of information to the database.

data for discriminability. However, the user may have reasons to alter this prior to decision processing. In the example the value of 30 for age provides a good discrimination for marital status with the probabilities distributed as shown, but the user may be interested in whether it is worth targeting 40 year olds with inducements to take out family protection loans as survey data might have shown. By adjusting the value using a slider and doing a database recount with the new category values a new pattern of dependency between the relevant categories can be shown and its effect on some goal attribute established. By adding or deleting boundaries at will the user may arrive at a model that predicts the likely effect of targeting 35–40 year olds. The graphical slider and the accompanying textbox are coupled such that updating either automatically updates the other. This is useful in cases of changes in the law, such as raising the school leaving age to 16, where typing in a number to adjust a boundary may be easier than adjusting a slider.

So far, we have discussed only some features implemented in the GUI which is essentially intended to be used by business modellers to aid decision making. However, we should close by noting that our system is intended to go beyond this to allow the model which has been built and tested to be more generally used. For this, software was written which takes the classification rules implicit in the data model which predict a goal variable of interest and translates them into the format used by an expert system shell (see Oates and Gammack 1992).

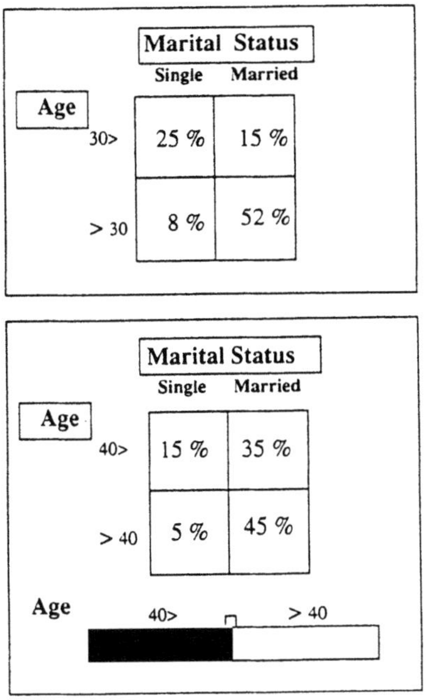

Fig. 4. Adjustments to the database.

The advantage of this is that it allows the automatic generation of an expert system from information available in a database, reporting such information in a natural-language like manner through an already familiar interface. This enables a business model to be ported to personal computers in branch offices or onto, say, smart cards. This automatic generation allows the development of the end-user interface to be restricted to filling in the appropriate textual explanations cutting down the knowledge acquisition effort.

The IDIOMS environment represents one approach to intention based interfaces in which the environment of application development and use is adapted to the users' intentions and situated judgements. Allowing users to design the use of systems as they develop represents a change from designs based on the third party assumptions of a system designer. We hope to extend this philosophy through our research on the integration of language and vision in interface design, in bringing intelligence to the default settings and configuration of the interface, through learning about user characteristics and modelling local semantics to anticipate the user's intent. Although groupware systems such as the *Coordinator* (see Winograd and Flores 1986) based on speech act theory have been perceived as too constraining and inflexible the introduction of more sophisticated processing and transmission of intentions will surely enhance communication.

6. CONCLUSION AND FUTURE WORK

We started out with the assumption that the optimum human-computer interface will be one which maximises communication between users and computers. We claimed that the analysis of human intentions will be a method by which communication is maximised. It was pointed out that intention analysis will be maximised in an environment where there are a number of media of communication between the human and computer.

We discussed the fact that communication media can be categorised into two major types: verbal and nonverbal. The analysis of intention in verbal communication was discussed with respect to work on a computer program called OSCON which answers questions about computer operating systems. Then we discussed nonverbal communication with respect to recognising emotions in facial expressions and indicated the potential of this work for intelligent interfaces with integrated semantic processors and user modelling capability. We argued for a philosophy of interface design which brings the human and computer closer to analysing each other's intentions. Finally, we discussed the IDIOMS project and an example case study of loan application where verbal and nonverbal intention analysis could be incorporated.

Future work will involve designing an interface which will enable the computer to analyse intentions in utterances, facial expressions, touch, and sound. Representations which assimilate all these means of communication of intent will need to be developed. This will help in enabling the computer to better analyse human intentions. This work can then be incorporated into interfaces such as Le-Mail which acts a an animated/iconic network communication E-mail system across language boundaries (see Yazdani 1995) and integrated with iconic languages such as Icon-Text (see Beardon 1995).

The analysis of intention can be used to build better computer programs which can communicate with people through dialogue whether that dialogue be in natural language or otherwise. With such techniques people will be nearer to communicating with computers in their own natural ways rather than having to learn some abstract computer language. The hope is that, if they are communicating in the same language, computers will be better able to understand people's intentions, and likewise, people will be able to use computers more effectively.

ACKNOWLEDGEMENTS

This research was supported in part by grants from the Chinese National Science Foundation (NSF) and from the British Council. The authors would like to thank Dr. Carolyn Begg for helpful discussions during preparation of this paper.

NOTES

* Paul Mc Kevitt is currently funded for five years on an Engineering and Physical Sciences Research Council (EPSRC) Advanced Fellowship under grant B/94/AF/1833 for the Integration of Natural Language, Speech and Vision Processing.

[1] Such correspondences can be extended and, for example, in Japan the radiator grilles on cars are sometimes perceived as faces expressing say, *aggression*, and car sales have been affected by this. (Equinox, –Zen on Wheels, British Television, channel 4, 1/11/92).
[2] Sinix is a version of UNIX developed by Siemens AG in Germany.
[3] UNIX is a trademark of AT&T Bell Laboratories.
[4] MS-DOS is a trademark of Microsoft Corporation.
[5] ParseCon uses a grammar, in the Definite Clause Grammar (DCG) formalism of Prolog. Definite Clause Grammars (DCG's) were first developed by Pereira and Warren (1980) as a tool to be used in Prolog for natural-language processing.
[6] The IDIOMS project is being undertaken by the Bristol Transputer Centre at West of England University (formerly Bristol Polytechnic), The National Transputer Centre at Sheffield, Strand Ltd., and a well-known British high street retail bank.

APPENDIX A

Face icons used with E-mail

This Appendix shows ASCII face icons which can be used by computer users while sending E-mail messages. The smileys are available on a smiley server from DaviD W. Sanderson (dws@cs.wisc.edu) (© Copyright 1991 by DaviD W. Sanderson) as shown (see Sanderson 1993). We have only shown around 100 of the full set here.

```
From pa.dec.com!decwrl!uunet!sparky!kent Tue Oct 22 12:55:00 PDT 1991
Article: 2864 of comp.sources.misc
Newsgroups: comp.sources.misc
Path: pa.dec.com!decwrl!uunet!sparky!kent
From: dws@cs.wisc.edu (DaviD W. Sanderson)
Subject:  v23i102:  smiley - smiley server, version 4, Part01/01
Message-ID: <1991Oct22.033215.1939@sparky.imd.sterling.com>
Followup-To: comp.sources.d
X-Md4-Signature: 30ae782918b11808204e363618389090
Sender: kent@sparky.imd.sterling.com (Kent Landfield)
Organization: Sterling Software, IMD
Date: Tue, 22 Oct 1991 03:32:15 GMT
Approved: kent@sparky.imd.sterling.com
Lines: 2158

Submitted-by: dws@cs.wisc.edu (DaviD W. Sanderson)
Posting-number: Volume 23, Issue 102
Archive-name: smiley/part01
Environment: UNIX
Supersedes: smiley: Volume 20, Issue 73

smiley(1) is a "smiley server" I wrote for my own pleasure.
Its list of smileys is more comprehensive than any other I have seen;
it subsumes all the smiley lists I have ever seen posted to the net.

This version has about fifty more smileys than version 3,
(589 faces, 818 definitions) and a better README file.
Keep those smileys coming!

DaviD W. Sanderson (dws@cs.wisc.edu)
```

:-) Willie Shoemaker
-(always should wear safety glasses, especially in the laser burn-in room [entropy@fluke.UUCP]
!-(black eye
!.'v (profile) flat top
#-) partied all night
#:-) smiley done by someone with matted hair [figmo@lll-crg.ARpA]
#:-o "Oh, nooooooo!" (a la Mr. Bill) [figmo@lll-crg (Lynn Gold)]
#:-o smiley done by someone with matted hair
#:o+= Betty Boop
$-) Alex P. Keaton (from "Family Ties")
$-) won big at Las Vegas
$-) won the lottery
$-) yuppie
%') after drinking a fifth for lunch
%*@:-(hung over
%*} very drunk [jeanette@randvax]
%+{ lost a fight
%-(I) laughing out loud
%-) Elephant man
%-) after staring at the terminal for 36 hours
%-) broken glasses
%-) cross-eyed
%-) drunk with laughter
%-) long bangs
%-6 braindead
%-<I> drunk with laughter
%-\ hungover
%-^ Picasso
%-{ sad variation
%-| been working all night
%-} humor variation
%-~ Picasso
%\v Picasso
&-| tearful
&.(.. crying
&:-) curly hair
'-) one eyed man
'-) only has a left eye, which is closed
'-) wink
':-) accidentally shaved off one of his eyebrows this morning
':-) one eyebrow
'~;E unspecified 4-legged critter
(o) (o) hooters
(-) needing a haircut
(-) needs a haircut
(-: Australian
(-: Don Ellis from Tektronix
(-: left-handed
(-::-) Siamese twins
(-:|:-) Siamese twins
(-E: wearing bifocals [jeanette@randvax]
(-_-) secret smile
(-o-) Imperial Tie Fighter ("Star Wars")
(00) mooning you
(8-) wears glasses

(8-o Mr. Bill
(8-{)} glasses, moustache and a beard
(: (=| wearing a ghost costume
(:)-) likes to scuba dive
(:)-) scuba diving
(:+) big nose
(:- unsmiley frowning
(:-# I am smiling and I have braces (watch out for the glare!)
(:-# said something he shouldn't have
(:-$ ill
(:-& angry
(:-(frowning
(:-(unsmiley frowning
(:-) big-face
(:-) no hair
(:-) smiley big-face
(:-) surprised
(:-) wearing bicycle helmet
(:-* kissing
(:-... heart-broken
(:-D blabber mouth
(:-I egghead
(:-\ VERY sad
(:-{~ bearded
(:-|K- formally attired
(:<) blabber mouth
(:=) TWO noses (?)
(:>-< thief: hands up!
(:I egghead
(:^(broken nose
(@ @) You're kidding!
(O--< fishy
(V)=| pacman champion
([(Robocop
) Cheshire cat
)8-) scuba smiley big-face
):-(unsmiley big-face
):-) smiley big-face
!#!^*&:-) a schizophrenic
*-(Cyclops got poked in the eye
*-) shot dead
*8-) Beaker (the Muppet lab assistant) (from James Cameron)
: fuzzy
*:** fuzzy with a fuzzy mustache
*:o) Bozo the Clown
*<.'v (profile) wearing snow cap
*<:-) Santa Claus
*<|:-) Santa Claus (Ho Ho Ho)
*<|:-)) Santa Claus
L blotto
+-(:-) Religious leader
+-(:-) the Pope
+-(:-) the pope
+-:-) priest
+:-) priest
+:-) smiley priest

APPENDIX B

Face icons for emotions

The following 70 face icons were used in an experiment to compare British and Chinese emotion classification (see Wang and Gammack 1995).

REFERENCES

Allen, James F. (1983). Recognising Intentions from Natural Language Utterances. In Brady, M. & Berwick, R. C. (eds.) *Computational Models of Discourse*, 107–166. MIT Press: Cambridge, MA.
Alshawi, Hiyan (1987). *Memory and Context for Language Interpretation*. Cambridge University Press: Cambridge, United Kingdom.
Appelt, Douglas E. (1981). *Planning Natural-language Utterances to Satisfy Multiple Goals*. Technical Note 259, SRI International, 333 Ravenswood Avenue, Menlo Park, California 94025, U.S.A.
Appelt, Douglas E. (1985). *Planning English Sentences*. Cambridge University Press: Cambridge, United Kingdom.
Austin, J. L. (1962). *How To Do Things With Words (Second Edition)*. Urmson, J. O. & Sbisà, Marina (eds.). Harvard University Press: Cambridge, MA.
Beardon, Colin (1995). Discourse Structures in Iconic Communication. In Mc Kevitt, Paul (ed.) *Artificial Intelligence Review, Special Issue on Integration of Natural Language and Vision Processing* **9**(2–3): 189–203.
Brown, John Seeley, Burton, Richard R. & Bell, Alan G. (1975). SOPHIE: A Step Towards Creating a Reactive Learning Environment. In *International Journal of Man-Machine Studies* **7**: 675–696.
Brunelli, R. & Poggio, T. (1993). Face Recognition: Features versus Templates. In *IEEE Transactions on Pattern Analysis and Machine Intelligence* **15**.
Burton, R. (1976). *Semantic Grammar: An Engineering Technique for Constructing Natural-language Understanding Systems*. BBN Report No. 3453, Bolt, Beranek & Newman, Cambridge, MA, U.S.A.
Carberry, Sandra (1989). A pragmatics-based Approach to Ellipsis Resolution. In *Computational Linguistics* **15**(2): 75–96, June.
Chin, David (1988). Exploiting User Expertise in Answer Expression. In Proceedings of *The Seventh National American Conference on Artificial Intelligence (AAAI-88)* **2**: 756–760, St. Paul, Minnesota, U.S.A., August.
Cohen, Phil R., Perrault, C. Raymond & Allen, James F. (1982). Beyond Question Answering. In Lehnert, Wendy G. & Ringle, Martin H. (eds.) *Strategies for Natural Language Processing*, 245–274. Lawrence Erlbaum Associates: Hillsdale, New Jersey.
Collen, A., Minati, G. & Ciapessoni, E. (1994). Logical Openness in Systems. In *Systems Research* **11**(2): 65–72.
Computer Weekly (1995). *Computer Weekly* **13**: June, p. 40.
Cytowic, R.E. (1992). *The Man Who Tasted Shapes*. Abacus: London, England.
Dale, Robert (1988). The Generation of Subsequent Referring Expressions in Structured Discourses. In Zock, M. & Sabah, Gérard (eds.) *Advances in Natural Language Generation, An Interdisciplinary Perspective, Communication in Artificial Intelligence Series*, 58–75. Pinter Publishers: London.
Dale, Robert (1989). Cooking Up Reference Expressions. In Proceedings of *the 27th Annual Meeting of the Association for Computational Linguistics*, 68–75. University of British Columbia, Vancouver, British Columbia, Canada, June.
Darwin, Charles (1872). *The Expression of the Emotions in Man and Animals*. Chicago University Press: Chicago, Illinois.
Davidson, C. (1993). *Visions of the Future*. The Guardian, England, Sep. 9.
Delvolvé, N. & Queinnec, Y. (1983). Operators' Activities at Terminals: A Behavioural Approach. In *Ergonomics* **26**: 329–346.
Eibl-Eibesfeldt, I. (1972). Similarities and Differences between Cultures in Expressive Movements. In Hinde, R. A. (ed.) *Nonverbal Communication*. CUP: Cambridge.
Ekman, P. (1993). Facial Expression and Emotion. 1992 Award Address. In *American Psychologist*, April, 384–392.
Fass, Dan (1988). *Collative Semantics: A Semantics for Natural-language Processing*. Ph.D. Dissertation, Department of Computer Science, University of Essex. Also, as Memorandum in

Computer and cognitive Science, MCCS-88-118, Computing Research Laboratory, Dept. 3CRL, Box 30001, New Mexico State University, Las Cruces, NM 88003-0001, U.S.A.
Fogarty, T. C., Ireson, N. S. & Battle, S. A. (1992). Generating Combinations of Attributes and Categories of Nominal Attribute Values for a Bayesian Classifier for Credit Control. In Proceedings of *Institute of Mathematics and Applications (IMA) International Conference on Control: Modelling, Computation, Information*. Glasgow Polytechnic, Glasgow.
Fowler, C. J. H. & Murray, D. (1987). Gender and Cognitive Style: Differences at the Human-computer Interface. In Bullinger, H. J. & Shackel. B. (eds.) *Human-Computer Interaction – INTERACT '87*. Elsevier Science Publications B.V./North-Holland: Amsterdam.
Gammack, J. G., Battle, S. A. & Stephens, R. A. (1989). A Knowledge Acquisition and Representation Scheme for Constraint Based and Parallel Systems. In Proceedings of *The IEEE Conference on Systems Man and cybernetics*, Hyatt Regency Hotel, Cambridge, Massachusetts, 1030–1035.
Gammack, J. G., Fogarty, T. C., Battle, S. A. & Miles, R. G. (1991). Management Decision Support from Large Databases: The IDIOMS Project. In Proceedings of *The Association of Modelling and Simulation Enterprises (AMSE) International Conference on Signals and Systems*, Institute of Transport, Warsaw, Poland, 213–219.
Gammack, J. G., Fogarty, T. C., Battle, S. A., Ireson, N. S. & Cui, J. (1992). Human Centred Decision Support: The IDIOMS Project. In *AI and Society* **6**(4): 345–366.
Gill, K.S. (1991). Summary of Human-centred Systems Research in Europe. In *Systemist* **13**(1–2), Feb and May.
Graves, Gaye L. (1993). *This Digital Baby Responds to Coos and Goos*. Tech. Watch, Computer Graphics World **16**, July.
Grosz, Barbara J. (1983). TEAM: A Transportable Natural Language Interface System. In Proceedings of *The 1983 Conference on Applied Natural Language Processing*, 39–45, Santa Monica, California, U.S.A., February.
Grosz, B., Joshi, A. & Weinstein, S. (1983). Providing a Unified Account of Definite Noun Phrases in Discourse. In Proceedings of *The 21st Annual Meeting of the Association for Computational Linguistics*, 44–50, Cambridge, Massachusetts, U.S.A. Also in Proceedings of *The International Joint Conference on Artificial Intelligence*, Cambridge, MA.
Grosz, B. J. & Sidner, C. L. (1986). Attention, Intentions and the Structure of Discourse. *Computational Linguistics* **12**(3): 175–204.
Hecking, M., Kemke, C., Nessen, E., Dengler, D., Gutmann, M. & Hector, G. (1988). *The SINIX Consultant – A Progress Report*. Memo No. 28, Department of Computer Science, University of Saarbrücken, D-6600 Saarbrücken 11, Germany, European Union (EU), August.
Hinkelman, Elizabeth & Allen, James (1989). Two Constraints on Speech Act Ambiguity. In Proceedings of *The 27th Annual Meeting of the Association for computational Linguistics*, 212–219, University of British Columbia, Vancouver, British Columbia, Canada, June.
Hobbs, Jerry (1979). Coherence and Coreference. In *Cognitive Science* **3**(1): 67–90.
Kemke, Christel (1986). *The SINIX Consultant – Requirements, Design, and Implementation of An Intelligent Help System for a UNIX Derivative*. Report No. 11, SC-Project, Department of Computer Science, University of Saarbrücken, Saarbrücken, Germany, European Union (EU), October.
Kemke, Christel (1987). Representation of Domain Knowledge in an Intelligent Help System. In Bullinger, H. J. & Shackel, B. (eds.) *Human-Computer Interaction – INTERACT '87*, 215–220. Elsevier Science Publications B.V./North-Holland: Amsterdam.
Kobsa, Alfred & Wahlster, Wolfgang (1988). *User Models in Dialog Systems*. Springer-Verlag: Berlin.
Libet, B. (1985). Unconscious Cerebral Initiative and the Role of Conscious Will in Voluntary Action. In *Behavioural and Brain Sciences* **8**(4): 529–539.
Litman, Diane & Allen, James (1984). A Plan Recognition Model for Clarification Subdialogues. In Proceedings of *The COLING-84*, 302–311.
Maes, P. & Nardi, D. (1987). *Meta-level Architecture and Reflection*. North Holland: Amsterdam.
Maruyama, M. (1986). Toward Picture-coded Information Systems. In *Futures*, June, 450–452.
Mc Kevitt, Paul (1986). *Object and Action Frames for Transfer Semantics*. Memorandum in

Computer and cognitive Science, MCCS-86-69, Computing Research Laboratory, Dept. 3CRL, Box 30001, New Mexico State University, Las Cruces, NM 88003-0001, U.S.A.
Mc Kevitt, Paul (1988). *Artificial Communicators: An Operating System Consultant*. Master's Thesis, Computer Science Department, Dept. 3CU, Box 30001, New Mexico State University, Las Cruces, New Mexico 88003-0001, U.S.A, March.
Mc Kevitt, Paul (1991a). Principles and Practice in an Operating System Consultant. In Partridge, Derek (ed.) *Artificial Intelligence and Software Engineering* **1**, Chapter on 'AI Mechanisms and Techniques in Practical Software'. Ablex Publishing Corporation: New York.
Mc Kevitt, Paul (1991b). *Analysing Coherence of Intention in Natural Language Dialogue*. Ph.D. Thesis, Department of Computer Science, University of Exeter, GB- EX4 4PT, U.K., EU.
Mc Kevitt, Paul & Wilks, Yorick (1987). Transfer Semantics in an Operating System Consultant: The Formalization of Actions involving Object Transfer. In Proceedings of *The Tenth International Joint Conference on Artificial Intelligence (IJCAI-87)* **1**: 569–575. Milan, Italy, European community (EC), August.
Mc Kevitt, P., Partridge, D. & Wilks, Y. (1992a). *Approaches to Natural Language Discourse Processing*. Technical Report 227, Department of Computer Science, University of Exeter, GB- EX4 4PT, England, EU.
Mc Kevitt, P., Partridge, D. & Wilks, Y. (1992b). *Analysing Coherence of Intention in Natural Language Dialogue*. Technical Report, Department of Computer Science, University of Exeter, GB- EX4 4PT, Exeter, England, EU.
Mc Kevitt, P., Partridge, D. & Wilks, Y. (1992c). *Why Machines Should Analyse Intention in Natural-language Dialogue*. Technical Report 233, Department of Computer Science, University of Exeter, GB- EX4 4PT, Exeter, England, EU.
Mc Kevitt, P., Partridge, D. & Wilks, Y. (1992d). *Experimenting with Intention in Natural-language Dialogue*. Technical Report 234, Department of Computer Science, University of Exeter, GB- EX4 4PT, Exeter, England, EU.
Normile, D. & Barnes-Svarney, P. (1993). Hold that Thought: Computers Read Minds. In *Popular Science*, June, p. 51.
Oates, T. & Gammack, J. G. (1992). Generating Knowledge for Expert Systems from Data-bases. In *Presentation at the Association of Modelling and Simulation Enterprises (AMSE) International Conference on Modelling, Simulation and Control*, Hefei, China, October.
Pentland, Alex (ed.) (1993). *Looking at People: Recognition and Interpretation of Human Action*. IJCAI-93 Workshop (W28) at The 13th International Conference on Artificial Intelligence (IJCAI-93), Chambéry, France, EU, August.
Pereira, Fernando & Warren, David (1980). Definite Clause Grammars for Language Analysis – A Survey of the Formalism and a Comparison with Augmented Transition Networks. *Artificial Intelligence* **13**: 231–278.
Radin, D. I. (1993). Neural Network Analysis of Consciousness Related Patterns in Random Sequences. In *Journal of Scientific Exploration* **7**(4): 355–373.
Sanderson, David W. (1993). *Smileys*. O Reilly & Associates, Inc., Sebastopol, California.
Sealre, John R. (1969). *Speech Acts: An Essay in the Philosophy of Language*. Cambridge University Press: London.
Schank, Roger C. (1972). Conceptual Dependency: A Theory of Natural Language Understanding. In *Cognitive Psychology* **3**(4): 552–631.
Schank, Roger C. (1973). Identification and Conceptualizations Underlying Natural Language. In Schank, R. & Kolby, K. (eds.) *Computer Models of Thought and Language*. W.H. Freeman and Co.: San Francisco, CA.
Schank, Roger C. (1975). *Conceptual Information Processing*. Fundamental Studies in Computer Science **3**. North-Holland: Amsterdam.
Schank, Roger C. & Abelson, Robert P. (1977). *Scripts, Plans, Goals and Understanding: An Inquiry into Human Knowledge Structures*. Lawrence Erlbaum Associates, Hillsdale, NJ.
Sheehy, N. P., Chapman, A. J. & Forrest, M. A. (1987). Communication Failure in Dialogue: Non-verbal Behaviour at the User Interface. In Megaw, E. D. (ed.) *Contemporary Ergonomics. Proc. Ergonomic Society's 1987 Annual Conference*. Taylor and Francis: London.
Sidner, Candace L. (1983). What the Speaker Means: The Recognition of Speakers' Plans in

Discourse. In *International Journal of Computers and Mathematics, Special Issue in Computational Linguistics* **9**(1): 71–82.
Sidner, Candice L. (1985). Plan Parsing for Intended Response Recognition in Discourse. *Computational Intelligence* **1**(1): 1–10, February.
Suchman, Lucy (1987). *Plans and Situated Actions: The Problem of Human-machine Communication.* Cambridge University Press: Cambridge, United Kingdom.
Tao, Li (1989). *How To Read Faces.* Hamlyn: London.
von Bertalanffy, L. (1950). The Theory of Open Systems in Physics and Biology. In *Science* **3**, Jan. 13th.
Wang, Z.-M. (1993). Editorial: Strategies for Ergonomics in Developing Countries. *Ergonomics* **36**: 597–599.
Wang, Z.-M. & Gammack, J. G. (1995). *Faces and Interfaces: Towards the Computer Mediated Communication of Affect.* Technical Report, Department of Computing and Information Systems, University of Paisley, Paisley, Scotland.
Webber, Bonnie (1978). *A Formal Approach to Discourse Anaphora.* Doctoral Dissertation. Also in, BBN Report No. 3761, Bolt, Beranek & Newman, Cambridge, MA, U.S.A.
Wilensky, Robert (1983). *Planning and Understanding.* Addison-Wesley: Reading, MA.
Wilensky, R., Arens, Y. & Chin, D. (1984). Talking to UNIX in English: An Overview of UC. *Communications of the ACM* **27**(6): 574–593, June.
Wilensky, R., Mayfield, J., Albert, A., Chin, D., Cox, C., Luria, M., Martin, J. & Wu, D. (1986). *UC – A Progress Report.* Report No. UCB/CSD 87/303, Computer Science Division (EECS), University of California, Berkeley, California 94720, U.S.A., July.
Wilensky, R., Chin, D. N., Luria, M., Martin, J., Mayfield, J. & Wu, D. (1988). The Berkeley UNIX Consultant Project. *Computational Linguistics* **14**(4): 35–84, December.
Wilks, Yorick (1973). An Artificial Intelligence Approach to Machine Translation. In Schank, R. & Kolby, K. (eds.) *Computer Models of Thought and Language.* Wh Freeman and Co., San Francisco, CA.
Wilks, Yorick (1975a). Preference Semantics. In Edward, Keenan (ed.) *Formal Semantics of Natural Language.* Cambridge University Press: Cambridge, United Kingdom. Also as, Memo AIM-206, Artificial Intelligence Laboratory, Stanford University, Stanford, California, U.S.A., July 1973.
Wilks, Yorick (1975b). An Intelligent Analyzer and Understander of English. *Communications of the ACM*, **18**(5): 264–274, May. Also in Grosz, B., Jones, K. S. & Webber, B. (eds.) *Readings in Natural Language Processing*, 193–204. Morgan Kaufmann, 1986: Los Altos, California.
Wilks, Yorick (1975c). A Preferential, Pattern-seeking Semantics for Natural Language Inference. *Artificial Intelligence* **6**: 53–74.
Winograd, Terry & Flores, Fernando (1986). *Understanding Computers and Cognition: A New Foundation for Design.* Ablex Publishing Corporation: Norwood, New Jersey.
Yazdani, Masoud & Mealing, Stuart (1995). Communicating Through Pictures. In Mc Kevitt, Paul (ed.) *Artificial Intelligence Review, Special Issue on Integration of Natural Language and Vision Processing* **9**(2–3): 205–213.

Artificial Intelligence Review **10**: 299–319, 1996.

Multimodal Interfaces

ALEX WAIBEL[1,2], MINH TUE VO[1], PAUL DUCHNOWSKI[2] and STEFAN MANKE[2]

[1] *School of Computer Science, Carnegie Mellon University, Pittsburgh, PA 15213-3890, U.S.A.;* [2] *University of Karlsruhe, Computer Science Department, ILKD, Am Fasanengarten 5, 76128 Karlsruhe, Germany; Email: ahw@cs.cmu.edu, tue@cs.cmu.edu, paul_d@ira.uka.de, manke@ira.uka.de*

Abstract. In this paper, we present an overview of research in our laboratories on Multimodal Human Computer Interfaces. The goal for such interfaces is to free human computer interaction from the limitations and acceptance barriers due to rigid operating commands and keyboards as the only/main I/O-device. Instead we move to involve all available human communication modalities. These human modalities include Speech, Gesture and Pointing, Eye-Gaze, Lip Motion and Facial Expression, Handwriting, Face Recognition, Face Tracking, and Sound Localization.

Key words: multimodal interfaces, speech recognition, lip-reading, gesture recognition, handwriting recognition, neural networks.

1. INTRODUCTION

Recent developments in the computer and communication industries are accelerating the pace and variety of forms in which information is delivered to users worldwide. This, in turn, multiplies the problems associated with managing and interacting with the new wealth of data and information. The combination of sound, images, and text is already available on Multimedia PC's and publishing companies are advancing their goal of delivering multimedia information to everyone as the "Information Super-Highway" unfolds. While the multiplicity and amount of information expands, ways to access it or communicate with it remain limited. Relatively primitive input devices and interfaces, such as keyboard and mouse still dominate as interfaces. In contrast, human-to-human communication takes advantage of a wealth of hints and signals, explicit or implicit, that are lost in human-computer interaction. Meeting "face-to-face", having "eye-contact", "reading one's lips", "handwaving", "pointing one's finger at someone or something", as well as "plain talk" make human communication richer than simple text transmittal. Speech and writing represent perhaps the most direct expressions of language, but are routinely complemented by other mostly visual modalities (e.g., "body-language"). These will need to be processed also if one hopes to achieve truly natural human-computer interaction. To increase their effectiveness, human-computer interfaces should, therefore, include and combine visual as well as spoken or textual language to represent the full spectrum of human communication.

In this paper, we present our efforts toward developing richer human-computer and computer mediated human-human interfaces that attempt to embrace and take advantage of *all* communication modalities. The INTERACT project involves a number of research projects in progress at our labs at Carnegie Mellon University in Pittsburgh, U.S.A., and University of Karlsruhe, Germany. They are aimed at interpreting the visual and acoustic instantiations of language as we use them to communicate day to day. The modalities of interest in our work at both labs are: speech understanding (and translation), sound source localization, gesture recognition, lipreading, handwriting recognition, eye- and face tracking. Our research involves improving recognition accuracies of the modality specific component processors, as well as development of optimal combination of multiple input signals to deduce user intent more reliably in cross-modal "speech"-acts. More specifically, we aim to combine visual, acoustic and textual cues, including:

- Speech recognition with lipreading for more robust recognition
- Gesture with speech for multimodal interpretation
- Speech with Handwriting for more flexible, redundant input
- Face- and eyetracking with sound source localization for robust speech extraction in adverse acoustic environments (the cocktail-party effect)
- Face- and eyetracking with speech recognition for focus of attention (who is the user talking to? What is he/she referring to?)

We have begun attacking these advanced goals along a rather broad front of activity. The present paper reviews where we currently stand in three of these subtopics: lipreading (as a complement to speech recognition), gesture recognition (as a complement to speech) and on-line handwriting character recognition. Wherever possible, we develop learning strategies (mostly connectionist and statistical), to ensure scalability and portability to larger and different application domains. In the following we discuss these three efforts and report on initial results of cross-modal integration.

2. AUTOMATIC LIP-READING AND SPEECH RECOGNITION

Lip movement is a visual information source tightly and synchronously coupled to the acoustic speech act and hence can be naturally viewed as an integral part of a speech recognition effort. This is in contrast to other communication modalities described later in this article, such as gestures or handwriting, which may be invoked independently of speech.

Most approaches to automated speech recognition (ASR) that consider solely acoustic information are very sensitive to background noise or fail totally when two or more voices are present simultaneously (cocktail-party effect), as often happens in offices, conference rooms, outdoors, and other real-world environments. Humans deal with these distortions by considering additional sources such as directional, contextual, and visual information, primarily lip movements. This latter source is subconsciously involved in the recognition process and is used extensively by hearing-impaired individuals, but also contributes significantly to normal hearing recognition. The usefulness of lip movement stems in large part from its rough complementariness to the acoustic signal: the former is most reliable for distinguishing the place of articulation (ex. Jackson 1993), the latter conveys most robustly manner and voicing information (ex. Miller and Nicely 1955).

The task of exploiting lip-reading in an automatic speech recognition system requires the solution of two conceptually distinct but not independent problems: suitable representation and recognition of the visual signal and the integration of thus obtained visual evidence with the acoustic side. Clearly, a given type of visual pre-processing will constrain the options available for further combination of the two sources.

2.1. *Related Research*

The first significant attempt to supplement acoustic ASR with lip-reading was the system built by Petajan and applied to a speaker-dependent isolated-word (vocabulary of 100 words) recognition task (Petajan 1984). Four static features were extracted from each image frame and a linear time-warping procedure was used to identify the most probable word. By combining the output of the optical recognizer with that of a commercial ASR system the recognition rate was improved from 65 to 78%. In a follow-up effort (Petajan *et al.* 1988) simplified optical processing was used to achieve near real-time performance. The image of the speaker's mouth area was captured by a camera and lighting system installed in a head-mounted harness, circumventing some image-processing problems. The combination of optical and acoustic decisions was achieved via a set of 30 heuristic rules. The overall performance was similar to the earlier system.

Mase and Pentland (1991) chose to parameterize the oral cavity image by computing average optical flow vectors in four regions of the picture designed to capture the movement of particular facial muscles. The regions were selected manually by the experimenters. They used template matching (on optical data alone) to recognize strings of three to five digits from three speakers. Average word recognition rate was roughly 75%.

Neural networks were used by Yuhas *et al.* (1989) with both optical and acoustic input to distinguish among 9 vowel phonemes under varying acoustic signal-to-noise ratio (SNR). Only static images (not sequences) were used as the optical input. Furthermore, the relative contribution of visual and acoustic information was adjusted according to the SNR by an "omniscient controller" (i.e., the value of the SNR is explicitly given). The visual input was shown to compensate for noise-induced performance drop in purely acoustic recognition.

Stork *et al.* (1992) measured the position of ten reflective markers placed on the lips of the talker thus significantly simplifying the issue of optical data capture. From these measurements they derived five parameters as the visual input. Separate Time Delay Neural Networks (TDNN) processed acoustic and optical data to render a decision on one of 10 English letters spoken in isolation. Visual and acoustic-alone recognition was 51% and 64%, respectively. By combining the outputs in a Bayesian framework, they achieved overall performance of 91%.

Goldschen (1993) used 13 visual features extracted from processed image frames acquired with a head-mounted camera as in (Petajan *et al.* 1988) to identify one out of 150 possible TIMIT sentences spoken by a single talker. It appears that the sentences were treated essentially as very long words in this setup. Vector quantization of the input allowed the use of discrete Hidden Markov Models (HMM) in the recognition process. The system using generalized "triseme" models achieved 25% recognition rate (visual information only).

2.2. *Initial System*

Our integrated acoustic/visual continuous-speech ASR system was first reported in (Bregler *et al.* 1993). It was developed for a spelling task using the German alphabet. Training and test utterances comprise spelled (without pauses) names and nonsense letter sequences of arbitrary and unknown to the recognizer lengths. The task is thus equivalent to continuous recognition with a small but highly confusable vocabulary.

2.2.1. *System Description*

We record acoustic and visual data in parallel and pre-process them as illustrated in Figure 1. The acoustic signal is sampled at 16 kHz with 12-bit resolution. A fairly standard front-end then divides the data stream into overlapping windows (Hamming windows) at 10-msec frame rate and transforms the data to frequency domain by computing 16 numbers (the so-called Melscale Fourier coefficients) for each frame.

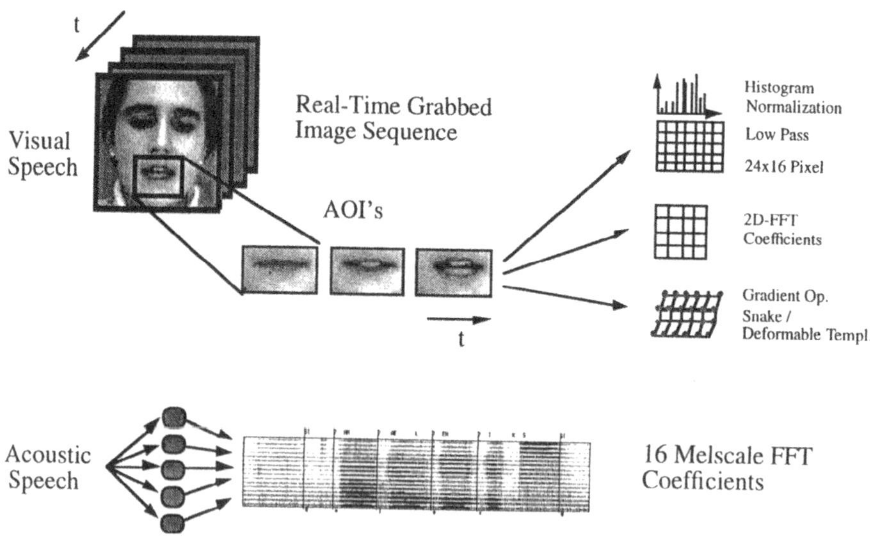

Fig. 1. Bimodal Data Acquisition for Speech Recognition and Lip-reading

Visual data was initially captured as 256 × 256 pixel images with 8-bit gray level resolution per pixel. A smaller area of 144 × 80 pixels centered on the mouth was then manually extracted and, after low-pass filtering, downsampled to a 24 × 16 pixel image. The resulting 384 gray level values were then normalized for each frame to lie between −1.0 and 1.0 and constituted the visual evidence available to the classification algorithms.

We make use of a concept called "viseme" in our system. A "viseme" is the rough correlate of the phoneme, i.e., the smallest visually distinguishable unit of speech. In general, and for our purposes, visemes are defined by a many-to-one mapping from the set of phonemes. This reflects the fact that many phonemes (for instance: /p/, /b/, /m/) are essentially indistinguishable from visual information alone.

We use a modular Multi-State Time Delay Neural Network (MS-TDNN) (Hild and Waibel 1993) to perform the actual recognition. Figure 2 shows the architecture. Through the first three layers (input-hidden-phoneme/viseme) the acoustic and visual inputs are processed separately. The third of these layers produces activations for 65 phoneme states on the acoustic side and 42 viseme states on the visual side. In our system phoneme-to-phoneme (and thus viseme-to-viseme) transitions were included as separate phone (viseme) states.

The outputs of the phoneme and viseme layers are integrated in the units of the combined layer (this layer does not exist in the basic MS-TDNN). The activation of each combined phone-state is the weighted sum of the activations of the corresponding phoneme-state and viseme-state units. Some visemes will therefore influence more than one of the combined layer units. In the final layer (which copies the activations from the combined layer) a one stage Dynamic Time

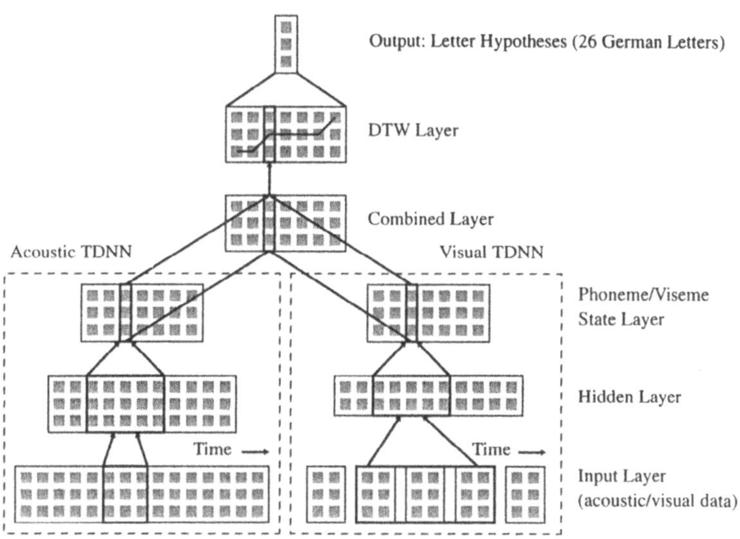

Fig. 2. Network Architecture for the Audio/Visual ASR System.

Warping algorithm (Ney 1984) is applied to find the optimal path through the phone-hypotheses that corresponds to a sequence of letter models.

Network training is done in two phases. First, the acoustic and visual sub-nets are trained separately to fit phoneme/viseme targets. Second, the complete network is trained to fit letter targets. Error backpropagation is used to find the connection weights resulting in optimal recognition of the training data. The weights determining the combination of the two sub-nets are not trained this way, rather they are computed dynamically during recognition to reflect the apparent reliability of the sub-net outputs. Specifically, the activations of the phoneme and viseme layers are normalized to represent probabilities and the entropy of each sub-net's output is computed. Low entropy signifies probability concentrated in a few units, i.e., relative confidence in the respective sub-net's identification. Conversely, high entropy corresponds to near equal probability of most phonemes or visemes. Accordingly, we symmetrically weight the acoustic and visual contributions to the combined layer in inverse proportion to their respective entropies.

2.2.2. *Results*

Table 1 shows recognition performance originally achieved on a speaker-dependent task (Bregler *et al.* 1993). Training data consisted of 75/200 training and 39/150 testing sequences for two speakers (identified by their initials msm and mcb in Table 1). Misclassified, omitted and inserted letters were counted as errors. The rows marked with "noisy" correspond to experiments in which the acoustic data was corrupted with broadband noise until the acoustic-alone performance was significantly reduced.

Table 1. Word accuracy (in %) of Speech/Lip System.

Speaker	Acoustic	Visual	Combined
msm/clean	89	32	93
msm/noisy	47	32	76
mcb/clean	97	47	97
mcb/noisy	59	47	70

The results show that adding visual information can significantly boost overall recognition rate despite the relatively poor performance on visual input alone. The improvement is naturally most evident when the acoustic speech is noisy.

Further experiments were carried out on a database of 6 speakers (2 female, 4 male) to test the performance on a multispeaker task (Bregler 1993). 80 sequences per speaker were used for training and 10 for testing. Visual-alone mode achieved only 12% word accuracy. Nonetheless, by adding it to the acoustic-mode we reduced the error rate by almost 9% for clean speech and 29% for 30 dB SNR.

2.3. *Current Development Directions*

At present we are seeking to improve the performance of the system on the letter spelling task, with the view of extending it to continuous speech recognition. We have been concentrating on the visual side of the system since the acoustic technology is much more mature at this point.

2.3.1. *Robustness*

In a practical system, manual extraction of the mouth region from the face image is not acceptable. As a first step away from this method we have recorded new data where the speaker is asked to position himself such that his lips are visible within a rectangle shown on the workstation screen. The image in that frame is then used directly.

We have been experimenting with this system to understand the principal weaknesses and sources of "fragility". Contrary to initial suspicion, the processing appears relatively insensitive to reasonable variation in lighting conditions. We have implemented a different version of the gray-level normalization procedure that further protects the performance under varying average image brightness. Severe illumination gradients would still pose a problem and might be alleviated through adaptive histogram equalization. However, this would significantly increase the computational load.

The shift of the lip image within the frame has been found to cause a more serious degradation as shown in the following experiment. We trained the network on 180 newly recorded sequences from one speaker. The images in the training sequences that the network recognizes perfectly were then diagonally shifted within the frame by three pixels. The direction of shift was chosen at random for each successive image (even in the same sequence). This shift is equivalent to the speaker moving his face by only about 2 millimeters. Yet the word accuracy dropped to 87%. With a six-pixel shift the recognition was 66%. Even more severe losses were observed when the shift was effected in a constant direction.

We are investigating several approaches to counteract this effect. First, we are designing a detector to automatically and precisely locate the lips within a picture. In addition to compensating for the likely shifts, this would obviate the need for the speaker to hold his head in a constant orientation. Initial, speaker-dependent results indicate that a neural network detector can reliably locate the lip region under varying image size, lighting and backgrounds.

To further increase robustness, we are training the visual TDNN on several copies of the training images artificially shifted and scaled. The idea is to let the network learn the patterns as they may occur in different locations and sizes within the frame. With 600 training sequences (created with artificial image translation but at constant size) the system already shows insensitivity to image shifts, approaching the performance levels observed on originally hand-excised frames. Finally, we are investigating different parameterizations of the input that might already exhibit shift invariance. The magnitude of the Fourier Transform of the image is one such representation.

2.3.2. *Parameterization*

There is almost certainly much irrelevant and/or redundant information in the 384 gray level values currently used as the visual input. Also, such a large parameter count increases significantly the number of network weights that need to be estimated. A smaller parameter set should lead to better generalization (particularly for speaker-independent recognition) and computational load reduction. We would like to reduce the number of visual parameters without invoking heuristics for image segmentation or feature extraction; the TDNN is expected to form its own internal representation of the relevant features.

Preliminary experiments show that we can represent the images by their first 32 principal components, thus reducing the data by a factor of 6, without visibly undermining performance. It should be noted that this representation (relying as it does on the correlations among the original data points) is sensitive to image shifts, as also found in other studies (ex. Turk and Pentland 1991). We are also investigating linear discriminant analysis, a related technique, which might prove better for image classification (as opposed to representation).

2.3.3. *Acoustic/Visual Integration*

There is evidence that humans combine acoustic and visual information before classification, i.e., without making separate decisions based on each modality (Summerfield 1983; Braida 1991). An automatic system should also benefit from integration at a low level, thanks to the availability of cross-modal features (for instance, temporal relationships between events in the two modalities). This is of course contingent on the availability of sufficient training data to robustly train the magnified network that results from increasing the size of the input vector. Preliminary experiments (Bregler 1993) suggest that this approach to modality integration is, in fact, not feasible without visual data reduction. This observation supplies more motivation still for the work described in Section 2.3.2.

Low level modality integration allows us also to avoid the tricky problem of viseme specification. While it is reasonably straightforward to specify the phoneme-to-viseme mapping in discrete syllables, the same is not true for continuous speech, especially when considering segmentation and coarticulation effects. However, if we are lead to maintain integration at the phoneme/viseme level, the combination scheme will be expanded. The units in the combined layer would likely benefit from drawing inputs from more than just the corresponding phoneme and viseme. For instance, the identity of the "second guess" of each sub-net should prove relevant.

3. ON-LINE CURSIVE HANDWRITING RECOGNITION

The recognition of cursive (or continuous) handwriting, as it is being written on a touch screen or graphics tablet, has not only scientific but also significant practical value, e.g. for note pad computers or for integration into multi-modal systems. Several different preprocessing and recognition approaches both for optical character recognition (OCR) and on-line character recognition (OLCR) have been developed during the last decades. The main advantage of OLCR is the temporal information of handwriting, which can be recorded and used for recognition. In general this dynamic writing information (the coordinate sequence) is not available in OCR, where input consists of scanned text (bitmaps). By contrast, in OLCR systems, the spatial context and proximity of the strokes of characters are distorted or lost, when one merely retains and uses pen coordinates as a function of time.

We have developed an input representation for OLCR, which combines the advantages of bitmaps used in OCR with the dynamic writing information of OLCR. In this input representation characters and words are represented as a sequence of so called *context bitmaps*, which are basically low resolution descriptions of the coordinate's neighborhood.

This input representation is used with a connectionist recognizer, which is well suited for handling temporal sequences of patterns as provided by this kind of input representation. This recognizer, a Multi-State Time Delay Neural Network (MS-TDNN) (Haffner and Waibel 1991), integrates the segmentation and recognition of words into a single network architecture. The MS-TDNN, which was originally proposed for continuous speech recognition tasks (Hild and Waibel 1993; Bregler *et al.* 1993), combines shift invariant high accuracy pattern recognition capabilities of a TDNN (Waibel *et al.* 1989; Guyon *et al.* 1991) with a non-linear time alignment procedure (dynamic time warping) (Ney 1984) for aligning strokes into character sequences.

Figure 3a shows the basic architecture of our on-line handwriting recognition system. This recognition system is integrated into the example application, which is shown in Figure 3b. The following sections describe the preprocessing techniques, the MS-TDNN architecture, and present recognition results for

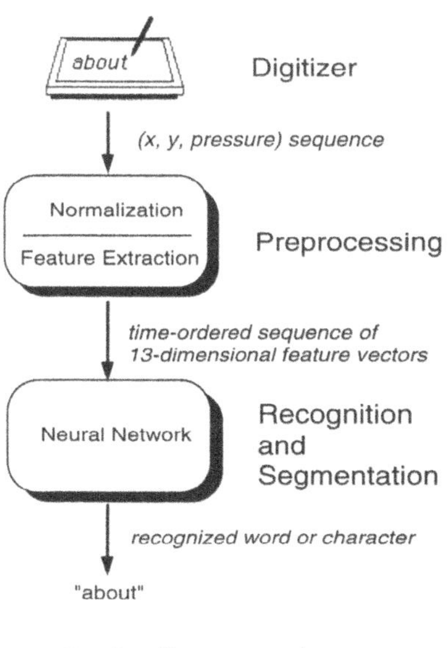

Fig. 3a. System overview.

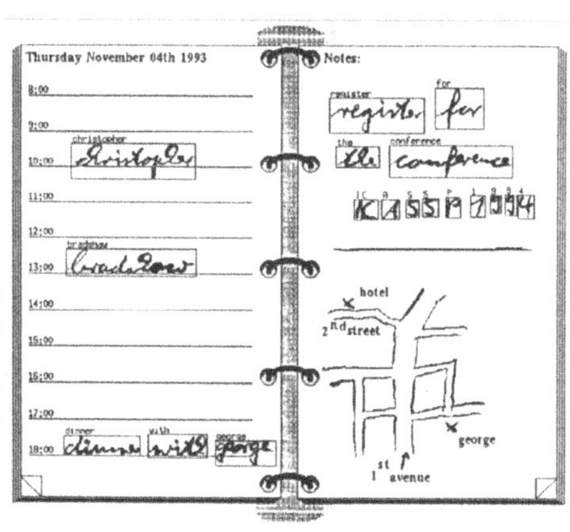

Fig. 3b. Example application.

writer-independent, single-character recognition tasks and large-vocabulary, writer-dependent, cursive handwriting recognition tasks with vocabulary sizes from 400 up to 20000 words.

3.1. *Preprocessing*

Preprocessing of the time-ordered coordinate sequence provided by the digitizer is performed in two successive steps: normalization and feature extraction.

3.1.1. *Normalization*

Normalization is performed to remove irrelevant variability occurring in the raw coordinate sequence. To compensate for varying writing speeds of different writers and of a single writer within a single word or character, the coordinate sequence is resampled, so that all successive coordinates are equally spaced. Then the resampled coordinate sequence is smoothed, using a moving average window, which mainly removes undesired sampling noise.

After that a baseline normalization of the word is performed. In a two stage process the word is first rotated according to the linear regression through all points, to get a rough correction of the word's orientation. Then, in a second fine adjustment the word is rotated according to the linear regression with respect to all local minima only. Finally, the word or character is linearly rescaled to a fixed height.

3.1.2. *Feature Extraction*

The second step of our preprocessing is the extraction of features along the pen trajectory yielding a sequence of time-ordered feature vectors. The basic idea of our feature extraction is to refer to low level topological features of the trajectory only and leave the extraction of high level features to the connectionist recognizer.

We started with a set of strictly local features similar to those in (Schenkel *et al.* 1994) and (Guyon *et al.* 1991). Each frame consisted of information on the pen position (x, y coordinates), directional features (Δx, Δy), curvature, speed and pen-up/pen-down indicator. But an inspection of the confusion matrices of networks trained on these features revealed significant problems in discriminating between cursive letters like "*a*" and "*u*" or "*g*" and "*y*", which look very similar and differ only in small regions of the characters (see Figure 4 for examples). These problems arise due to the fact that the features are strictly local, which

"a" "u" "g" "y"

Fig. 4. Differences between cursive characters, which are hard to detect, if only local information is used.

means that they are local both in space and time. Therefore they are inadequate for modeling temporal long range context dependencies occurring in the pen trajectory.

The basis for the new set of features is a bitmap representation of the digitizer input. After normalization of the input we map the sequence of points (x_t, y_t) to a grey scale bitmap $B = \{b(i, j)\}$, where $b(i, j)$ indicates the number of points (x_t, y_t) falling into pixel (i, j).

In contrast to the limitations of optical character recognition, where bitmaps are the only source of information, we also know the time sequence of the points. This leads to the following method of combining spatial and temporal sources: Assume (x_t, y_t) falls into bitmap pixel (i, j). Consider a local $d \times d$ section of bitmap B centered around (i, j) (Figure 5b) and derive a 3×3 grey scale bitmap L_t by averaging this section (Figure 5c). That means, we derive a temporal sequence of low resolution bitmaps L_t centered around (x_t, y_t) (Figure 5a). These bitmaps plus directional information $(\Delta x, \Delta y)$ and the pen-up/pen-down feature form the new set of input features we use for recognition.

These features are still local in space but no longer local in time. Each point of the trajectory is visible from each other point of the trajectory in a small neighborhood. Therefore, we call the local bitmaps L_t *context bitmaps*. They seem to be appropriate for modeling temporal long range and spatial short range phenomena as observed in pen trajectories.

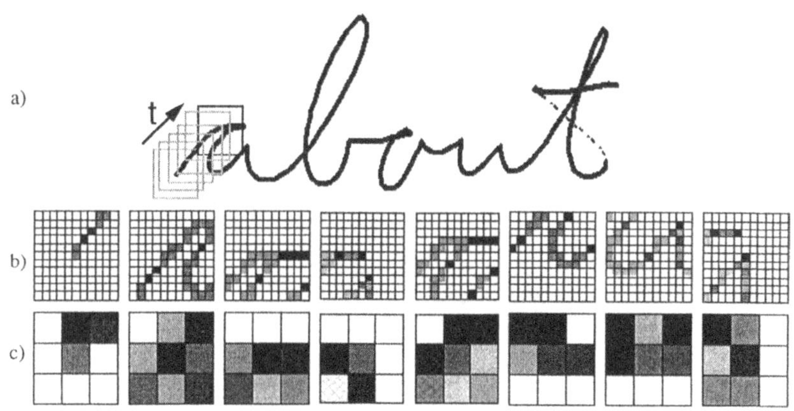

Fig. 5. Calculation of Context Bitmaps.

3.2. *The Multi-State Time-Delay Neural Network Architecture*

The input representation, which is described in the previous section, is used with a connectionist recognizer both for single character and cursive handwriting recognition tasks. This recognizer integrates the recognition and segmentation of words into a single network architecture, the Multi-State Time Delay Neural Network (MS-TDNN). Words are represented as a sequence of character, where each character is modeled by one or more states. For the results in this paper, each character is modeled by 3 states, representing the initial, middle, and final sections of a character.

The basic MS-TDNN architecture is shown in Figure 6. Only a brief description of its operation with respect to handwriting recognition is given here; references (Haffner *et al.* 1991), (Haffner and Waibel 1992), and (Hild and Waibel 1993) describe in detail the MS-TDNN and its applications in continuous speech recognition.

The first three layers constitute a standard TDNN with sliding input windows of certain sizes. This TDNN computes scores for each state and for each time frame in the states layer. In the dynamic time warping layer (DTW layer) each word of the vocabulary is modeled by a sequence of states, the corresponding scores are simply copied from the states layer into the word models of the DTW layer. An optimal alignment path is found by the DTW algorithm for each word and the sum of all activations along this optimal path is taken as the score for the word output unit.

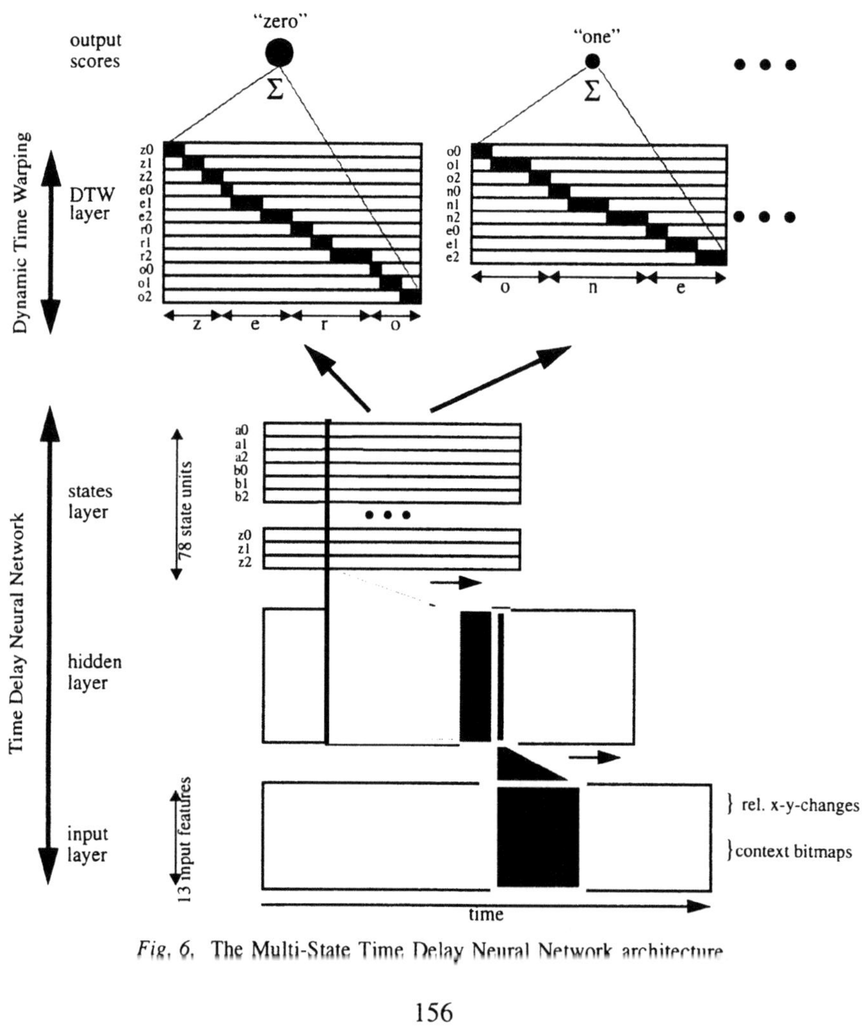

Fig. 6. The Multi-State Time Delay Neural Network architecture

Once the network is trained on a particular vocabulary other vocabularies of varying sizes can be used without retraining, just by replacing the word models in the DTW layer.

All network parameters such as the number of states per character, the size of the input windows, or the number of hidden units are optimized manually for the results presented in this paper, but can also be optimized automatically by the Automatic Structure Optimization (ASO) algorithm that we have proposed elsewhere (Bodenhausen *et al.* 1993). By using the ASO algorithm, no time-consuming manual tuning of these network parameters for particular handwriting tasks and training set sizes is necessary while achieving optimal recognition performance.

3.3. *Experiments and Results*

We have tested the input representation together with the MS-TDNN architecture both on single character recognition tasks and cursive (continuous) handwriting recognition tasks. The handwriting databases used for training and testing of the MS-TDNN were collected at the University of Karlsruhe. All data is recorded on a pressure sensitive graphics tablet with a cordless stylus, which produces a sequence of time ordered 3-dimensional vectors (at a maximum report rate of 205 dots per second) consisting of the x-y-coordinates and a pressure value for each dot. All subjects had to write a set of single words from a 400 word vocabulary, covering all lower case letters, and at least one set of isolated lower case letters, upper case letters, and digit. For the continuous handwriting results presented in this paper only the data of one of the authors was used. All data is preprocessed as described before.

Table 2 shows results for different writer independent, single character recognition tasks (isolated characters). Writer dependent recognition results for cursive handwriting (isolated words) can be found in Table 3. The network used for the results in Table 3 is trained with aprox. 2000 training patterns from a 400

Table 2. Single character recognition results (writer independent).

Task	Training patterns	Test patterns	Recognition rate (%)
0_9	1600	200 (20 writers)	99
A_Z	2000	520 (20 writers)	95
a_z	2000	520 (20 writers)	93

Table 3. Results for different writer dependent cursive handwriting tasks.

Task	Vocabulary size (words)	Test patterns	Recognition rate (%)
msm_400_a	400	800	98
msm_400_b	400	800	97
msm_1000	1000	2000	95
msm_10000	10000	2000	87
msm_20000	20000	2000	83

word vocabulary (msm_400_a) and tested without any retraining on different vocabularies with sizes from 400 up to 20000 words. Vocabularies msm_400_b, msm_1000, msm_10000, and msm_20000 are completely different from the vocabulary on which the network was trained and were selected randomly from a 100000 word vocabulary (Wall Street Journal Vocabulary). First experiments on writer independent, cursive handwriting databases have shown recognition rates of more than 76% on a 400 word vocabulary.

These result show that the proposed input representation and MS-TDNN architecture can be used both for single character recognition and cursive handwriting recognition tasks with high recognition performance. The MS-TDNN performs well not only on the vocabulary it was trained for (see task *msm_400_a*), but also for other vocabularies it has never seen before (see task *msm_400_b*), even on much larger vocabularies (see tasks *msm_1000, msm_10000*, and *msm_20000*).

4. GESTURE RECOGNITION

We have been investigating pen-based gestures drawn using a stylus on a digitizing tablet. This kind of gesture is simpler to handle than hand gestures captured with a camera but still allows for rich and powerful expressions, as any editor who has to mark up manuscripts knows. Pen-based gestures are becoming popular on hand-held computers, but the focus of our research is mainly on how gestures can be effectively combined with other input modalities, because using gestures as the sole input channel seems to be a still clumsy way of issuing commands to computers. In order to pursue this direction of investigation, we developed a multimodal text editor capable of recognizing speech and gesture commands (Vo and Waibel 1993).

The initial multimodal editor we developed currently uses 8 editing gestures (see Table 4). Some of these were inspired by standard mark-up symbols used by human editors. Others, such as the "delete" symbols, are what most people would automatically use when correcting written text with normal pencil and paper.

Table 4. Text-editing gestures.

○	Select	(	Begin selection
×	Delete	)	End selection
/	Delete	∽	Transpose
∧	Paste	_S‾	Split line

We use a temporal representation of gestures. A gesture is captured as a sequence of coordinates tracking the stylus as it moves over the tablet's surface, as opposed to a static bitmapped representation of the shape of the gesture. This dynamic representation was motivated by its successful use in handwritten character recognition (Section 3 and Guyon *et al.* 1991). Results of experiments described in (Guyon *et al.* 1991) suggest that the time-sequential signal contains more information relevant to classification than the static image, leading to better recognition performance.

In our current implementation, the stream of data from the digitizing tablet goes through a preprocessing phase (Guyon *et al.* 1991). The coordinates are normalized and resampled at regular intervals to eliminate differences in size and drawing speed; from these resampled coordinates we extract local geometric information at each point, such as the direction of pen movement and the curvature of the trajectory. These features are believed to hold discriminatory information that could help in the recognition process and thus can give the neural network recognizer appropriate information to find temporal regularities in the input stream.

4.2. *Gesture Classification Using Neural Networks*

We use a TDNN (Waibel *et al.* 1989) (see Figure 7) to classify each preprocessed time-sequential signal as a gesture among the predefined set of 8 gestures. Each gesture in the set is represented by an output unit. Each data point in the input stream is represented by 8 input units corresponding to the 8 features extracted during the preprocessing phases; these include pen coordinates and pressure as well as local geometric information as mentioned above. The network is trained on a set of manually classified gestures using a modified backpropagation algorithm (Waibel *et al.* 1989).

During training, the 10 units in the first hidden layer essentially become "feature detectors" that extract low-level patterns from the input, and the 8 hidden units in the next layer learn to spot those features that contribute to the recognition of each of the 8 gestures. Each output unit integrates over time the

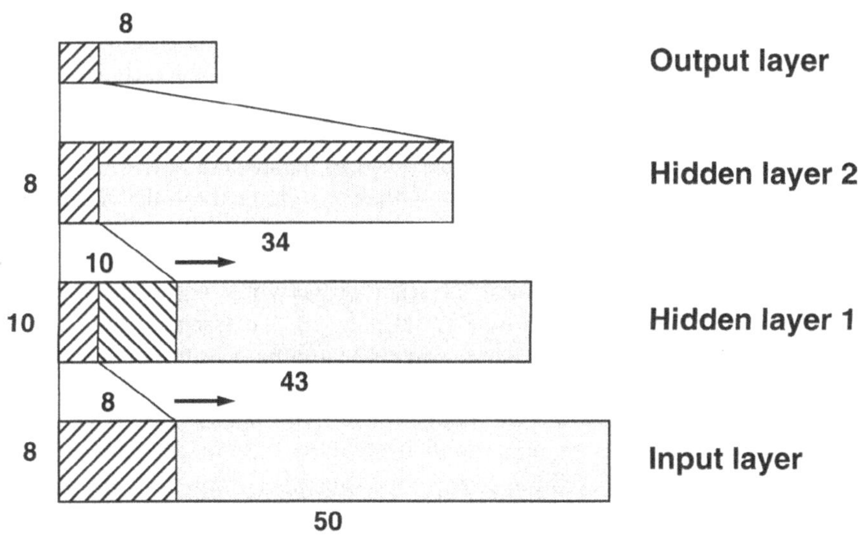

Fig. 7. TDNN architecture for gesture recognition.

evidence from the corresponding unit in the second hidden layer. The output unit with the highest activation level determines the recognized gesture.

The data samples used to train and evaluate the gesture recognizer were collected from a single "gesturer." Among the collected samples, 640 samples (80 per gesture) form the training set, and 160 samples (20 per gesture) form an independent test set which was never seen by the network during training. Our gesture recognizer achieves almost 99% recognition rate on both the training data and the test set.

4.3. *Learning in Gesture/Handwriting Recognition*

The usefulness of gesture and handwriting recognition depends largely on the ability to adapt to new users because of the great range of variability in the way individuals write or make gestures. No matter how many tokens we put in the training database to cover different gestures that mean "delete text", for example, there may always be totally different gestures that are not yet part of the gesture vocabulary. This is particularly troublesome for neural-network-based systems because usually the network has to be retrained using all the old training data mixed with a large number of new examples, in order to be able to recognize new patterns without catastrophically forgetting previously learned patterns. Because of the large number of examples needed and the long retraining time, this clearly cannot be done on-line in a way that would enable the user to continue to work productively. A good system should be able to query the user for correction and remember the particular input pattern that caused the error in order to make intelligent guesses when similar inputs occur. Such a fallback method would offer a reasonable level of performance until the network can be retrained off-line.

We have developed a method to accomplish this using an Incremental TDNN (ITDNN) architecture (Vo 1994). We start by training a regular TDNN using all the available data to obtain a base network. When a recognition error occurs during use, the system queries the user for the correct output and creates template-matching hidden units that influence the output units via excitatory or inhibitory connections (see Figure 8). Template matching is accomplished by making the weight matrix of the extra unit proportional to the activation matrix of the first hidden layer; this was deemed better than matching the input layer directly because during training by backpropagation the units of the first hidden layer have learned to spot input features relevant to classification.

In order to retain the time-shift invariant property that makes the TDNN such a powerful classifier of time-sequential patterns, we assemble the extra units out of subunits, each one having weights matching a different section of the activation template, that is, the activation matrix of the first hidden layer. Thus the extra "units" can in fact be thought of as extra hidden layers. The purpose of this is to enable these subunits to slide along the time dimension just like the regular TDNN units. Since consecutive subunits (within the same extra unit) will tend to have high activations in consecutive time slices, we employ a time-warping technique to compute match scores (see Figure 9). If a subsequent input pattern is similar to the template used to create an extra unit, the extra

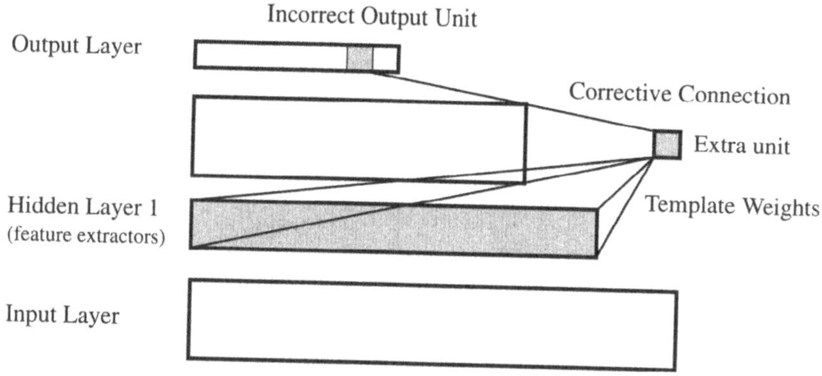

Fig. 8. The incremental TDNN architecture.

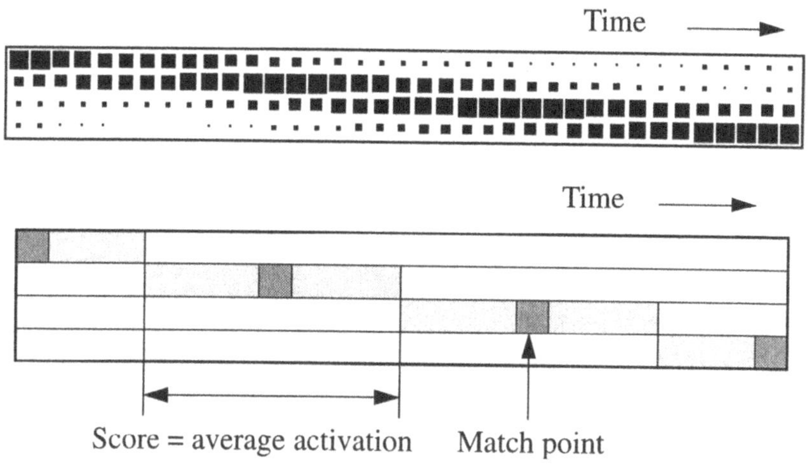

Fig. 9. Activation trace of an extra unit composed of four subunits.

unit is turned on and thus able to influence the corresponding output unit. We use extra units to fix recognition errors by lowering outputs that are incorrectly high via inhibitory (negative weight) connections, and by boosting outputs that are incorrectly low via excitatory (positive weight) connections.

We tested the incremental learning capability of the ITDNN in a series of experiments involving simple handwritten digit recognition (Vo 1994). This task was chosen because it is simple enough so that we can easily eliminate the influence of factors extraneous to what we want to measure: what is the degradation in performance on old input patterns when the ITDNN is trained on new input patterns. Although the development of the ITDNN was motivated by our gesture recognition research, handwriting recognition is very similar and poses the same problems as gesture recognition, hence the results of the experiments described here are still relevant.

We trained a base network with examples of handwritten digits, each written in a consistent way. We then tested the network on a different variation of one digit (namely the digit 6 written in a clockwise direction rather than counter-clockwise as in the training set). The base TDNN was unable to recognize any of the new examples. When a single extra unit was added, the resulting ITDNN was able to correctly classify 99% of the new examples while "forgetting" only 0.6% of the old training examples.

These experiments show that the ITDNN is capable of quickly adding coverage for a new input variation without forgetting previously learned information and thus is a good candidate for systems requiring on-line, immediate recognition improvements during use, such as gesture and handwriting recognizers for pen-based computers. Systems capable of incremental learning will be able to adapt quickly to a new user at a reasonable level of performance while allowing productive work to continue. During subsequent work sessions new data can be unobtrusively collected for off-line training of a full network with regular architecture. This presumably superior network can then replace the patched one.

4.4. *The Language of Speech and Gesture*

Figure 10 shows a block diagram of the multimodal interpreter module in our speech- and gesture- based text editor.

The TDNN-based gesture recognizer was described in Section 4.2. For the speech component we use many alternative speech recognition strategies; these include a keyword spotter developed by Zeppenfeld (1992, 1993) as well as full-scale continuous speech recognition modules such as Sphinx (Huang *et al.* 1993) and Janus (Wosczyna *et al.* 1993). The speech recognition module is coupled with a Recursive Transition Network parser (Ward 1991) using a semantic grammar developed for the editing task. For the keyword-spotting version, the word spotter was trained to spot 11 keywords representing editing commands such as *move, delete, . . .* and textual units such as *character, word, . . .* The effect is to let the user speak naturally without having to worry about grammar and vocabulary, as long as the utterance contains the relevant keywords. For example, an utterance such as "Please delete this word for me" is equivalent to "Delete word". In the case of continuous speech recognition, the semantic-fragment parser

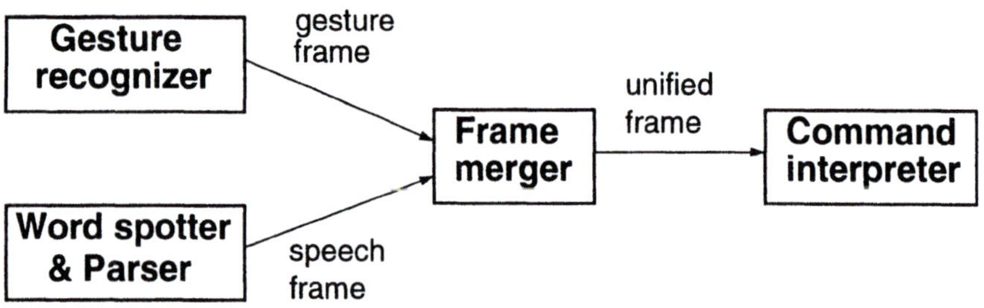

Fig. 10. Joint interpretation of gesture and speech.

achieves essentially the same effect by matching fragments of the recognized speech against predefined templates to find semantically meaningful parts of the text. It then creates a frame consisting of slots representing various components of a plausible semantic interpretation, and fills in any slot it can using semantic fragments found in the hypothesized sentence.

The interpretation of multimodal inputs was based on semantic frames and slots representing parts of an interpretation of user intent. The speech and gesture recognizers produce partial hypotheses in the form of partially filled frames. The output of the interpreter is obtained by unifying the information contained in the partial frames.

In the system each frame has slots named *action* and *scope* (what to operate on.) Within *scope* there are subslots named *type* and *textual-unit*. The possible scope types include "point" and "box"; the textual units include "character," "word," "line" . . .

Consider an example in which a user draws a circle and says "Please delete this word". The gesture-processing subsystem recognizes the circle and fills in the coordinates of the "box" scope in the gesture frame as specified by the position and size of the circle. The word spotter produces "delete word", from which the parser fills in the *action* and *textual unit* slot in the speech frame. The frame merger then outputs a unified frame in which *action* = delete, *scope.type* = box, and *scope.textual-unit* = word. From this the command interpreter constructs an editing command to delete the word circled by the user.

One important advantage of this frame-based approach is its flexibility, which will facilitate the integration of more than two modalities, and across acoustic, visual, and linguistic ones. All we have to do is define a general frame for interpretation and specify the ways in which slots can be filled by each input modality.

5. CONCLUSIONS

In this paper, we have presented research that is aimed at producing more natural, more robust (redundant) and more efficient human-computer interfaces, by exploring the combination of several different human communication modalities. Such combinations naturally involve acoustic but also visual and gestural expressions of human intent and form a multimodal "language" we seek to decode. We have shown that more robust recognition can indeed be achieved by combining speech with lipreading, i.e., visual and acoustic modalities. We have also shown an on-line handwritten character recognizer, that could be combined with speech and gesture. Finally, we have demonstrated that speech and gesture can be joined to provide more natural, robust interpretation of user intent, as speech and gesture both deliver complementary cues to complete the semantics of a multimodal "speech" act. Further research currently in progress includes exploring eye- and face- tracking and sound source localization, to deliver multimodal cues more accurately, even when a person is moving about the room, and to determine focus of attention and reference of human interaction.

ACKNOWLEDGEMENTS

The authors would like to gratefully acknowledge support by the NSF and ARPA-MTO for work on basic neural network modeling in speech and gesture recognition and for work on the combination of speech/gesture and language. We would also like to thank the state of Baden-Wuerttemberg, Germany, (Landesschwerpunkt Neuroinformatik) for supporting our work in character recognition and lip-reading. This research would have been impossible without these sponsors' support.

Special thanks to Herman Hild, Chris Bregler, Arthur McNair, Torsten Zeppenfeld, Michael Finke, Wayne Ward, and many others for their invaluable help and the use of their code.

REFERENCES

Baluja, S. & Pomerleau, D. (1994). Non-Intrusive Gaze Tracking Using Artificial Neural Networks. To appear in *Advances in Neural Information Processing Systems 6*, Morgan Kaufmann Publishers.

Bodenhausen, U., Manke, S. & Waibel, A. (1993). Connectionist Architectural Learning for High Performance Character and Speech Recognition. In Proceedings of *ICASSP'93*, Vol. 1, 625–628. Minneapolis, MN, U.S.A.

Braida, L. D. (1991). Crossmodal Integration in the Identification of Consonant Segments. *The Quarterly Journal of Experimental Psychology* **43**A(3): 647–677.

Bregler, C., Hild, H., Manke, S. & Waibel, A. (1993). Improving Connected Letter Recognition by Lipreading. In Proceedings of *ICASSP'93*, Vol. 1, 557–560, Minneapolis, MN, U.S.A.

Bregler, C. (1993). *Lippenlesen als Unterstützung zur robusten automatischen Spracherkennung.* M.S. Thesis. Fakultaet für Informatik, Universität Karlsruhe.

Goldschen, A. J. (1993). *Continuous Automatic Speech Recognition by Lipreading*. Ph.D. Dissertation, George Washington University.

Guyon, I., Albrecht, P., LeCun, Y., Denker, J. & Hubbard, W. (1991). Design of a Neural Network Character Recognizer for a Touch Terminal. *Pattern Recognition* **24**(2): 105–119.

Haffner, P., Franzini, M. & Waibel, A. (1991). Integrating Time Alignment and Neural Networks for High Performance Continuous Speech Recognition. In Proceedings of *ICASSP'91*, Vol. 1, 105–108. Toronto, Canada.

Haffner, P. & Waibel, A. (1991). Multi-State Time Delay Neural Networks for Continuous Speech Recognition. *Advances in Neural Network Information Processing Systems 4*, 135–142. Morgan Kaufmann Publishers.

Hauptmann, A. (1989). Speech and Gestures for Graphic Image Manipulation. In Proceedings of *CHI'89*, 241–245. Austin, TX, U.S.A.

Hild, H. & Waibel, A. (1993). Connected Letter Recognition with a Multi-State Time Delay Neural Network. *Advances in Neural Information Processing Systems 5*, 712–719. Morgan Kaufmann Publishers.

Huang, X., Alleva, F., Hon, H., Hwang, M., Lee, K. & Rosenfeld, R. (1993). The SPHINX-II Speech Recognition System: An Overview. *Computer Speech and Language* **7**(2): 137–148.

Jackson, P. L. (1988). The Theoretical Minimal Unit for Visual Speech Perception: Visemes and Coarticulation. *The Volta Review* **90**(5): 99–115.

Manke, S. & Bodenhausen, U. (1994). A Connectionist Recognizer for On-Line Cursive Handwriting Recognition. In Proceedings of *ICASSP'94*, Vol. 2, 633–636. Adelaide, Australia.

Miller, G. A. & Nicely, P. E. (1955). An Analysis of Perceptual Confusions Among Some English Consonants. *Journal of the Acoustical Society of America* **27**(2): 338–352.

Ney, H. (1984). The Use of a One-Stage Dynamic Programming Algorithm for Connected Word Recognition. In *IEEE Transactions on Acoustics, Speech and Signal Processing* **32**(2): 263–271

Nodine, C., Kundel, H., Toto, L. & Krupinski, E. (1992). Recording and Analyzing Eye-position Data Using a Microcomputer Workstation. *Behavior Research Methods, Instruments & Computers* **24**(3): 475–584.

Mase, K. & Pentland, A. (1991). Automatic Lipreading by Optical-Flow Analysis. *Systems and Computers in Japan* **22**(6): 67–76.

Petajan, E. D. (1984). *Automatic Lipreading to Enhance Speech Recognition*. Ph.D. Thesis, University of Illinois.

Petajan, E. D., Bischoff, B. & Bodoff, D. (1988). An Improved Automatic Lipreading System to Enhance Speech Recognition. In Proceedings of *CHI'88*, 19–25. Washington, DC, U.S.A.

Pomerleau, D., (1992). *Neural Network Perception for Mobile Robot Guidance*. Ph.D. Thesis, Carnegie Mellon University, CMU-CS-92-115.

Rose, R. & Paul, D. (1990). A Hidden Markov Model Based Keyword Recognition Systems. In Proceedings of *ICASSP'90*, Vol. 1, 129–132. Albuquerque, NM, U.S.A.

Rubine, D., (1991). *The Automatic Recognition of Gestures*. Ph.D. Thesis, Carnegie Mellon University.

Rubine, D., (1991). Specifying Gestures by Examples. *Computer Graphics* **25**(4): 329–337.

Schwartz, R. & Austin, S. (1991). A Comparison of Several Approximate Algorithms for Finding N-best Hypotheses. In Proceedings of *ICASSP'91*, Vol. 1, 701–704. Toronto, Canada.

Schenkel, M., Guyon, I. & Henderson, D. (1994). On-Line Cursive Script Recognition Using Time Delay Neural Networks and Hidden Markov Models. In Proceedings of *ICASSP'94*, Vol. 2, 637–640. Adelaide, Australia.

Schmidbauer, O. & Tebelskis, J. (1992). An LVQ-based Reference Model for Speaker-Adaptive Speech Recognition. In Proceedings of *ICASSP'92*, Vol. 1, 441–444. San Francisco, CA, U.S.A.

Stork, D. G., Wolff, G. & Levine, E. (1992). Neural Network Lipreading System for Improved Speech Recognition. In Proceedings of *IJCNN'92*, Vol. 2, 289–295. Baltimore, MD, U.S.A.

Summerfield, Q. (1983). Audio-visual Speech Perception, Lipreading and Artificial Stimulation. In Lutman, M. E. & Haggard, M. P. (eds.) *Hearing Science and Hearing Disorders*, Academic Press: New York.

Tebelskis, J. & Waibel, A. (1993). Performance Through Consistency: MS-TDNNs for Large Vocabulary Continuous Speech Recognition. In *Advances in Neural Information Processing Systems 5*, 696–703. Morgan Kaufmann Publishers.

Turk, M. & Pentland, A. (1991). Eigenfaces for Recognition. *Journal of Cognitive Neuro-Science* **3**(1): 71–86.

Vo, M. T. & Waibel, A. (1993). A Multimodal Human-Computer Interface: Combination of Speech and Gesture Recognition. In *Adjunct Proc. InterCHI'93*. Amtersdam, The Netherlands.

Vo, M. T. (1994). Incremental Learning using the Time Delay Neural Network. In Proceedings of *ICASSP'94*, Vol. 2, 629–632. Adelaide. Australia.

Waibel, A., Hanazawa, T., Hinton, G., Shikano, K. & Lang, K. (1989). Phoneme Recognition Using Time-Delay Neural Networks. *IEEE Transactions on Acoustics, Speech, and Signal Processing* **37**(3): 328–339.

Waibel, A., Jain, A., McNair, A., Saito, H., Hauptmann, A. & Tebelskis, J. (1991). JANUS: A Speech-to-speech Translation System Using Connectionist and Symbolic Processing Strategies. In Proceedings of *ICASSP'91*, Vol. 2, 793–796. Toronto, Canada.

Ward, W. (1991). Understanding Spontaneous Speech: The Phoenix System. In Proceedings of *ICASSP'91*, Vol. 1, 365–367. Toronto, Canada.

Ware, C. & Mikaelian, H. (1987). An Evaluation of an Eye Tracker as a Device for Computer Input. In *SIGCHI Bulletin, Spec. Issue, CHI+GI'87*, 183–188. Toronto, Canada.

Woszczyna, M. *et al.* (1993). Recent Advances in Janus: A Speech Translation System. In Proceedings of *EUROSPEECH'93*, Vol. 2, 1295–1298. Berlin, Germany.

Yuhas, B. P., Goldstein, M. H., Sejnowski, Jr. & T. J. (1989). Integration of Acoustic and Visual Speech Signals Using Neural Networks. *IEEE Communications Magazine* **27**(11): 65–71.

Zeppenfeld, T., & Waibel, A., (1992). A Hybrid Neural Network, Dynamic Programming Word Spotter. In Proceedings of *ICASSP'92*, Vol. 2, 77–80. San Francisco, CA, U.S.A.

Zeppenfeld, T., Houghton, R., & Waibel, A. (1993). Improving the MS-TSNN for Word Spotting. In Proceedings of *ICASSP'93*, Vol. 2, 475–478. Minneapolis, MN, U.S.A.

Artificial Intelligence Review **10:** 321–344, 1996.

Picture Semantics For Integrating Text And Diagram Input

RAMAN RAJAGOPALAN
Department of Computer Sciences, University of Texas at Austin, Austin, Texas, 78712.
Author's current address: Intel Corporation, MS EY3-06, 5200 N.E. Elam Young Parkway, Hillsboro, OR 97124-6497, USA
E-mail: Raman_Rajagopalan@ccm.hf.intel.com

Abstract. The saying 'a picture is worth a thousand words' exemplifies the great value of pictures in describing a scenario. Pictures convey spatial information in a compact form, allowing textual descriptions to concentrate on the non-spatial (henceforth, *contextual*) properties of objects. The difficult task in integrating text and diagrammatic input to a system is to establish *coreference* – matching object references in the text to objects in the diagram.

We show that the coreference problem can be greatly simplified if limited contextual information can be provided directly in diagrams. We present a methodology, the Picture Semantics description language, for associating contextual information with objects drawn through graphical editors. Then, we describe our implemented research tool, the Figure Understander, which uses this methodology to integrate the differing information in text and graphically-drawn diagrammatic input into a single unified knowledge base description. We illustrate the utility of our methods through examples from two independent domains.

Key words: picture semantics, coreference, diagram and text integration, spatial reasoning

1. Introduction

Maps, schematic diagrams, and pictures accompanying stories are three examples of the many ways in which pictorial information is used in human communication. Larkin and Simon describe the benefits of using both diagrams and text to describe a scene in their classic paper, "Why a Diagram is (Sometimes) Worth 10,000 Words" (Larkin et al., 1987). Pictures can be used to *compactly* describe the spatial properties of objects in a scene. This allows any accompanying textual descriptions to concentrate on the non-spatial domain-specific and problem-specific (henceforth, *contextual*) properties of objects. To clarify our terminology, the rectangular object in the diagram of Figure 1 has the *spatial* property that it is rectangular, and the *contextual* property that it is a magnetic field.

1.1. *The coreference problem*

Diagrams and text typically describe the same object in different ways. Figure 1 shows the diagram and text statement for a Physics problem (Resnick et

– **Diagram:**

754 / Faraday's Law of Induction

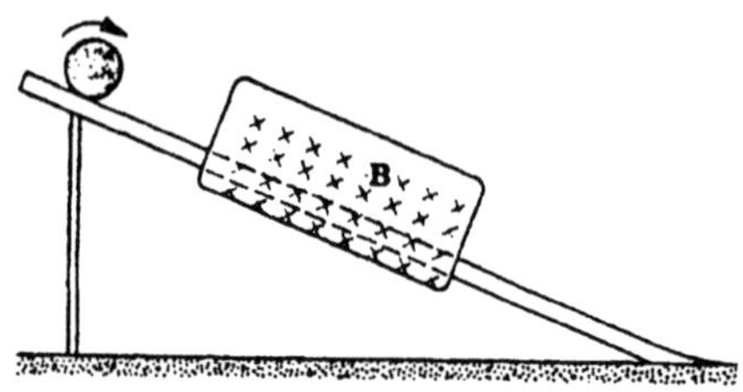

Figure 13 Question 7:

– **Text:** Figure 13 shows an inclined wooden track that passes, for part of its length, through a strong magnetic field. You roll a copper disk down the track. Describe the motion of the disk as it rolls from the top of the track to the bottom.

Figure 1. A problem from Resnick and Halliday's (1988) textbook, *Fundamentals of Physics*.

al., 1988). The diagram objects are lines, polygons, and circles. The text problem statement uses domain-specific terms, such as 'disk' and 'track', to describe the same objects. Each form of input, diagram and text, contains unique information. In Figure 1, the diagram shows the position and shape of the circular object, but it is the word 'disk' in the text that reveals that it is a solid object, and it is the word 'copper' that reveals that it is a conducting object.

The *coreference* problem (Novak et al., 1993) is to associate object references in text with the appropriate diagram objects. Solutions to the coreference problem are important because the unique information in each form of input, diagrams and text, can be integrated only after the mappings between diagram and textual objects are identified.

To solve the coreference problem, human readers can make use of a large "commonsense" knowledge base to quickly visualize the spatial properties of an object mentioned in a text description and identify the appropriate object(s) in a picture. Similar strategies have been adopted in previous work to automate the ability to solve the coreference problem. One approach is to use model libraries which map domain-specific terms to a spatial model for the object (Novak et al., 1993), such as the model that a 'car' is a rectangle with four circles attached to it. Another approach is to use an image database to directly associate a picture with a textual term (Rowe et al., 1993; Srihari, 1994).

Both approaches face problems with the completeness of the model library or image database and ambiguities in assessing the quality of a match against a given input. Unfortunately, a given object or collection of objects in a diagram may map to several models in a model library, or objects in the input may have a different shape or orientation, and thus appear to be different, than objects in an image database.

For example, in interpreting the diagram in Figure 1, a human reader can easily recognize that the sloping portion of the triangular base forms the 'track', that the vertical piece forms the support for the track, and that the horizontal line is the ground. In a model library, a possible mapping for the word 'track' is that it is a line object in a diagram.

In the text of Figure 1, there is only one reference to a 'line' object – the track. The diagram contains three line objects - the track, the support, and the ground. In this case, we would either need a model for a 'supported track' in the library which would include all three line objects in the diagram, or the underlying system would have to perform complex reasoning about the information in the text to associate only the sloping line with the word 'track'.

1.2. *Overview of our goals and solution*

In previous work, researchers have addressed the problem of automatically interpreting text and pictorial input *intended for human use*, such as Srihari's interests in identifying persons in newspaper photographs based on clues in an associated text caption (Srihari, 1994), or Novak and Bulko's (1993) interest in solving textbook Physics problems using the exact text problem statement and associated diagrams that are available to the human reader. These problem assumptions do not allow any automation-friendly modifications in either the diagram or text input, thus preserving the full complexity of the coreference problem, and making the solutions difficult to implement and use.

For example, in previous work, it is assumed that the pictorial input is provided in visual (raster) form, such as a camera image. In such cases, it becomes necessary to perform visual scene interpretation (Ballard et al., 1982) simply to identify the pictorial objects of interest. There can be many ambiguities. In Figure 1, for example, it may be non-trivial to infer that the X's form a pattern to be associated with the rectangular object, or to infer that the label 'B' is attached to the rectangular object, as opposed to the track or to the diagram as a whole.

1.2.1. *Our goal*

Our goal is to provide a simpler methodology which allows the combined use of text and diagrams to compactly provide the spatial and contextual properties of a scene as input to a given system (Rajagopalan et al., 1994; Rajagopalan, 1994b). This need was forced on us as we pursued another goal, the development of a problem solver for the magnetic fields domain which performs qualitative reasoning about changes in both spatial and non-spatial properties to solve problems (Rajagopalan, 1994a). As we considered how to input a description of the initial state, we found that special purpose text forms were too cumbersome for providing a complete description of the spatial properties, and that diagrams were a far more natural method of providing the same information. However, we still required text input to describe certain non-spatial properties of the initial state, including changes that may be taking place. Thus, we encountered the coreference problem.

1.2.2. *Our approach*

We have developed a novel solution to the coreference problem based on two observations: (1) Annotations are often used in drawings to allow human readers to associate non-spatial contextual information with objects. For example, Figure 1 contains two means to identify the rectangular object as a magnetic field: the label, B, and the pattern of Xs; (2) Graphical drawing tools provide several methods, such as colors, filling patterns, and brush types, to highlight objects.

Our solution to the problem of compactly providing both spatial and non-spatial information as input to a given reasoning system has been to automate the ability to associate contextual information with the use of highlighting colors, patterns, and brush types for objects in diagrams drawn through graphical drawing tools. We have developed a special description language, the *Picture Semantics*, for this purpose.

1.2.3. *Advantages of our approach*

Our approach has two favorable consequences for the coreference problem: (1) The need for additional text input can sometimes be completely eliminated, thus trivially solving the coreference problem; (2) When the need for additional text input persists, our approach allows constraints on both the spatial and contextual properties of objects to be used when matching textual and diagram objects.

Our solution is straightforward to implement and use. The assumption that the pictorial input is given through a graphical editor greatly reduces the complexity of diagram interpretation – anything drawn as a distinct object in the diagram can be readily identified as a distinct object from the output of the graphical editor. Further, properties such as brush types, filling patterns,

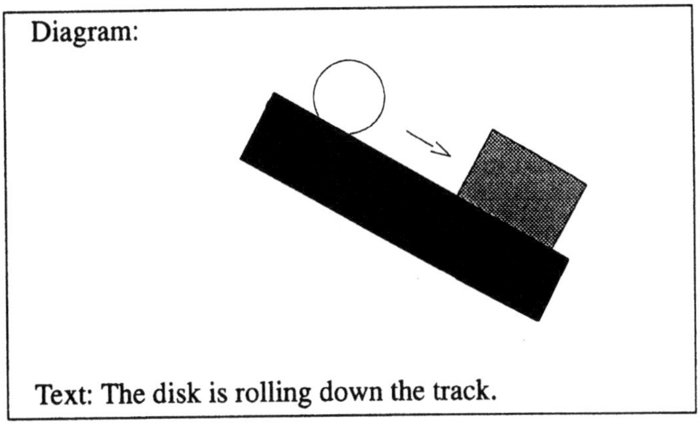

Figure 2. Input given to the Figure Understander for the textbook problem shown in Figure 1.

and colors can be directly associated with objects, thus eliminating a source of ambiguity present in interpreting visual input in raster form.

The remainder of this paper is organized as follows. In section 2, we describe the Picture Semantics language for describing contextual properties directly within a diagram, and illustrate its use in solving the coreference problem for the magnetic fields problem described in Figure 1. In Section 3, we describe the Figure Understander, our implemented tool for automatically interpreting and integrating the information in text and diagram input. In Section 4, we illustrate the utility of our approach through additional examples involving the interpretation of dialogue about an urban scene.

2. The Picture Semantics description

The diagram and text input to the Figure Understander for the problem of Figure 1 is given in Figure 2. The cruder diagram and greatly simplified text form are sufficient to capture all the necessary input information for the problem. This simplification is possible because of the power of our Picture Semantics description, illustrated in Figures 3 and 4, which allows contextual properties to be associated with the use of brush types, filling patterns, and colors in diagrams.

Incidentally, text labels could also be used in the Picture Semantics if the graphical editor provides a means to directly attach the label to other diagram objects. Otherwise, the task of associating the text label with a diagram object can itself be a challenging problem (He et al., 1994) particularly when the diagram contains overlays. Since the graphical editor we use, the

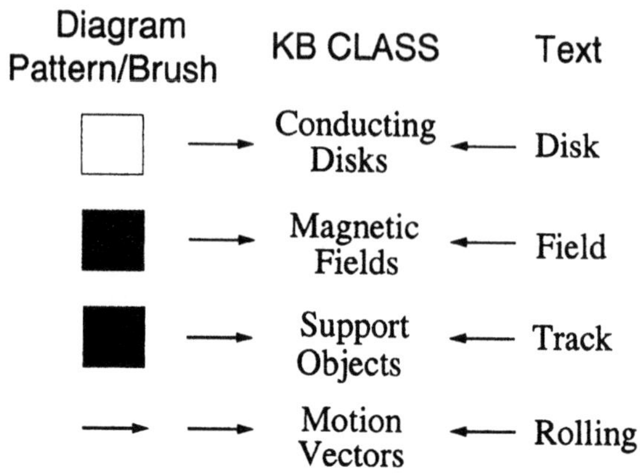

Figure 3. Diagram and text semantics for Figure 2.

`InterViews` drawing editor, treats text as a separate object, we shall not consider text labels any further in this paper.

In our approach, we first process the diagram before processing the text input. The result is a partial knowledge base with instantiations for each diagram object under the appropriate knowledge base class. For the diagram in Figure 2, we use the Picture Semantics form to provide the following associations between diagram objects and knowledge base (KB) classes, as illustrated in Figure 3: white objects are conducting disks, gray objects are magnetic fields pointed into the page, black objects are supports, and vectors with the light brush type used in the diagram are motion vectors.

In our application, we always provide a vector in the diagram to provide the direction of motion of objects, intrinsic front directions, and the directions of any forces acting on the objects. In the example of Figure 2, the diagram does not specify which object is in motion, since the vector is floating in free space. This information is obtained from the text input, "the disk is rolling down the track".

2.1. *Solving the coreference problem in Figure 2*

After processing the text input in Figure 2, we learn that there must be a mobile, conducting disk in the diagram which is in motion (from 'disk is rolling'). Further, we learn that there is contact between the disk and a supporting track (from 'down the track'). From our application-wide assumption described above, we also infer that there must be a motion vector present.

The coreference problem in processing the diagram and text in Figure 2 is to identify the conducting disk, motion vector, and supporting track in the diagram, even though the diagram primitives are only lines, circles, and polygons.

The problem is quickly solved by use of the Picture Semantics description, since, when processing the diagram, we have already extracted the information that there are instances of conducting disks, magnetic fields, supporting objects, and motion vectors in the diagram. Thus, once the text processing identifies the need for finding a conducting disk, motion vector, and supporting track, we can directly search against the knowledge base for diagram objects with these contextual properties.

Since there is only one object of each KB class in the diagram, the matching process becomes straightforward, and we can assert the direction of motion specified by the vector into the KB description of the disk. In more complex scenes, when there are multiple instances of a given object type in the diagram, spatial constraints in the text, such as the clue that the conducting disk and supporting track must be in contact, can be used to isolate the specific instances of interest. In Section 4, we present an urban scene interpretation example where there are multiple instances of each object type.

2.2. *Features of the Picture Semantics description*

Figure 4 shows a partial Picture Semantics description for our magnetic fields problems. There are four main blocks. Under `:patterns-for-2d--objects` and `:brush-types-for-vector-objects`, the user can assign a meaningful label, such as the label 'mobile-conducting-disk' assigned to the solid-white pattern, for each of the color, filling pattern, and vector types allowed by the graphical editor used to draw the diagram.

The second block (`:object-groups`) allows the user to organize individual labels into groups and to specify the root to be used for the names of the knowledge base instantiations of diagram objects of this group. For example, the group 'magnetic-fields' is defined to include diagram objects with a solid-gray pattern and those with a horizontal line pattern. The first diagram object encountered with this pattern will have a knowledge base instantiation with the name 'F'. The second will be named F-1, the third F-2, and so on.

The third block specifies the knowledge base assertions to be made for each individual object type (`:individual-object-semantics`) and for groups as a whole (`:object-group-semantics`). All contextual information is expressed in terms of predicates in the Algernon knowledge representation language (Crawford et al., 1991).

For example, under `:object-group-semantics`, we have specified that all diagram objects of the group 'conducting-disks' are members of the knowledge base class 'conducting-disks', and that they have the prop-

```
(defpict pictures-for-mag-fields
    :patterns-for-2d-objects
      ; Graphical Editor Pattern      ; Label For Object
      ((solid-gray                    field-into-page)
       (horizontal-line               horizontal-field)
       (solid-black                   track)
       (solid-white                   mobile-conducting-disk)
       (light-cross-mesh              immobile-conducting-disk))

    :brush-types-for-vector-objects
      ; Graphical Editor Brush Type   ; Label For Object
      ((vl-s-vector-out               mot-dir-vect))

    :object-groups
      ; Label For Group   ; Root Name For KB objects  ; Objects In Group
      ((magnetic-fields         F      (field-into-page horizontal-field))
       (conducting-disks        D      (mobile-conducting-disk
                                        immobile-conducting-disk))
       (support-objects         S      (track))
       (motion-vectors          MV     (mot-dir-vect)))

    :object-group-semantics
      ((conducting-disks ; Group Label
        ; Properties of group to be asserted into the KB.
         ((member conducting-disks ?obj) ; membership in KB class.
          (is-solid ?obj TRUE)))
       (magnetic-fields
         ((member steady-uniform-magnetic-fields ?obj)
          (source-of-field ?obj permanent)))
       (motion-vectors
         ((member motion-vectors ?obj))))

    :individual-object-semantics
      ((conducting-disk  ; Group Label
        (mobile-conducting-disk  ; Object Label
         ; special properties of object type to assert into the KB.
         ((mobility-of ?obj mobile))))
       (magnetic-fields
        (field-into-page
         ((field-direction-of ?obj '(0 0 -1))))))

    :special-procedures (connect-vectors-to-objects))
```

Figure 4. A partial Picture Semantics description for our magnetic fields problems.

erty of being solid objects. Under `:individual-object-semantics`, we specify that diagram objects with a solid-white pattern (label 'mobile-conducting-disks') have the additional property that they are mobile.

The fourth block (`:special-procedures`) specifies user-defined, special-purpose procedures to be run after diagram processing is completed. For example, the special procedure 'connect-vectors-to-objects' associates a vector in the diagram with the object which contains the tail of the vector whenever an unambiguous match can be found. The vector in Figure 2 is intentionally not attached to the conducting disk. However, we could have eliminated the need for text input completely by moving the tail of the vector into the disk, allowing the fact that the disk is moving to be extracted directly from the diagram!

3. The Figure Understander

The Figure Understander is an implemented research tool for integrating the information in text and *graphically drawn* diagrammatic input into a single knowledge base description. The intended use of the Figure Understander is to support applications, such as map understanding systems, story understanding systems, or automated problem solving systems, that will benefit from the ability to *compactly* describe the spatial state of the world through a diagram, and yet may require additional text-based input to describe the domain properties of the diagram objects and any dynamic changes that are taking place.

The input to the Figure Understander includes a diagram produced through an object-oriented drawing editor (currently, the `Postscript` file for a diagram produced using the `Interviews` drawing editor), a Picture Semantics description for the diagram, one or more sentences of descriptive text, and an Algernon (Crawford et al., 1991) knowledge base. It outputs an integrated description of the information in each form of input, diagram and text, into the knowledge base.

3.1. *Diagram processing*

The strength of the Figure Understander lies in its diagram interpretation capabilities. As the diagram is processed, a knowledge base (KB) object is created for each diagram object. Both the contextual information given in the Picture Semantics and the qualitative spatial properties of interest are attached to the KB description of the object. The spatial properties extracted include the spatial extent (size, shape, and position), connectivity, and orientation of individual objects, and topological and directional spatial relations between objects. For example, the connectivity of a polygon is stored by creating knowledge base structures for all the edges and vectors, and storing the connections between the edges and vertices. Incidentally, the Figure Understander also contains heuristics to allow for human errors in drawing the diagrams, such as adjusting for an unintentional gap of a few pixels between objects intended to be touching each other.

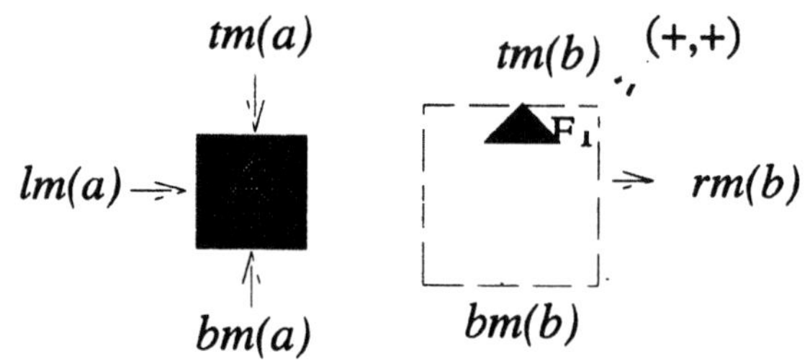

Figure 5. Modeling spatial extent and orientation using extremal points.

3.1.1. *The spatial model*

The Figure Understander extracts and reasons with a *qualitative* internal description of the initial spatial state. Our spatial representation, described in greater detail in (Rajagopalan, 1994a), has been used to solve problems involving static scenes as well as problems involving translational and rotational motion. For the purposes of this paper, we will assume that all objects are 2-dimensional and are confined to the XY plane.

Spatial relations between objects are evaluated using 'ideal meanings', as defined by Herskovits (1985). More specifically, for problems involving static scenes or only translational motion, we use a minimum bounding rectangle, similar to Chang, et al., (1987) and Jungert (1992), to approximate the spatial extent of each object. Two objects are assumed to satisfy a spatial relation if their bounding rectangles satisfy the relation.

The minimal bounding rectangle is drawn around the extremal edges or vertices of an object: its rightmost (rm), leftmost (lm), topmost (tm), and bottommost (bm) vertices or edges, as shown in Figure 5. Then, as shown in Figure 6, we define eight regions around the bounding box of each object. The relative positions of two objects are determined based on the regions around the bounding box of a reference object that are intersected by bounding box of the second object.

We model both directional (e.g., right-of, left-of) and topological (e.g., next-to, adjacent, intersecting) spatial relations between objects in terms of *qualitative inequality constraints* on the X-coordinate values of the rightmost and leftmost extremal edges of their bounding boxes, and the Y-coordinate values of the topmost and bottommost extremal edges of the bounding boxes. The inequality relations that define the relative positions of objects in an input diagram are extracted automatically by the Figure Understander.

The list of binary spatial relations recognized by the Figure Understander is given in Figure 7.

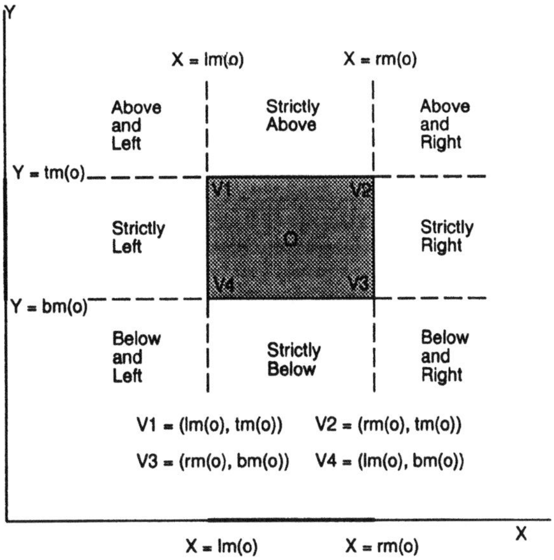

Figure 6. Regions defined by a rectangular bounding box with vertices V1, V2, V3, and V4.

Right-of	Strictly-right-of	Touching	Adjacent
Left-of	Strictly-left-of	Touching-right	Adjacent-right
Above	Strictly-above	Touching-left	Adjacent-left
Below	Strictly-below	Touching-above	Adjacent-above
Ahead-of	Strictly-ahead-of	Touching-below	Adjacent-below
Behind	Strictly-behind	Disconnected	Overlapped
Intersecting	Intersecting-right	Intersecting-left	Intersecting-top
Equals	Encloses	Enclosed-in	Intersecting-bottom

Figure 7. The spatial relations recognized by the Figure Understander.

While space limitations do not permit a formal definition to be presented for all of these spatial relations, here are three examples. For two bounding boxes, A and B:

- Left-of(A,B) iff $rm(A) < lm(B)$, where $rm(A)$ is the X-coordinate value of the rightmost edge of A, and $lm(B)$ is the X-coordinate value of the leftmost edge of B.
- Aligned-X(A,B) iff $tm(A) > bm(B) \wedge bm(A) < tm(B)$, where $tm(A)$ and $tm(B)$ are the Y-coordinate values of the topmost edges of A and B, and $bm(A)$ and $bm(B)$ are the Y-coordinate values of the bottommost edges of A and B. The region defined by the Aligned-X relation contains

the points where motion in the X direction could cause an intersection between A and B.
– Strictly-left-of(A,B) iff $Left\text{-}of(A,B) \wedge Aligned\text{-}X(A,B)$.

We model the orientation of an object in two ways: (1) the surface normal direction of each distinct surface (edge) of the object, as used by Nielsen (1988), and (2) the angle between the plane of the object and each of the planes formed by the coordinate axes. The latter is required only for reasoning about rotation and will not be discussed further here.

For (1), we can obtain the surface normal direction of any edge or arc of a convex object from knowledge of the *identities* of the vertices and edges which form the extremal points/surfaces of the object. For example, if an edge or arc lies between the topmost and rightmost extremal points/surfaces, such as edge E1 in Figure 5, then its surface normal direction will have positive X and Y components. We similarly model all 8 qualitative orientations in 2-dimensional space as presented by Freksa (1992) and Mukerjee and Joe (1990).

The distinction in our work is that while the 'idealized' minimum bounding rectangles are used as the basis for describing the relative positions of objects, for reasoning about orientation, we maintain knowledge of the actual orientation of the surfaces of an underlying object. This is necessary to model such properties as the direction of current flow along a particular surface of an object, the directions of magnetic forces acting on an object, and the intrinsic front direction of an object.

Further details of the advantages and limitations of our spatial model, its extensions for reasoning about translational and rotational motion, and details of its implementation within the framework of existing qualitative modeling and simulation systems (Kuipers, 1994) may be found in our AAAI-94 article (Rajagopalan, 1994a).

3.2. *Text processing*

The task of attaching semantic information given in any accompanying text sentences to diagram objects requires one to first locate the appropriate diagram objects to which the information is to be attached. We require that the text must provide sufficient information to *uniquely* locate the diagram objects to which the information is to be attached.

The Figure Understander performs text processing after processing the diagram. Since the Picture Semantics provides the conceptual class for each diagram object, if we can obtain the conceptual class of each text object, text and diagram objects could be matched based on their conceptual class. We use domain-dependent semantic interpretation functions, as illustrated in Figure 8, to provide the conceptual class for any nouns or pronouns that may be used

```
(defparameter *semantic-functions*
  '((disk (lambda ()
          (let ((?vl (make-variable)))
               `(:the ,?vl (member conducting-disks ,?vl)))))

    (track (lambda ()
           (let ((?vl (make-variable)))
                `(:the ,?vl  (member support-objects ,?vl))))) ))
```

Figure 8. Examples of semantic interpretation functions used to obtain the conceptual class for textual objects.

```
Interpreting text sentence:
 (THE DISK IS ROLLING DOWN THE TRACK)

 The following Algernon path shall be asserted:

((:THE ?V1 (MEMBER CONDUCTING-DISKS ?V1) (MOBILITY-OF ?V1 MOBILE))
 (:THE ?V2 (MEMBER SUPPORT-OBJECTS ?V2) (TOUCHING ?V1 ?V2))
 (:THE ?V3 (MEMBER MOTION-VECTORS ?V3) (VECTOR-DIRECTION-OF ?V3 ?VECT))
 (VELOCITY-VECTOR ?V1 ?VECT))
```

Figure 9. Algernon query and assert form generated for the text in Figure 2.

in the text as reference objects. In Figure 8, the function `make-variable` is used to return a variable name, such as ?V1 or ?V2, to be substituted into the `:the` from.

Algernon's (Crawford et al., 1991) definite description facility `(:the)` is used to connect object references in text to objects in the knowledge base (KB). The form `(:the ?vl (member conducting-disks ?vl))` asks Algernon to find a *unique* object, to be bound to the variable ?v1, that is a member of the knowledge base class `conducting-disks`. If it is the case that there is more than one conducting disk in the knowledge base, we can use any additional constraints, such as spatial relations, obtained from processing the text to narrow the search of the knowledge base.

The text processing is accomplished by first parsing a sentence through an ATN grammar, and then interpreting the parse output through a domain-dependent semantic interpreter. For each supported sentence type, the semantic interpreter examines the subject, verb, direct object, etc., and assembles a query-and-assert form in the syntax of the Algernon language for locating the appropriate diagram objects in the knowledge base (query) and attaching any new information given in the text about the object (assert).

Figure 9 shows the Algernon form generated after processing the sentence 'The disk is rolling down the track'. There are three queries (:the) and one new assertion. The queries search for diagram objects using both spatial properties and contextual properties. The first form, `(:the ?v1 (member conducting-disks ?v1) (mobility-of ?v1 mobile))`, is a query to locate a *unique* diagram object which is a member of the knowledge base (KB) class 'conducting-disks', and which is also a mobile object. The second query is to locate a member of the KB class 'support-objects' such that the conducting disk and support object are touching each other. The third query searches for a motion vector and retrieves its direction. The assert then assigns the direction of the motion vector as the velocity vector of the rolling disk.

4. A scene interpretation example

In Section 2, we discussed the use of the Picture Semantics description to provide contextual information, such as the knowledge base (KB) class for each diagram object, directly within the diagram. We showed that when each diagram object is of a unique KB class, the solution to the coreference problem of matching text and diagram objects becomes straightforward. In this section, we consider solution strategies for the coreference problem when there are multiple objects of the same contextual class in the diagram. Essentially, in such cases, the Figure Understander expects additional constraining information in the text to uniquely identify the appropriate diagram object. One useful source of additional constraints is the use of spatial relations in the text.

Figure 10 shows an input diagram for an urban scene that consists of many lines, rectangles, and ellipses. To assist the reader, Figure 10 includes a key which visually presents the Picture Semantics for the diagram. The Picture Semantics form shown in Figure 11 provides the contextual knowledge that the objects are buildings, streets, vehicles, and pedestrians. The goal for this example is to process the text sentences in Figure 12 to attach additional contextual properties to descriptions of the diagram objects.

The text sentences in Figure 12 make heavy use of spatial relations to assist the reader in locating the diagram objects of interest. By convention, the text interpretor for the urban scene understanding application interprets references to the directional spatial relations right of, left of, ahead of, and behind as strictly right of, strictly left of, strictly above, and strictly behind. For example, to interpret sentence 2, "The name of the building that is to *my right* is Welch Hall", the Figure Understander uses the fact that the word 'my' refers to the speaker, locates the only speaker (O) in the diagram, and then uses the spatial relation 'building *strictly to the right* of the speaker' to locate

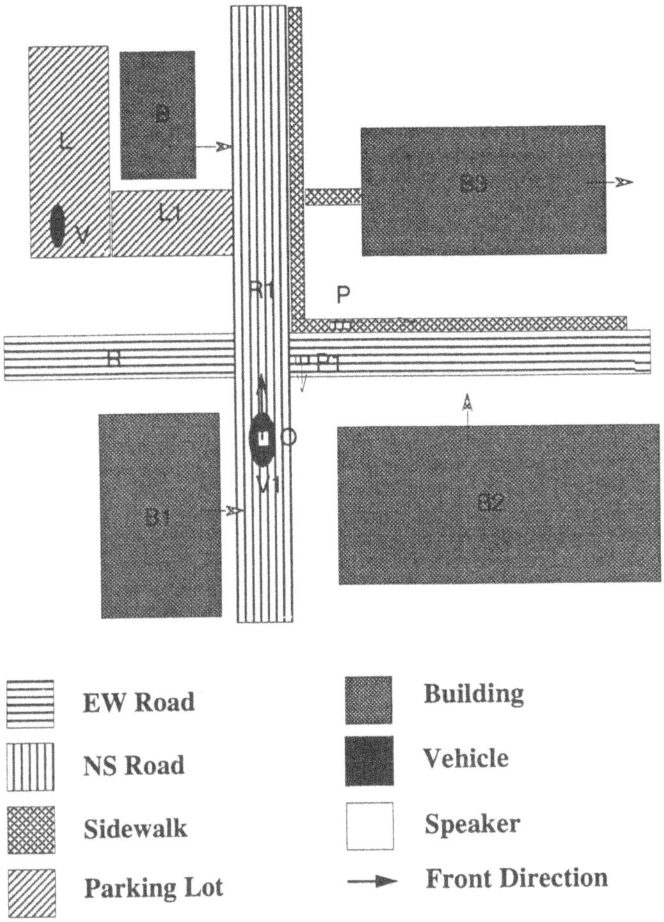

Figure 10. An urban scene – buildings, streets, vehicles, and pedestrians. The labels identify the internal names of the knowledge base objects created for each diagram object. The key shows the domain class for each diagram object.

the only building (B2) that satisfies the 'strictly right of' relation with respect to the speaker and labels that as 'Welch Hall'.

4.1. *Intrinsic/Deictic frames of reference*

Retz-Schmidt (1988) discusses that in human use of spatial prepositions, extrinsic, intrinsic, or deictic frames of reference could be used. The Figure Understander reasons about spatial relations with respect to the extrinsic frame of reference of the diagram. However, to allow reasoning about deictic and intrinsic frames of reference, the Figure Understander's spatial reasoning

```
(defpict roads-and-buildings
    :patterns-for-2d-objects
      ;Graphical Pattern  Domain Object Type
      ((solid-white          speaker)
       (solid-black          vehicle)
       (solid-gray           building)
       (slash                parking-lot)
       (horizontal-line      NS-road)
       (vertical-line        EW-road)
       (wide-rect-mesh       pedestrian)
       (light-cross-mesh     sidewalk))

    :brush-types-for-vector-objects
      ;Graphical Brush Type, Domain Object Type
      ((vl-s-vector-out      int-front-vect))

    :object-groups
      ; Domain-Class-Name     Abb-Name   Member-Object-Type
      ((sidewalks               S           (sidewalk))
       (speakers                O           (speaker))
       (pedestrians             P           (pedestrian))
       (roads                   R           (EW-road NS-road))
       (buildings               B           (building))
       (int-front-vectors       IF-V        (int-front-vect)))

    :object-group-semantics
      ; Semantics given as Algernon predicates.
      ((buildings     ((member buildings ?obj)))
       (roads         ((member roads ?obj)))
       (pedestrians   ((member people ?obj)))
       (speakers      ((member speakers ?obj))))

    :individual-object-semantics
    ; format: (class-name (obj-type semantics) (obj-type semantics) ..)
      ((roads
        (EW-road ((direction-of ?obj EW)))
        (NS-road ((direction-of ?obj NS)))))

    :special-procedures ((connect-vectors-to-objects))  )
```

Figure 11. Example of a partial Picture Semantics for urban scene interpretation.

module allows queries about directional spatial relations to carry a frame of reference argument, and automatically determines an equivalent relation to prove in terms of the extrinsic frame of reference of the diagram. In Figure 10, the vectors define the front direction for each object. Currently, the Figure Understander only considers intrinsic and deictic frames of reference that are orthogonal to that of the diagram.

In general, when processing text sentences, it is possible that there can be ambiguity concerning whether spatial relations are specified with respect to

1. My name is Raman.
2. The name of the building that is to my right is Welch Hall.
3. The name of the building that is in front of Welch Hall is Taylor Hall.
4. The name of the building that is behind Taylor Hall is the Aerospace-Engineering building.
5. The name of the building that is to the right of the Aerospace-Engineering building is the Biology building.
6. I am traveling on Twenty-Fourth street.
7. Speedway street intersects Twenty-Fourth street.
8. Ben is crossing Speedway street.

Figure 12. A collection of descriptive sentences for the scene depicted in Figure 10.

an intrinsic or deictic frame of reference. To avoid this ambiguity, the Figure Understander follows the convention that only objects mentioned explicitly in text sentences can serve as the frame of reference. Thus, in processing sentence 2, the deictic frame of reference of the speaker is used as the frame of reference, based on the use of the phrase 'my right'. However, in processing sentences 3-5, the intrinsic frames of reference of Welch Hall, Taylor Hall, and the Aerospace-Engineering building, respectively, are used instead, since those sentences contain such phrases as 'in front of Welch Hall' and 'behind Taylor Hall'.

4.2. *Annotated demonstration*

In the remainder of this section, we shall demonstrate the combined use of contextual and spatial constraints in text to solve the coreference problem in processing the diagram in Figure 10 and the text in Figure 12. All computer generated output is shown in typewriter font.

```
> (parse-figure "speedway-24th.ps"       ; input diagram
'((my name is Raman))    ; input text
'roads-and-buildings)    ; picture semantics form

**************************************************
***            Parsing The Figure            ***
**************************************************

Extracting spatial information from the figure.
Executing user defined special procedures.
Interpreting text sentence:
 (MY NAME IS RAMAN)

 The following Algernon path shall be asserted:
((:THE ?V1 (MEMBER SPEAKERS ?V1))
 (NAME-OF ?V1 'RAMAN))
```

The Figure Understander is invoked through the `parse-figure` function. The diagram is provided in the form of a PostScript file produced by the InterViews drawing editor. The input also includes a list of the sentences to be processed and the picture semantics form to be used. As the Figure Understander processes the diagram, it creates knowledge base objects for all the diagram objects, and stores both the spatial information about the objects and the semantic information given through the picture semantics.

After processing the diagram and the text sentence 'My name is Raman', database entries will exist for all the objects in the diagram, and their internal names will correspond to the abbreviations given in the picture semantics. The internal names for the larger objects in the scene are given as labels in Figure 10.

Let us now query the entire set of two dimensional objects in the knowledge base to identify the objects with bindings for the name-of relation. This is accomplished through Algernon's `ask` function. A list of bindings for the variables (symbols with the initial character, `?`) used within the `ask` function is retrieved using the `:collect` argument.

```
algy> (ask '((member convex-2-d-objects ?x)
             (name-of ?x ?y)) :collect '(?x ?y))
  ((O RAMAN))
```

Note that the only object with a domain-specific name is the speaker, O, whose name is Raman. Next, we shall proceed to process sentences 2-5 from Figure 12. Below, we show the Algernon query-and-assert form generated for the sentence 'The name of the building that is behind Taylor Hall is the Aerospace-Engineering building.' The query is to find two objects: first, to find a convex 2-dimensional object, `?V1`, whose name is `'(Taylor Hall)`, and second, to find a building `?V2` that is strictly behind the object `?V1`. The query further specifies that the 'strictly behind' relation is to be interpreted in terms of the intrinsic front direction of object `?V1` if it has one. If object `?V1` does not have an intrinsic front direction, then the query will be interpreted in terms of the extrinsic frame of reference of the diagram. If such a building `?V2` is found, the assert says to name the building as the Aerospace Engineering building.

In processing this query and assert form, since the intrinsic front direction of Taylor Hall points to the right, as given by the vector attached to object B3 in Figure 10, the relation 'behind' is determined with respect to this new frame of reference to identify the building labeled B in Figure 10 as the Aerospace Engineering building.

```
algy> (interpret '(The name of the building that is behind Taylor Hall
                   is the Aerospace-Engineering building))
```

```
The following Algernon path shall be asserted:

((:THE ?V1 (MEMBER CONVEX-2-D-OBJECTS ?V1) (NAME-OF ?V1 '(TAYLOR HALL)))
 (:THE ?V2 (MEMBER BUILDINGS ?V2)
          (:BIND ?VECT (GET-INTRINSIC-FRONT-DIRECTION-IF-ANY '?V1))
          (GET-DIRECTIONAL-RELATION-USING-ALTERNATE-FRAME-OF-REFERENCE
            STRICTLY-BEHIND ?V2 ?V1 ?VECT))
 (NAME-OF ?V2 '(AEROSPACE-ENGINEERING BUILDING)))
```

Set of named objects after processing sentences 2-5 in Figure 12:

```
algy> (ask '((member convex-2-d-objects ?x) (name-of ?x ?y))
           :collect '(?x ?y))
  ((B (AEROSPACE-ENGINEERING BUILDING)) (B1 (BIOLOGY BUILDING))
   (B2 (WELCH HALL)) (B3 (TAYLOR HALL)) (O RAMAN))
```

Now let us proceed to name the streets. Below, we show the Algernon query forms generated for sentences 6 and 7 in Figure 12. Notice that there are no attempts to identify an intrinsic frame of reference since the spatial relations to be proven, enclosed-in and intersecting, are not directional relations. The 'ask' query at the end reveals that streets R and R1 have been named.

```
algy> (interpret '(I am traveling on Twenty-Fourth street))

 The following Algernon path shall be asserted:

((:THE ?V1 (MEMBER SPEAKERS ?V1))
 (:THE ?V2 (MEMBER ROADS ?V2) (ENCLOSED-IN ?V1 ?V2))
 (NAME-OF ?V2 '(TWENTY-FOURTH STREET))
 (ACTION-OF ?V1 'TRAVELING))

algy> (interpret '(Speedway street intersects Twenty-Fourth street))

 The following Algernon path shall be asserted:

((:THE ?V1 (MEMBER ROADS ?V1) (NAME-OF ?V1 '(TWENTY-FOURTH STREET)))
 (:THE ?V2 (MEMBER ROADS ?V2) (INTERSECTING ?V2 ?V1))
 (NAME-OF ?V2 '(SPEEDWAY STREET)))
```

Set of named roads in the KB after processing sentences 6-7 in Figure 12:

```
algy> (ask '((member convex-2-d-objects ?x)
             (isa ?x roads) (name-of ?x ?y)) :collect '(?x ?y))
((R (SPEEDWAY STREET)) (R1 (TWENTY-FOURTH STREET)))
```

Let us now consider the last sentence in Figure 12, 'Ben is crossing Speedway Street'. This sentence names one of the pedestrians after uniquely identifying the street that the pedestrian is crossing. Note that in addition to the name of the street, Speedway, we could have instead specified the direction of the street, NS or EW, since that is also a known property (given in the picture semantics) that distinguishes the two streets in Figure 10. Since it can be inferred that Ben is not the speaker, the query looks for a person other than the speaker.

```
algy> (interpret '(Ben is crossing speedway street))

 The following Algernon path shall be asserted:

((:THE ?V1 (MEMBER ROADS ?V1) (NAME-OF ?V1 (:QUOTE (SPEEDWAY STREET))))
 (:THE ?V2 (MEMBER PEOPLE ?V2)
          (:UNP (ISA ?V2 SPEAKERS)) (ENCLOSED-IN ?V2 ?V1))
 (NAME-OF ?V2 (:QUOTE BEN)))

algy> (ask '((member people ?x) (name-of ?x ?y)) :collect '(?x ?y))
  ((P1 BEN) (O RAMAN))
```

5. Discussion

This paper has addressed the question "Are there any simple, but unrestrictive, methods that allow diagrams and text to be used as computer input?". The goal is to take advantage of the power of diagrams for describing a spatial state (Larkin et al., 1987; Narayanan et al., 1994) and yet retain the ability to use text-based input to describe other contextual properties of interest. This goal requires the development of solutions to the *coreference problem* - matching object references in text to objects in the diagram.

Previous work in this area has resulted in the development of methods for automating the ability to understand text and diagrammatic input intended for *human communication* (He et al., 1994; Novak et al., 1993; Rowe et al., 1993; Srihari, 1994). This assumption makes the coreference problem particularly complex and difficult for several reasons: (1) There can be hidden assumptions on the background knowledge of the human reader which may be not be available to an automated reasoning system; (2) Even the task of independently understanding each form of input may be difficult. Understanding pictorial input in visual (raster) form requires visual scene interpretation (Ballard et al., 1982), and processing text intended for human-to-human communication can require a sophisticated natural language processing system to resolve the ambiguities that may be present.

We have described a simpler methodology, the Picture Semantics description, and an implemented tool, the Figure Understander, which allows multimedia input to a knowledge base in the form of a graphically-drawn diagram and a collection of text sentences to be integrated into a single unified description.

By using graphical editors to provide diagrammatic input, we gain two advantages over systems that have to deal with visual input. First, graphical editors directly identify the objects of interest by providing a *geometric description* of the objects in the scene. If the additional constraint that diagram objects must be in one-to-one correspondence with the objects to be created in the knowledge base is enforced, there is no need for visual scene interpretation.

Second, graphical editors allow additional properties to be attached to objects such as patterns, colors, and brush types. Our system uses a special input form, the Picture Semantics, to associate contextual knowledge with these graphical properties. This approach provides a simple and elegant solution to the coreference problem by allowing text and diagram objects to be matched based on both spatial and domain-specific contextual information.

5.1. *Applicability of our solution*

We impose strict restrictions on the contents of both the diagram and the text. For example, unlike the work of Srihari (1994), we do not consider the possibility that there may be object references in the text for which there is no corresponding object in the diagram. To avoid ambiguity in establishing coreference, we also require that there is at least one unique object in the diagram which can be matched against a text object based on its Picture Semantics description alone. We further assume that it will be possible to use spatial relations in the text between such uniquely identifiable objects and the non-unique diagram objects to isolate any specific non-unique diagram object.

The reader may ask, 'Aren't these requirements too restrictive?'. The answer is yes, if, as with the work of Srihari (1994), Rowe (1993), and Novak (1993), the goal is to automatically process text and diagram input intended for human use, such a problem statement in a textbook, or a newspaper photograph. That is why their solutions to the coreference problem are necessarily more complex.

The solutions provided in this paper are intended for users who simply wish to take advantage of diagrams to compactly input the many spatial properties of a spatial scene, but who need another means, such as text, to provide additional domain-specific information about the objects in the diagram. In these situations, it is quite reasonable to assume that the user has a great interest in providing ambiguity-free input descriptions.

Just as we are making use of the Figure Understander to process diagram and text descriptions of a problem in our work on qualitative reasoning about the effects of magnetic fields (Rajagopalan, 1994a), the work of Hari Narayanan, et al. (1994) and He et al. (1994) could also benefit from the simple approach presented in this paper for using diagrams and text as computer input.

Further, although the focus of this paper has been on our solutions for the coreference problem, the reader may find the diagram processing and spatial reasoning capabilities of the Figure Understander to be worthy of further study. The Figure Understander automatically chooses bounding shape abstractions for objects in diagrams, can choose a frame of reference for a diagram to maximize the alignments of vectors and object surfaces with the coordinate axes, and automatically compensates for simple human errors in drawing a diagram, such as slight misalignments between objects. The Figure Understander also automatically extracts a qualitative description of a spatial scene from an input diagram, including the shapes (if the shape is simple) of objects, the connectivity (in terms of edges and vertices) of polygons, the relative positions of objects, and the orientation of objects.

Although the Figure Understander reasons about a static input scene, we have also developed methods for qualitatively reasoning about simultaneous dynamic changes in both the spatial and non-spatial properties of a physical system. The interested reader may consult (Rajagopalan, 1994a) or (Rajagopalan, 1995) for further details.

5.2. *Related issues*

This paper has focused on a very specific problem – providing an efficient method for using text and diagrams as computer input. Some related research issues include the generation of explanations using both text and graphical input (Feiner et al., 1990), generating a pictorial description from a text description of a scene (Gapp, 1994; Latecki et al., 1992; Olivier et al., 1994), and generating a text description from a visual image of a scene (Maass, 1994).

The solutions to these issues focus less on associating pictorial objects with text objects, and instead, concentrate on the modeling and use of spatial relations. For example, Gapp (1994), Latecki and Pribbenow (1992), and Olivier, et al., (1994) have all pointed out that the interpretation of distance-based topological relations, such as near and far, and those relating two paths, such as along, can be highly context dependent. They have defined both heuristic and quantitative methods for evaluating the applicability of such topological relations to a set of objects in a given spatial scene.

Acknowledgements

I wish to thank Professor Benjamin Kuipers, Paul Mc Kevitt, and the anonymous reviewers for their many suggestions in developing and clarifying the ideas presented in this paper. This work has taken place in the Qualitative

Reasoning Group at the Artificial Intelligence Laboratory, The University of Texas at Austin. Research of the Qualitative Reasoning Group is supported in part by NSF grants IRI-8904454, IRI-9017047, and IRI-9216584, and by NASA contracts NCC 2-760 and NAG 9-665.

References

Ballard, D.H. and Brown, C.M. (1982). *Computer Vision*, Prentice Hall.

Chang, S. K., Shi, Q. Y., and Yan, C. W. (1987). Iconic Indexing by 2-D Strings *IEEE Transactions on Pattern Recognition and Machine Intelligence*, **9:** 413–428.

Crawford, J. and Kuipers, B. (1991). Algernon – A Tractable System for Knowledge-Representation. In Working Notes of *The AAAI Spring Symposium on Implemented Knowledge Representation and Reasoning Systems*, Palo Alto, CA: American Association for Artificial Intelligence.

Feiner, S. and McKeown, K. (1990). Coordinating Text and Graphics in Explanation Generation. In Proceedings of *The Eighth National Conference on Artificial Intelligence*, 442–449, Boston, MA: American Association for Artificial Intelligence.

Freksa, C. (1992). Using Orientation Information for Qualitative Spatial Reasoning. In Frank, A., Campari, I., and Formentini, U. (Eds.) *Theories and Methods of Spatio-Temporal Reasoning in Geographic Space*, 162–178, Springer-Verlag: Berlin.

Gapp, K. (1994). Basic Meanings of Spatial Relations: Computation and Evaluation in 3D Space. In Proceedings of *The Twelfth National Conference on Artificial Intelligence*, 1393–1398, Seattle, WA: American Association for Artificial Intelligence.

He, S., Abe, N., and Kitahashi, T. (1994) Assembly Plan Generation by Integrating Pictorial and Textual Information in an Assembly Illustration. In Paul Mc Kevitt (Ed.) Working Notes of *The AAAI-94 Workshop on Integration of Natural Language and Vision Processing*, 66–73, Seattle, WA: American Association for Artificial Intelligence.

Herskovits, A. (1985). Semantics and Pragmatics of Locative Expressions. *Cognitive Science* **9:** 341–378.

Jungert, E. (1992). The Observer's Point of View: An Extension of Symbolic Projections. In Frank, A., Campari, I., and Formentini, U. (Eds.) *Theories and Methods of Spatio-Temporal Reasoning in Geographic Space*, 179–195, Springer-Verlag: Berlin.

Kuipers, B. (1994) *Qualitative Reasoning: Modeling and Simulation with Incomplete Knowledge*. MIT Press: Cambridge, MA.

Landau, B. and Jackendoff, R. (1993). "What" and "Where" in Spatial Language and Spatial Cognition". *Behavioral and Brain Sciences* **16:** 217–265.

Larkin, J. and Simon, H. (1987). Why a Diagram is (Sometimes) Worth 10,000 Words. *Cognitive Science* **11:** 65–99.

Latecki, L. and Pribbenow, S. (1992). On Hybrid Reasoning for Processing Spatial Expressions. In Proceedings of *The Tenth European Conference on Artificial Intelligence*, 389–393, Vienna: European Coordinating Committee for Artificial Intelligence.

Maass, W. (1994). From Visual Perception to Multimodal Communication: Incremental Route Descriptions. *AI Review Journal*, **8.**

McKevitt, P. (Ed.) (1994) *Working Notes of the AAAI Workshop on Integration of Natural Language and Vision Processing*. American Association for Artificial Intelligence: Menlo Park, CA.

Mukerjee, A. and Joe, G. (1990). A Qualitative Model for Space. In Proceedings of *The Eighth National Conference on Artificial Intelligence*, Boston, MA: American Association for Artificial Intelligence.

Narayanan, N. Hari (Ed.) (1992). *Working Notes of the AAAI Spring Symposium Series, Symposium: Reasoning with Diagrammatic Representations*. American Association for Artificial Intelligence: Menlo Park, CA.

Narayanan, N. Hari, Suwa, M., and Motoda, H. (1994). How Things Appear to Work: Predicting Behaviors from Device Diagrams. In Proceedings of *The Twelfth National Conference on Artificial Intelligence*, 1161–1166, Seattle, WA: American Association for Artificial Intelligence.

Nielsen, P. (1988). A Qualitative Approach to Mechanical Constraint. In Proceedings of *The Seventh National Conference on Artificial Intelligence*, 270–274, Saint Paul, MN: American Association for Artificial Intelligence.

Novak, G. S., and Bulko, W. (1993). Diagrams and Text as Computer Input. *Journal of Visual Languages and Computing* **4:** 161–175.

Olivier, P., Maeda, T., and Tsujii, J. (1994). Automatic Depiction of Spatial Descriptions In Proceedings of *The Twelfth National Conference on Artificial Intelligence*, 1405–1410, Seattle, WA: American Association for Artificial Intelligence.

Rajagopalan, R. (1994a). A Model for Integrated Spatial and Dynamic Reasoning about Physical Systems. In Proceedings of *The Twelfth National Conference on Artificial Intelligence*, 1411–1417, Seattle, WA: American Association for Artificial Intelligence.

Rajagopalan, R. (1994b). The Figure Understander: A Tool for the Integration of Text and Graphical Input to a Knowledge Base. In Proceedings of *The Sixth IEEE International Conference on Tools with Artificial Intelligence*, 80–87, New Orleans, LA: IEEE Computer Society.

Rajagopalan, R. (1995). *Qualitative Reasoning about Dynamic Change in the Spatial Properties of a Physical System*. Ph.D. Diss., Department of Computer Sciences, University of Texas at Austin, Austin, TX.

Rajagopalan, R. and Kuipers, B. (1994). The Figure Understander: A System for Integrating Text and Diagram Input to a Knowledge Base. In Proceedings of *The Seventh International Conference on Industrial and Engineering Applications of Artificial Intelligence and Expert Systems*, 211–220, Austin, TX: International Society of Applied Intelligence.

Resnick, J., and Halliday, D. (1988) *Fundamentals of Physics*, John Wiley and Sons: New York.

Retz-Schmidt, G. (1988). Various Views on Spatial Prepositions. *AI magazine* **9:** 95–105.

Rowe, N. and Guglielmo, E. (1993). Exploiting captions in retrieval of multimedia data. *Information Processing and Management* **29:** 453–461.

Srihari, R. (1994). Use of Captions and other Collateral Text in Understanding Photographs. *AI Review Journal* **8:** 349–369.

Artificial Intelligence Review **10:** 345–368, 1996.

Dynamic Conceptualization in a Mechanical-Object Assembly Environment

I. WACHSMUTH & B. JUNG
Faculty of Technology, University of Bielefeld
D-33501 Bielefeld, Germany
E-mail: {ipke,jung}@techfak.uni-bielefeld.de

Abstract. In an experimental setting of mechanical-object assembly, the CODY ("Concept Dynamics") project is concerned with the development of knowledge representations and inference methods that are able to dynamically conceptualize the situation in the task environment. A central aim is to enable an artificial agent to understand and process natural-language instructions of a human partner. Instructions may build on the current perception of the assembly environment on the one hand, and on the other on the knowledge-based understanding of grouped structures in the developing construct. To this end, a dynamic conceptualization must integrate information not only describing the types of the objects involved, but also their changing functional roles when becoming part of structured assemblies.

We have developed an operational knowledge representation formalism, COAR ("Concepts for Objects, Assemblies, and Roles"), by which processes of dynamic conceptualization in sequences of assembly steps can be formally reconstructed. Inferences concern the assertion or retraction of aggregate representations in a dynamic knowledge base, as well as the computation of role changes for individual objects associated herewith. The structural representations integrate situated spatial features and relations, such as position, size, distance, or orthogonality, which are inferred on need from a geometry description of the task environment. The capacity of our approach has been evaluated in a 3D computergraphics simulation environment.

Key words: knowledge representation, hybrid structural and spatial representations, situated communication

1. Introduction

Artificial agents that act in an environment must be able to maintain knowledge about objects undergoing change in the course of a situation. Let us assume an agent that has sensors to perceive input from a task environment (e.g., images and speech), and actuators to affect the outside world. Let us further assume that we want to communicate with the agent, for instance, issue natural language instructions to direct the agent's actions. For instance, we could want the agent to change a configuration of objects as this is typically encountered in robot assembly tasks. Then the agent has to build an internal representation of its environment which forms the basis of understanding what instructions refer to, and which can be manipulated to explore the effect of actions before they are actually attempted in the task environment.

In order to conceptualize a changing task environment, the agent must draw on certain world knowledge, for instance, knowledge which describes the possible roles that an object can take on in an assemblage. On the other hand, the world knowledge at the agent's disposal can never be complete with respect to the multitude of situations to which the agent could be exposed. Hence, being coupled to its environment by way of sensors and actuators, the agent needs to *exploit the actual situation*, as a source of information, for example, to integrate visual input while processing a natural language instruction. And it is crucial for the agent to modify its conception of the environment as it changes, in other words, the task environment must be "dynamically conceptualized" by the agent.

1.1. *SFB 360 - Reference Situation*

The work reported here is part of the Collaborative Research Centre SFB 360 *"Situated Artificial Communicators"* at the University of Bielefeld. One of the long-term aims of the research in SFB 360 is the construction of an artificial system that is able to communicate and cooperate with a human partner in the accomplishment of assembly tasks. In our reference situation from mechanical-object assembly, which touches all projects in SFB 360 (see site description, Rickheit & Wachsmuth, this volume), complex aggregates, such as a model airplane, are to be constructed from the components of a wooden construction kit, named "Baufix" (Figure 1). The human partner who has a diagram of the target aggregate takes on the part of an *instructor* and directs the system to carry out particular assembly steps. An artificial communicator - in the long range an assembly robot - takes on the part of a *constructor* and carries out the necessary actions. This reference situation is referred to as "instructor-constructor scenario".

Natural communication among human partners to a great extent grounds on their current perception of the situation in the environment, i.e., is situated. When both partners in the instructor-constructor scenario share an environment which they both can (at least partially) observe, verbal instructions will likely make reference to what can be seen in the current situation. What can be 'seen' in an assembly environment could also include how constructed aggregates are perceived as structured assemblies by the cooperating partners. Furthermore, while some of an object's properties may remain unchanged in the course of an assemblage, others will depend on the actual situation. Thus, when processing the verbal instructions of the instructor, the constructor needs to draw on what is currently true in a changing situation.

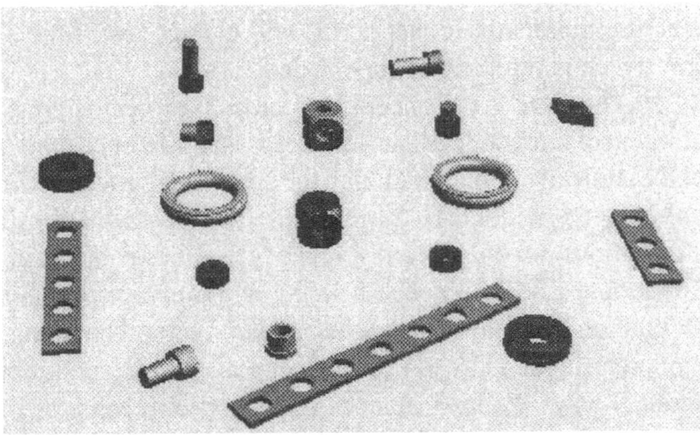

Figure 1. Baufix construction kit (sample parts)

If we want artificial communicators to make better profit of the ways humans communicate, the artificial communicator needs to be able to process situated verbal instructions by integrating what is *said* with what is *seen* (a *situated artificial communicator*). Much work in SFB 360 is spent on the reception, processing, and understanding of acoustic and visual information and on how the visually available information and spoken information are to be put in relation with each other (Fink et al., 1994; Fuhr et al., 1995; Moratz et al., 1995). Besides of sensori-motor and communicative abilities, the artificial communicator must have at its disposal a repertoire of suitable background knowledge and inference capabilities. Most crucially, the constructor must be able to process instructions and accomplish construction steps in a continually altered environment. This is why we need dynamic conceptualization.

1.2. *Dynamic Conceptualization - The CODY Project*

A conceptualization is an abstract, simplified view of a world represented for some purpose (Genesereth & Nilsson, 1987 ; Gruber & Olsen, 1994). By *dynamic conceptualization*, roughly, we mean that an agent maintains and updates an internal view of a changing environment (Jung & Wachsmuth, 1994). To accomplish this, internal representations must be coupled with the environment, and they must be created, modified, and deleted as the current situation demands. The purpose of dynamic conceptualization in SFB 360's instructor-constructor scenario is that instructor and constructor can communicate about a dynamic scene. While a construction is in progress, internal representations are to be updated dynamically by the constructor, in the same way as the human instructor is assumed to have a dynamic mental model which adapts to the changing characteristics of the task environment

(Rickheit & Strohner, 1994). Thus, the knowledge representations needed by the artificial communicator (constructor) will change over time and involve information which is replaced or superseded.

In SFB 360, the CODY ("Concept Dynamics") project is concerned with the development of knowledge representations and inference methods that are capable of dynamically conceptualizing the situation in a task environment of mechanical-object assembly. To this end, internal representations must accumulate informations not only describing the types of the objects involved, but also the functional role of objects in larger assembly groups. For instance, a *bar* may take on the role of a *propeller blade* when becoming part of an airplane undercarriage. Thus, object conceptualizations cannot be modeled in the 'classical way', i.e. as instances of a long-term repertoire of generic concepts. Rather, they have a life cycle in which they undergo changing classifications, associated with changing feature attributions, where role aspects tend to prevail as construction is progressing.

As a core part of CODY, we have developed and implemented a knowledge representation formalism, COAR, by which processes of dynamic conceptualization in sequences of assembly steps can be formally reconstructed. COAR builds on ideas of semantic networks but provides more than classic instantiation: Internal representations are constructed, maintained and restructured along with the changes that occur when assemblies are constructed from a variety of multi-function construction objects. COAR representations integrate taxonomic, partonomic, and functional information of objects and aggregates used in assembly, and they can access situated spatial information from the task environment. *Long-term concepts*, serving as background knowledge, describe mechanical objects, assemblies, and roles. *Short-term concepts*, serving as temporal descriptions of individual entities in dynamic conceptualization, bear current classifications of entities with respect to object type and role type. Whereas object-type classification persists, role-type classification is dynamic, i.e. it may change over time and thus evoke changing feature attribution. Inferences on short-term concepts concern the assertion or retraction of representations for constructed aggregates in a dynamic knowledge base, and the computation of role changes for individual objects combined herewith.

The capacity of our approach is so far evaluated in a 3D computergraphics simulation environment, the Virtual Constructor, in which the assemblage of model airplanes and similar constructs from a construction kit can be simulated. The Virtual Constructor is briefly described in Section 2, before we go into detail explaining the CODY representation language, COAR, in Section 3. The usage of COAR representations for dynamic conceptualization in Section 4, where coherence conditions specifying the creation, modification, and retraction of short-term concepts are described. In concluding, we discuss our achievements, their current and prospective applications, and where we want to go next.

2. The CODY Virtual Constructor

In order to probe our work in a task environment accessible to perception and action (not yet available as a full technical system integrating all necessary components), we currently work with a computergraphics environment, the Virtual Constructor (Jung et al., 1995). The CODY Virtual Constructor is a knowledge-based simulation system for the interactive assembly of complex aggregates from 3D objects. The external scene is reproduced, somewhat simplified, as a virtual scene, the *virtual assembly workbench*, on which the assemblage of model airplanes and similar constructs from a construction kit can be simulated.[1]

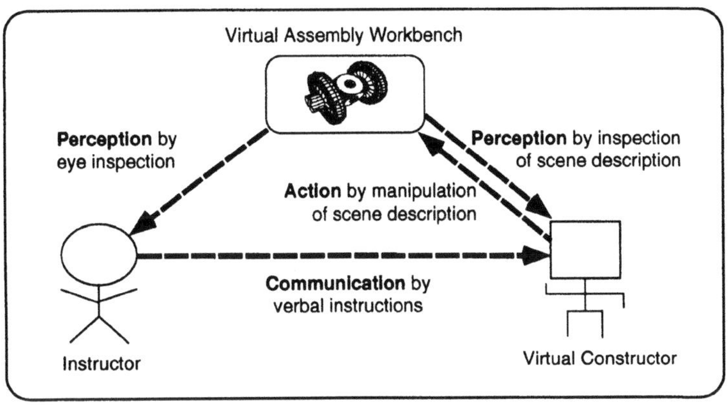

Figure 2. Instructor-constructor scenario with virtual assembly workbench

The virtual scene can be inspected by both communicators, i.e., is a commonly perceived world situation. The (human) instructor can view the scene from changing perspectives, whereby the (artificial) constructor has knowledge of the instructor's current field of view. The instructor can issue simple (written) natural-language commands. The Virtual Constructor can change the world situation by manipulating the geometry scene description (cf. Figure 2).

As a sample application for the Virtual Constructor we chose the assembly of a simple target aggregate - a model airplane - from the parts of construction kit (cf. SFB 360 reference situation, Section 1.1). These parts, e.g. bolts, blocks, and bars of different sizes, can be assembled in various ways. Any aggregate that can be built from Baufix building parts, but no aggregate that is physically impossible, can be assembled on the virtual assembly workbench. For instance, the partially assembled model airplane shown in Figure 3 (left) was produced on the virtual assembly workbench. In Figure 3, also, the effect of the instruction *"attach the propeller to the fuselage"* is illustrated (right).

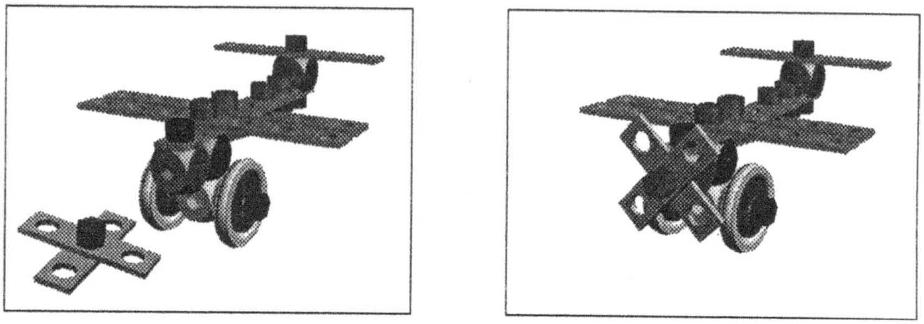

Figure 3. "Attach the propeller to the fuselage"

Instructions to the Virtual Constructor may refer to object types (e.g. *bolt*, *bar*, etc.), to objects' current functional roles in the evolving airplane (e.g., *axle*, *propeller blade*, etc.), to visual object properties such as color, form, and size, and finally, to object locations (e.g. *"upper left"*). Besides single parts, also assembled aggregates can be referred to, and any part or aggregate may be referred to as *"thing"*. In some cases, the instructor can alter the situation reached in the preceding action of the constructor by issuing a follow-up instruction which is correcting the previous one. Some sample instructions are given below.

> *put the left bolt through the red disc*
> *attach the thing to the left to the bottom of the block*
> *mount the wheel on the axle*
> *attach the long bolt to the top of the undercarriage*
> *detach the tire from the drum*
> *rotate the bar crosswise to the tail unit*
> *no, the other way round*

Instructions typically make reference to the current object configuration in the environment as it is perceived from the current perspective. Spatial expressions in instructions can be evaluated by accessing an internal camera model describing the current user perspective and the geometric scene description of the virtual environment. The geometric scene description, contains among other information the position and orientation of objects and aggregates in three-dimensional space. To find reference objects for natural language expressions like *"the left bolt"*, the Virtual Constructor will evaluate the geometric scene description and the camera model to select the bolt that is most to the left as seen from the current user perspective.

While a key idea is to exploit the geometric scene description to the greatest extent possible for instruction processing, this alone does not suffice. Instead, the geometric scene description is enriched with a layer of structural symbolic representations that account for the Virtual Constructor's current conceptualization of the environment. They describe which aggregates are formed in the current situation and which functional roles objects have assumed in the evolving airplane. Only by integrating the geometric scene description (including the camera model) with these dynamic knowledge representations, natural-language expressions like *"the left axle"* or *"the wheel on the right"* can be understood. By using the Virtual Constructor, we are in the position to satisfactorily evaluate the effect of dynamic conceptualization, even when an integrated system with sensori-motor components is not yet available.

3. A Concept Language for Objects, Assemblies, and Roles

The concept language COAR ("Concepts for Objects, Assemblies, and Roles") was developed as a formal basis for dynamic conceptualization in assembly tasks. Concepts for mechanical objects, assemblies that can be built from these objects, and finally, the changing roles that objects can take on in larger assemblies can be modeled. Main design goals of COAR were to supply language constructs that enable the classification of constructed aggregates as instances of predefined assemblies and which allow the assignment of roles to object representations, according to their current aggregate context.

The language provides means to describe concepts by their attributes and to relate different concepts to one another by a small set of semantic relations. COAR, roughly, is a synthesis of the semantic-network language ERNEST (Sagerer, 1990; Niemann et al., 1990), which is used in a number of SFB 360 projects, and the description logics for part-of hierarchies introduced in (Padgham & Lambrix, 1994). COAR further allows the integration of spatial knowledge in concept definitions, in that descriptions of aggregates, besides of has-part and connected-to relations, may include geometric relations between parts, e.g. $\texttt{orthogonal}_x$ or `touches`, which would have to be evaluated in a geometric scene description when establishing an instantiation (Jung & Wachsmuth, 1995).

3.1. *Object Types and Role Types*

In COAR, a distinction is made between two kinds of concepts: *Object types* are used to model mechanical objects, their subparts (e.g., their connection ports), and assemblies. *Role types* are used to model the specific functional aspects of objects in larger assemblies.

One motivation for introducing the object type – role type distinction is to clearly separate an object's essential (context-independent) properties from its specific functional properties in larger wholes. A further motivation is to exploit this distinction in the design of inference methods which update an agent's internal model as the external situation changes. While the object type of an individual representation will always remain the same, its role type may change over time. Therefore, inference mechanisms for updating an agent's internal model must never consider the reclassification of individual representations w.r.t. their object type but only w.r.t. their role type.

Distinctions similar to our separation of object types and role types have been proposed by Sowa (1988), Way (1991), and Guarino et al. (1994). Sowa, for example, distinguishes between *natural types* and *role types*, the latter being "subtypes of natural types in some particular pattern of relation-ships" (Sowa, 1988, p.120). In the assembly tasks considered here, this particular pattern of relationships is an object's aggregate context, i.e. objects may assume specific roles when used in larger assemblies. Sowa (1988), and also Guarino et al. (1994), have proposed to model object types and role types in a single generalization hierarchy, with role types subordinated to objects types. This is different in COAR, where object types and role types are modeled in two distinct hierarchies. Concepts in the different hierarchies are not in a specialization relationship but they are linked through a special semantic relation *role-of*. This allows, for example, that the same role may be assumed by objects of different types.

3.2. *The COAR Language*

COAR is an operational knowledge representation formalism, by which processes of dynamic conceptualization in mechanical assembly can be formally reconstructed. The COAR language is used to model *long-term concepts*, serving as static background knowledge, and *short-term* concepts, serving as temporal descriptions of individual entities in dynamic conceptualization.

Long-term concepts are generic descriptions in a frame-like notation. The abstract syntax for long-term concepts is as follows:

long-term concept: *conceptname*
    specialization-of: *conceptname**
    [role-of *relationname*: *conceptname*⁺]
    (part *relationname int*: *conceptname*)*
    (connection *min max*: *conceptname*)*
    (pp-constraint *relation* <*relationname*⁺ ><*relationname*⁺ >)*

(attribute *attributename*: *valuedomain*)*

Short-term concepts are modeled as instances of long-term concepts; however, they can change classification during their life cycle. The abstract syntax for short-term concepts is as follows:

short-term concept: *individualname*
instance-of: *conceptname*$^+$
[role-of *relationname*: *individualname*]
(part *relationname*: *individualname*)*
(connection: *individualname*)*
(attribute *attributename*: *value*)*

In detail, the language constructs in COAR expressions describing long-term concepts serve the following purposes:

The *specialization-of ("isa")* slot relates concepts to their superconcepts. All properties of a concept are inherited to its specializations. Multiple superconcepts can be defined. Object types will only be specializations of other object types, and role types will only be specializations of other role types.

The *role-of* slot relates role types with object types. That is role types, typically, will have their role-of slot filled with possibly several object types. Object types will have no role-of slot. If a role type is related to a certain object type, then all instances of this object type may be assigned that role type during their life cycle.

The *part* slot relates composite objects with their components. Different parts of composites are distinguished by their names. Also, number and type restrictions must be defined. Composites, typically, have a pp-constraint filled which defines structural conditions between their parts such that the existence of assembled composites can be inferred from the configuration of their parts. Parts of a composite can either be object types or role types. The latter case indicates that objects will assume a certain role when used as part of a composite.

The *connection* relation is used to define the possible physical connections between mechanical objects. Connection relations will only be defined for long-term concepts which are at the bottom of the part decomposition, i.e. in our case the mechanical objects' connection ports. For example, it can be defined that certain bolts can be fitted in the holes of certain bars by defining an appropriate connection relation between these objects' connection ports. Objects other than ports are assumed to be connectable to all other objects, where the establishment of actual connections between their instances will depend on connectability of their ports (and on collision tests checked in the geometric scene description).

With the *pp-(part-part)constraint* construct, relations can be stated which must hold between two parts of an instance. To specify these (possibly indirect) parts, two paths of part names are specified. Two kinds of constraints can be stated: (1) *connection constraints*, which require connection relations to be established between the corresponding instances; (2) *geometric constraints*, e.g. $\texttt{orthogonal}_x$, which trigger tests in the geometric scene description on an if-needed basis. That is, spatial knowledge derivable from the geometric scene description can be integrated in COAR concept definitions.

The *attribute* slot allows the definition of concept-inherent properties, i.e. properties that hold for an object or role in isolation rather than expressing its relations to other entities. Typical attributes are color and shape.

COAR also comes with a number of predefined top-level (long-term) concepts. The concept OBJECTTYPE serves as most general object-type concept, and the concept ROLETYPE serves as the most general role type. Furthermore, a concept AGGREGATE is defined as a specialization of OBJECTTYPE representing unstructured, "flat" aggregations of connected objects. Any set of connected objects can such at least be conceptualized as an AGGREGATE. Finally, a concept ASSEMBLYGROUP is defined as a specialization of AGGREGATE and serves as the most general concept describing structured assemblies. The reasoning processes described below will only attempt to infer the existence of instances of user-defined concepts that are specializations of the concept ASSEMBLYGROUP.

The language constructs for short-term concepts are to a large extent identical with the language constructs for long-term concepts. The *instance-of* slot indicates the current classification of short-term concepts w.r.t. long-term concepts. The instance-relation w.r.t. role-type concepts is dynamic and can change after any assembly step. When a short-term concept is classified as instance an of a long-term concept, then also all attributes defined in the long-term concept must be asserted and properly initialized in the short-term concept, i.e. short-term concepts can be assigned changing attribute sets during their life cycle. The *role-of* slot is used to relate short-term concepts representing the same external entity, where one short-term concept accounts for the entity's object-type conceptualization and the other one for its role-type conceptualization.

3.3. *Using COAR for Modeling Long-term Concepts*

Long-term concepts serve as static background knowledge for dynamic conceptualization of objects and assemblies in the task environment. In our current demonstration system, long-term concepts are defined in two knowledge bases. A knowledge base "Building Blocks" contains long-term concepts for the multi-functional mechanical objects, like bolts and bars, and their connection ports. A knowledge base "Airplane" contains long-term concepts describing the functional decomposition of the model airplane which serves as target aggregate in our scenario. The airplane's assembly groups may be further structured in subassemblies. Functional decomposition grounds with role-type concepts describing the function of single objects in assembly groups. Role-type concepts are linked to their corresponding object-type concepts in the knowledge base "Building Blocks" via the role-of relation.

The partitioning of the background knowledge into two knowledge bases reflects the different ontologies with respect to which the external objects can be conceptualized. As a further advantage, this modularization supports reuse of the modeled ontologies. For example, the knowledge base "Building Blocks" could be reused for other target aggregates, such as cars or scooters.

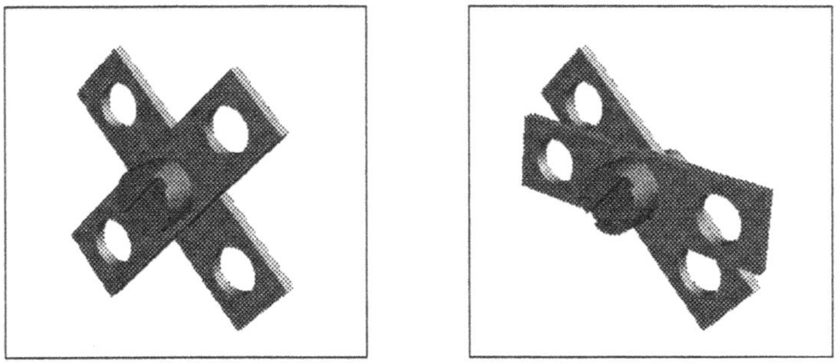

Figure 4. A propeller and an aggregate which is no propeller

In the following example, a long-term concept for the propeller of the model airplane is defined. As shown in Figure 4, a propeller consists of three parts: two propeller blades and the propeller hub. Furthermore, we want to define a propeller where the two propeller blades are orthogonal to each other. On the left of Figure 4, there is a propeller but the assembly on the right of Figure 4 is not considered an instance of the propeller concept since the two bars are not at a right angle.[2]

Figure 5 illustrates how such a propeller made of Baufix parts is modeled in COAR. The first concept, 3-HOLE-BAR, is a specialization of a general BAR and therefore, like the bar, an object-type concept. The 3-HOLE-BAR has three holes which are modeled as its parts. Each of the part slots has a unique name by which it can be distinguished from other parts. The PROPELLERBLADE is some role type which is a specialization of a general role type AIRPLANEPART. The role-of slot of the PROPELLERBLADE relates it to the 3-HOLE-BAR, which indicates that every instance of 3-HOLE-BAR can assume the role of PROPELLERBLADE. The concept PROPELLER is a specialization of the ASSEMBLYGROUP concept. Three parts are defined.

```
long-term concept: 3-HOLE-BAR                          // an object type
   specialization-of: BAR                              // in knowledge base
   part has-hole-1 #1: HOLE                            // "Building Blocks"
   part has-hole-2 #1: HOLE
   part has-hole-3 #1: HOLE
   attribute color: wood

long-term concept: PROPELLERBLADE                      // a role type
   specialization-of: AIRPLANEPART                     // in knowledge base
   role-of as-object: 3-HOLE-BAR                       // "Airplane"

long-term concept: PROPELLER                           // an object type
   specialization-of: ASSEMBLYGROUP                    // in knowledge base
   part has-propellerblade-1 #1: PROPELLERBLADE        // "Airplane"
   part has-propellerblade-2 #1: PROPELLERBLADE
   part has-propellerhub #1: PROPELLERHUB
   pp-constraint connection <has-propellerblade-1.as-object.has-hole-2>
                            <has-propellerhub.as-object.has-shaft>
   pp-constraint connection <has-propellerblade-2.as-object.has-hole-2>
                            <has-propellerhub.as-object.has-shaft>
   pp-constraint orthogonal_x <has-propellerblade-1> <has-propellerblade-2>
```

Figure 5. COAR definitions of long-term concepts (inherited slots not shown)

The first part slot, for example, must be filled with exactly one instance of the PROPELLERBLADE. Also, three pp-constraint constructs are defined that describe the arrangement of the these parts. The first pp-constraint, for example, requires the propeller hub to be connected with the second hole of the first propeller blade. The third pp-constraint requires the two propeller blades to be in orthogonal orientation to each other.

Besides the two knowledge bases "Building Blocks" and "Airplane", two additional knowledge bases are used to couple COAR instances to the geometric scene description. One of these additional knowledge bases provides generic geometry models of the mechanical objects used in the assembly environment. Besides containing purely presentational data like wireframe models, the generic geometry models also serve as analogical representations describing, e.g., the building blocks' intrinsic orientation and the exact positions and orientations of their connection ports. For instance, the rotation axis and the intrinsic orientation of bolts are kept with geometry models for each particular bolt type (e.g. short hexagon bolt). We are currently reworking the knowledge base to keep such information within generalized, parametric geometry models, called *imaginal prototypes* (e.g., of a general bolt). The geometric knowledge contained in these imaginal prototypes will be inherited to each particular geometry model; cf. Figure 6 for an illustration.

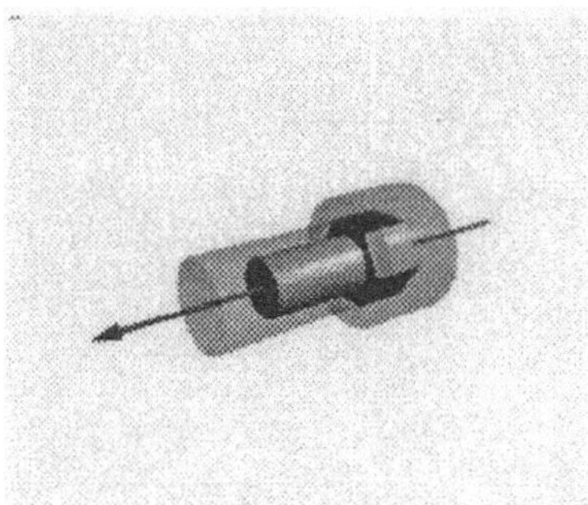

Figure 6. Imaginal prototype of a bolt superimposed on a concrete geometry model

The other additional knowledge base defines several qualitative spatial relations over the geometry models. In our current demonstrator system, the following spatial relations are defined: $\texttt{orthogonal}_x$, $\texttt{orthogonal}_y$, $\texttt{orthogonal}_z$ $\texttt{parallel}_x$, $\texttt{parallel}_y$, $\texttt{parallel}_z$, `touches`, and `near`. These spatial relations, as was described above, can be used in the pp-constraints of COAR concepts. Whether or not these relations hold between two individuals is tested in the geometric scene description. To this end, we use routines which keep track of varying situation parameters.

3.4. *Using COAR for Modeling Short-Term Concepts*

Short-term concepts serve as temporal conceptualizations of individual entities (objects and aggregates) in the current task environment. Dynamic conceptualization involves the step-keeping creation, modification, and retraction of short-term concepts as the external situation progresses. Short-term concepts account for the classification of entities with respect to object type and role type. They further mediate the derivation of situated spatial features of objects and aggregates, such as position, orientation, or size, and spatial relations between objects and aggregates, such as orthogonality or nearness, which are inferred on need from geometry descriptions in the task environment.

For a simple example, we illustrate how an individual entity in a certain role is modeled by way of two COAR short-term concepts. The descriptions shown in Figure 7 concern a bar, currently used as a propeller blade, which is connected to a bolt (like one of the bars of the propeller in Figure 4). In this example, the short-term concept bar-1 is an instance of the object type 3-HOLE-BAR. A connection relation is established from bar-1 to the short-term concept

```
short-term concept: bar-1
      instance-of: 3-HOLE-BAR
      part has-hole-1: bar-1/hole-1
      part has-hole-2: bar-1/hole-2
      part has-hole-3: bar-1/hole-3
      connection: bolt-1
      attribute color: wood

short-term concept: airplanepart-1
      instance-of: PROPELLERBLADE
      role-of as-object: bar-1
      connection: airplanepart-2
```

Figure 7. COAR descriptions of short-term concepts (explanation see text)

bolt-1. Via the role-of link, the short-term concept airplanepart-1 is related to bar-1. That is, airplanepart-1 and bar-1 represent the same geometric object where the short-term concept airplanepart-1 conceptualizes the object according to its function in the evolving airplane. Currently, airplanepart-1 is conceptualized as instance of the role type PROPELLERBLADE. This classification w.r.t. the role-type hierarchy corresponds to the object's current aggregate context as part of a propeller and could change if the object would be detached and used in a different assembly.

All short-term concepts in dynamic conceptualization are *grounded* in the the task environment, as given by the geometric scene description. In general, short-term concepts directly represent some associated geometric entity, for example, an object, aggregate, or connection port. As opposed to primitive objects and connection ports, geometric aggregate representations (grouped structures) do not exist from the beginning but are created and deleted dynamically whenever corresponding short-term concepts are. In some cases, short-term concepts do not directly represent geometric entities. These short-term concepts, however, have grounded representations as parts. In our current system, the only such indirectly grounded short-term concepts represent holes. At this time, holes do not exist in the geometry models. Instead, the two openings of holes (only tunnel-like holes occur in our scenario) are marked in the geometry models to distinguish between the sides from which some object can be fitted into a hole.

Being grounded in the geometric scene description, short-term concepts can access the spatial knowledge contained therein. For instance, geometry models of objects and aggregates give their current positions and orientations, or the length of the bounding box can be used to compute their approximate sizes. Furthermore, as described before, short-term concepts can infer spatial information when needed which thus need not explicitly be represented in them.

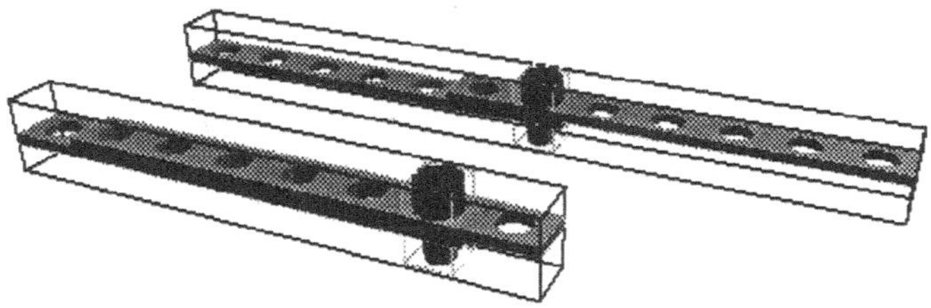

Figure 8. Geometric aggregate representations shown with their bounding boxes

As an example, Figure 8 illustrates how spatial knowledge can be extracted from the geometry scene. It shows two geometric aggregate representations, visualized by their bounding boxes, which were created after the existence of corresponding short-term concepts was inferred. By accessing these geometric representations, it can be inferred that one of the aggregates is in front of the other one and that they are in parallel orientation. By measuring their bounding boxes, it can be furthermore inferred that one of the two aggregates, which both consist of the same parts arranged differently, is larger than the other one.

As short-term concepts are grounded representations of objects and aggregates in the task environment, changes in the environment will be reflected in the short-term concept structure. For example, dynamic conceptualization involves the creation of new short-term concepts, when aggregates are assembled, or role-type instantiation of short-term concepts when objects are used as functional parts in the target assembly. These issues are further described in the next section.

4. Dynamics of Short-term Concepts

As complex aggregates are assembled, or are taken apart again, the constructor's internal view of the environment must be updated accordingly. This is at the heart of dynamic conceptualization. Inferences on short-term concepts concern the assertion or retraction of representations for constructed aggregates in a dynamic knowledge base, and the computation of role changes for individual objects combined herewith. Updates of short-term concepts, usually, will cause updates of other, related short-term concepts as well. For example, a connection relation introduced between two object representations implies the existence of some aggregate representation that has the former object representations as parts. Or becoming part of a structured assembly group determines an object's role-type classification and, hence, a reclassification should be triggered. To capture such dependencies, seven *coherence conditions* over the states of related short-term concepts are formulated below. Altogether these coherence conditions, whose validity is ensured by appropriate inference rules, define the framework for dynamic conceptualization in the assembly domain.

4.1. *Role-Type Instantiation*

In most cases, objects will assume different roles in the course of assemblage. The possible role types according to which a short-term concept can be classified are restricted by the role-of relations between role types and objects types in long-term memory:

(1) Restriction of role-type classification through role-of relation
The role-type classification of a short-term concept with object type classification O is always one of the role types $R_1, ..., R_n$, or a generalization thereof, where each of the R_i is related to O, or a generalization of O, via the role-of construct.

For example, in our reference situation a short-term concept representing a bolt will at all times be classified w.r.t. the role-type hierarchy as PROPELLERHUB or AXLE, or (general) as AIRPLANEPART. But it will never have the role type PROPELLERBLADE since only bars can assume this role.

In particular, a short-term concept will be assigned a role type when it is used as part of an assembly group. The classification of a short-term concept w.r.t. the role type hierarchy is tied to its aggregate context by the second coherence condition:

(2) Role-type classification according to aggregate context
If some short-term concept a is the part *partname* of a short-term concept b where b is an instance of the long-term concept B, and if the definition of B requires its part *partname* to be filled with an instance of A then a must be an instance of A.

For example, if a short-term concept representing a bolt is the part "has-propellerhub" of a propeller, then it must be an instance of the concept PROPELLERHUB (cf. the definition of PROPELLER given in Figure 5).

Role-type instantiation, in general, will fill the instance-of slot of a short-term concept with a certain long-term concept and, by inheritance from that long-term concept, will also add further attributes to the short-term concept.

4.2. *Assertion and Retraction of Connection Relations*

In an assembly environment, the connection relation is of central importance. The mechanical objects considered in our scenario have connection ports that allow them to be fitted together in various ways. If an instruction states that two objects are to be connected, then appropriate connection ports are determined which are the put in the connection relation. If two entities are connected to each other and if both of these entities are part of composite objects, then these composite objects themselves are connected as well. Thus, the third coherence condition grounds connections between composites on connections between their parts:

(3) Assertion and retraction of connection relations
Connection relations between composites can only be asserted if there is a connection relation asserted between some of their parts.

For example, a connection relation between the short-term concepts for a propeller and a fuselage can be asserted when there is already a connection relation asserted between the representations for the propeller hub (which is a part of the propeller) and the motor block (which is a part of the fuselage). Ultimately, all connection relations between short-term concepts are based on connections between representations of the objects' connection ports. Whether a connection relation should be asserted between port representations is tested in the geometry scene. Once a connection relation is asserted between two port representations, this information is propagated in the short-term concepts' part-of structure where dependent connection relations are asserted. Similarly, the retraction of a connection relation between port representations will cause the retraction of induced (propagated) connection relations. That is, the connection structure of the short-term concepts, and therefore their aggregate and role-type structure, are grounded in the geometry scene.

4.3. *Creation and Deletion of Aggregate Representations*

When two or more mechanical objects are assembled, they jointly form an aggregate which is to be represented by some short-term concept. Such short-term concepts are dynamically created and deleted during assemblage. The creation of new short-term concepts for assembled aggregates, or the deletion of aggregates representations whose parts are disconnected, respectively, is ensured by the following coherence conditions:

(4) Creation of aggregate representations
If a connection relation is established between two short-term concepts then there also exists some aggregate representation that has the former two short-term concepts as direct or indirect parts.

(5) Deletion of aggregate representations
An aggregate representation can only exist in short-term memory as long as all its parts are directly or indirectly connected to each other.

4.4. *Creation and Deletion of Assembly-Group Representations*

Assemblies built from the mechanical objects might form, or contain as subassemblies, structured (named) assembly groups of the target aggregate. When such an assembly group has been constructed in the geometry scene, a corresponding short-term concept is to be created. In order to decide whether or not some assembly group has been constructed, a relation *composes* between a short-term concept a representing some unstructured aggregate and a long-term concept B of a structured assembly group is defined: a *composes* B, if a has all the parts required in the definition of B, and further, all the required relations in the definition of B, as specified by the pp-constraints of B, hold between the parts of a.

The following coherence condition ensures that a maximal number of short-term concepts representing structured assembly groups are created:

(6) Creation of assembly group representations
There is no unstructured aggregate representation in short-term memory that *composes* some long-term concept of a structured assembly group.

Instances of assembly groups must be deleted when the necessary conditions for their existence no longer hold:

(7) Deletion of assembly group representations
An instance of a long-term concept A describing a structured assembly group can only exist in short-term memory as long as also all the parts required in the definition of A exist and are in the required relationship to each other, as specified by the pp-constraints of A.

The technique we employ to infer the existence of assembly-group instances is a variant of compositional inferencing (Padgham & Lambrix, 1994). Our methods differ from those introduced in (Padgham & Lambrix, 1994) in several ways. Most importantly, the creation of multi-level part-of hierarchies in short-term memory is possible, i.e. short-term concepts representing assembly groups may themselves have representations of subassemblies as parts.

Furthermore, our framework allows to have changing role-type classifications of short-term concepts as their aggregate context changes.

4.5. *Example*

The following example illustrates the updates of short-term concepts in response to changes in the assembly environment. These updates are brought about by inference rules that ensure the validity of the above coherence conditions. On the left of the Figures 9-11, the current state of an assembly is presented as a visualization of the geometry scene. On the right, the short-term concept structure representing the geometry scene is shown in a graphical notation. In the graphical notation, short-term concepts are presented as boxes, part relations as arrows, and connection relations as curved lines. For presentation purposes, pairs of short-term concepts representing the same object are displayed in one box. Port representations are not shown.

In the first situation (cf. Figure 9), four building blocks are present on the virtual assembly workbench. Three of these, the two bars and the bolt, are already connected. According the above coherence condition (4), there is an aggregate representation that has these three objects as parts. The aggregate cannot be interpreted as a structured assembly group of the model airplane and is therefore unstructured. Also, none of the role types of the four objects is determined at this stage.

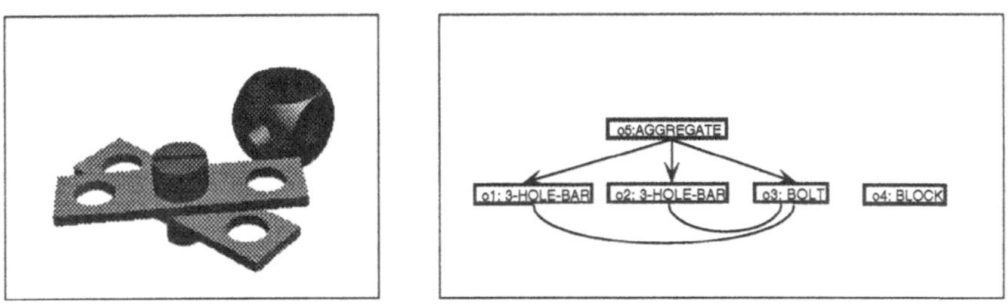

Figure 9. Assembly of a propeller (first situation)

In the following assembly step (cf. Figure 10), the bolt is fitted into the block, e.g. by the instruction: *"attach the bolt to the block"*. As after each assembly step, the system checks in the geometry scene if new connections between port representations have resulted. Assembly instructions cannot be translated directly into connection relations because, due to "physical" constraints, assembly operations can be subject to failures and side effects (e.g., more than one connection might result from one assembly step). In this situation, the system detects one new connection relation between the opening of the block's front hole and the shaft of the bolt and, accordingly, a new connection relation is asserted between the respective port representations (not shown in the graphs). This relation, according to the coherence condition (3), is then propagated in the short-term concepts' part-of structure and, eventually, a connection relation is asserted between the short-term concepts o4 and o3, representing the block and the bolt, respectively. According to coherence condition (4), the block and the bolt must both be part of the same aggregate, so the short-term concept o4 is added as a new part to the aggregate o5. It is then checked, according to coherence condition (6), if the aggregate now contains an assembly group. Since it does not, the short-term concepts are no further restructured.

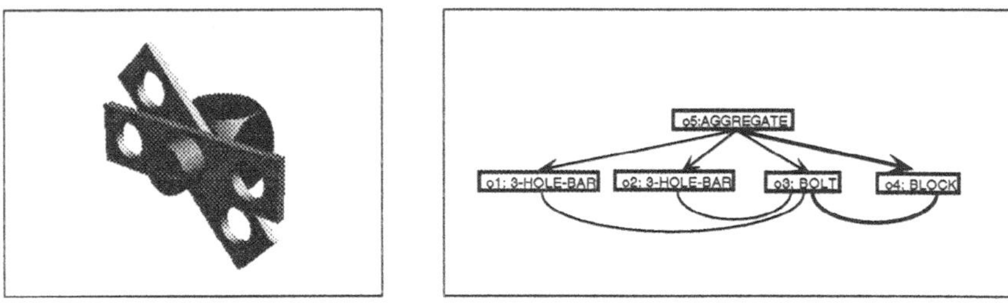

Figure 10. Assembly of a propeller (second situation)

In the next situation (cf. Figure 11), the two bars are brought into orthogonal orientation, e.g. by the instruction: *"rotate the front bar crosswise to the other bar"*. Rotation operations do not cause new connections nor do they detach previous connections. Yet they can induce new assembly groups, or destroy existing assembly groups. In the resulting situation, the system has to check, according to coherence condition (6), if the unstructured aggregate o5 composes some long-term concept of a structured assembly group. It does, in fact, compose the PROPELLER since it contains all of its parts in the required relationship. Therefore, a new short-term concept o6 is created as instance of the PROPELLER concept and inserted into the part hierarchy as part of o5, and with o1, o2, and o3 as parts. Then, according to coherence condition (3), the connection relation between the block o4 and the bolt o3 is propagated and a new connection relation between o4 and o6 is asserted. Finally, according to coherence condition (2), the role types of the propeller's parts are assigned: o1 and o2 are instantiated as PROPELLERBLADE, and o3 is instantiated as PROPELLERHUB.

Similarly, the above coherence conditions ensure updates of short-term concepts in all other situations where changes were made in the geometry scene. After any assembly step, the following operations are carried out:

- new connection relations between ports representations are extracted from the geometry scene and propagated in the part-of structure

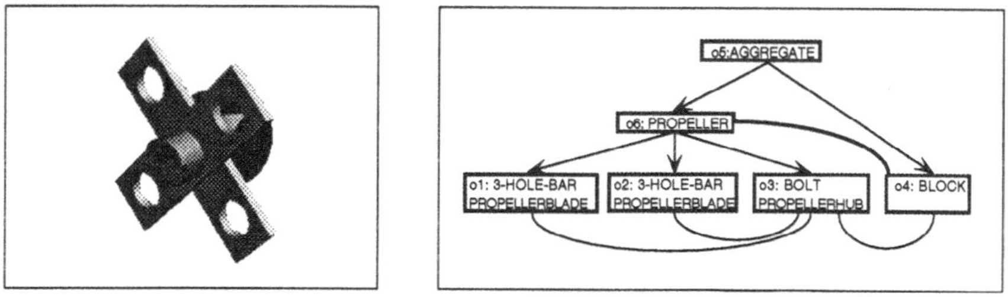

Figure 11. Assembly of a propeller (final situation)

- new unstructured aggregate representations are created and matched against the long-term concepts of assembly groups, and
- role-type classifications of short-term concepts are assigned according to their aggregate context.

After disassembly operations, connection relations are retracted and aggregate representations are deleted, whereby new aggregate representations could be created in case an aggregate is split. In response to rotation operations, assembly-group representations could either be created or deleted.

5. Conclusions and Future Work

In this paper, we introduced the notion of dynamic conceptualization and stressed its relevance for situated artificial communicators. Dynamic conceptualization is concerned with the fact that an agent's internal representation of the current situation must be adapted as its task environment changes. We have developed the knowledge representation language COAR which is tailored for the modeling of objects, assemblies, and roles in mechanical assembly. The language provides means to describe concepts by their attributes and to relate different concepts to one another by a small set of structural relations. COAR representations integrate taxonomic, partonomic, and functional information of objects and aggregates. Object types, used to model mechanical objects, and role types, used to model the specific functional aspects of objects in larger assemblies, are linked through a special semantic relation "role-of". Furthermore, geometric constraints can be integrated in concept definitions.

We also presented a framework for reasoning with COAR representations that further specifies dynamic conceptualization. Inferencing includes the creation and deletion of assembly representations and the reclassification of representations w.r.t. the role-type hierarchy depending on their changing aggregate context. Short-term concepts, serving as temporal conceptualizations of individual entities (objects and aggregates) in the current task environment, account for the classification of entities with respect to object type and role type. Whereas object-type classification persists, role-type classification is dynamic, i.e. it may change and evoke changing feature attribution. Being grounded in the task environment by way of the geometric scene description, short-term concepts can access the spatial knowledge contained therein which thus needs not be represented explicitly.

Our approach has so far been evaluated in the CODY Virtual Constructor, a knowledge-based system for the interactive assembly of simple building blocks in a virtual environment. In the Virtual Constructor COAR representations are coupled with the geometric scene description such that the processes of dynamic conceptualization are triggered by changes in the virtual environment. We anticipate several interesting applications for integrated knowledge-based graphics systems of this kind, e.g., in virtual prototyping and assembly planning.

Within SFB 360, the CODY system is currently being integrated in a demonstration system that comprises subsystems for image and speech understanding. We successfully coupled COAR representations with the geometric scene description produced by the vision component. As new input arrives from the vision component, dynamic conceptualization provides additional information about the objects' assembly structure and functional roles which can then be used in instruction processing. Furthermore, first experiments show that the knowledge about the legal connection structure of mechanical objects, defined by our system, can be used to correct physically impossible object configurations that are sometimes produced by the vision component due to camera tolerances (cf. Figure 12).

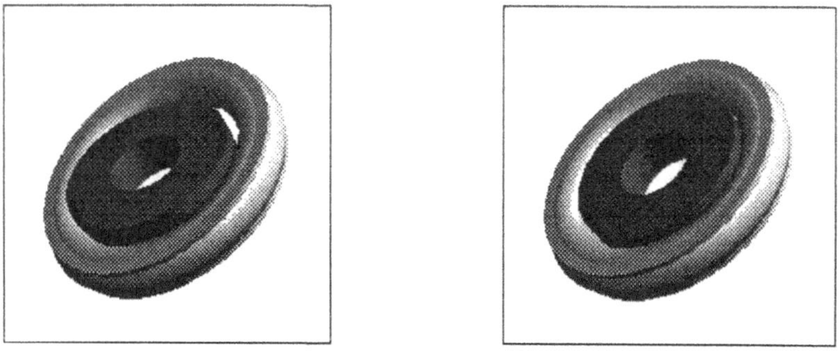

Figure 12. Raw reconstruction of a wheel as produced by the vision system (left) and its model-driven elaboration (right)

As a future extension of our knowledge representation formalism, we plan to add another, imaginal kind of representation to the structured representations we developed so far. These *imaginal prototypes*, that we already briefly described in Section 3 (cf. Figure 6), are parametric spatial representations of objects and aggregates whose realization will build on constructive solid geometry. They are useful, for example, to describe the generic shape of artifacts. Also, other space-related features, like intrinsic orientations, can be defined in imaginal prototypes. Like the structural descriptions of long-term concepts described in this paper, imaginal prototypes will be organized in a specialization hierarchy such that generic information can be dynamically inherited to all geometric instances in the mechanical-object assembly environment.

Acknowledgements

The CODY Project is part C1 of the Collaborative Research Centre *"Situated Artificial Communicators"* (see site description by Rickheit & Wachsmuth, this volume). Research in the CODY Project is partly supported by the German National Science Foundation (DFG). The authors are indebted to Britta Lenzmann, Martin Hoffhenke, Christian Pütter, and Stefan Kopp for various contributions to the research.

Notes

[1] A running demonstration of the virtual assembly workbench can be seen in our contribution to the IJCAI-95 Videotape Program, cf. (Cao et al., 1995).

[2] Some readers may still want to refer to this "false" propeller as a propeller. This is not the point in our current work. Our point is to provide means for recognizing a propeller that is correctly built according to its definition. Should the right-hand-side assemblage in Fig. 4 be recognizable as a propeller, we could allow for an according "slack" in the routine which evaluates orthogonality. Yet another point is how reference could be established to the right-hand-side assemblage by a description like "the propeller on the right". This topic concerns future work.

References

Y. Cao, B. Jung, and I. Wachsmuth: 1995. Situated verbal interaction in virtual design and assembly, IJCAI-95 Videotape Program. Abstract in *Proc. 14th International Joint Conference on Artificial Intelligence*, Morgan Kaufman, pages 2061–2062.

G.A. Fink, F. Kummert, and G. Sagerer: 1994. A close high-level interaction scheme for recognition and interpretation of speech. In *International Conference on Spoken Language Processing*, volume 4, Yokohama, Japan, pages 2183–2186.

Thomas Fuhr, Gudrun Socher, Christian Scheering, and Gerhard Sagerer: 1995. A three-dimensional spatial model for the interpretation of image data. In *IJCAI-95 Workshop on Representation and Processing of Spatial Expressions*, 14th Int. Joint Conf. on Art. Int. (IJCAI-95), Montréal, Canada, pages 93–102.

M. Genesereth and N. Nilsson: 1987. *Logical Foundations of Artificial Intelligence.* Morgan Kaufmann, Los Altos, CA.

Th. Gruber and G. Olsen: 1994. An ontology for engineering mathematics. In *Principles of Knowledge Representation and Reasoning*. Morgan Kaufmann, San Francisco, CA, pages 258–269.

N. Guarino, M. Carrara, and P. Giaretta: 1994. An ontology of meta-level categories. In *Principles of Knowledge Representation and Reasoning*. Morgan Kaufmann, San Francisco, CA, pages 270–280.

B. Jung, B. Lenzmann, and I. Wachsmuth: 1995. Interaktive Montage-Simulation mit wissensbasierter Grafik. SFB 360 Report 95/6, Universität Bielefeld.

B. Jung and I. Wachsmuth: 1994. Dynamische Konzeptualisierung. SFB 360 Report 94/9, Universität Bielefeld.

B. Jung and I. Wachsmuth: 1995. Integrating spatial and conceptual knowledge in virtual assembly. In L. Dreschler-Fischer and S. Pribbenow, editors, *KI-95 Activities: Workshops, Posters, Demos*. GI, pages 103–104.

R. Moratz, H.J. Eikmeyer, B. Hildebrandt, F. Kummert, G. Rickheit, and G. Sagerer: 1995. Integrating speech and selective visual perception using a semantic network. In *1995 AAAI Fall Symposium on Computational Models for Integrating Language and Vision*, Cambridge, MA, (to appear).

H. Niemann, G. Sagerer, S. Schröder, and F. Kummert: 1990. ERNEST: A semantic network for pattern understanding. *IEEE Transactions on Pattern Analysis*, 12(9), pages 883–903.

L. Padgham and P. Lambrix: 1994. A framework for part-of hierarchies in terminological logics. In *Principles of Knowledge Representation and Reasoning*. Morgan Kaufmann, San Francisco, CA, pages 485–496.

G. Rickheit and H. Strohner: 1994. Kognitive Grundlagen situierter künstlicher Kommunikatoren. In H.-J. Kornadt, J. Grabowski, and R. Mangold-Allwin, editors, *Sprache und Kognition: Perspektiven moderner Sprachpsychologie*. Spektrum Akademischer Verlag, Heidelberg, pages 73–92.

G. Rickheit and I. Wachsmuth: 1996. Collaborative Research Centre "Situated Artificial Communicators" at the University of Bielefeld. *This volume 10(3-4)*.

G. Sagerer: 1990. *Automatisches Verstehen gesprochener Sprache*. Bibliographisches Institut, Mannheim.

J. Sowa: 1988. Using a lexicon of canonical graphs in a semantic interpreter. In M. W. Evens, editor, *Relational Models of the Lexicon*. Cambridge University Press, Cambridge, UK, pages 112–137.

E. C. Way: 1991. *Knowledge Representation and Metaphor*. Kluwer, Dordrecht.

Book Review

Title: **'The Language Instinct' – Pinker's opinions concerning the innateness of language**	*Publisher/Date:* Penguin Books, London, 1994
Author: Steven Pinker	*Price:* P/b £8.99

Pinker presents a powerful argument to justify his opinion that the fundamental mechanisms of human language are innate. Emphasis is placed on the central role that syntax and grammars play in unravelling the mysteries of how humans learn, process, and augment language.

The language phenomenon is considered from a number of perspectives, such as Philosophy, Sociology, Psychology, Anthropology, and Linguistics. As the book develops it poses many questions which initially seem obscure and unrelated, but as the reader progresses the essence and power of Pinker's proposal begins to unwind in a highly coordinated fashion.

In the opinion of the reviewer, the best introduction to the quite unorthodox but ingenious format that this book takes is to drift through a substantial quantity of the questions and topics that Pinker describes, considering how these help to unravel Pinker's proposed solution to the mysteries of language.

The book opens discussing the miracle of communication using the language medium, describing the seemingly *logic defying* structure, and the phenomenal complexity of language. After discussing the initial proposal of language as a type of instinct by Darwin (1874), Pinker considers different languages (from the newly discovered dialects in New Guinea in the 1930's, to Harlem street-talk), the process called *creolisation* in which pidgin dialects evolve into highly grammatical languages, and the effect that brain disorders have on speech providing evidence of its innateness.

Pinker moves on to introduce the notion of a *mentalese* (also referred to as a metalanguage or interlingua), criticising the original clumsy word for word approaches to translation, and introducing psychological experiments which have produced interesting results, such as babies exhibiting the ability to carry out simple mental arithmetic. This leads onto a consideration of information representation within the brain.

The thrust changes to more scientific approaches, such as the description of Markov models and their limitations when attempting to formally define a language. Moving on to consider language as a grammar, and presenting concise descriptions of Chomsky's theories of language, this includes an excellent introduction to $\bar{X}$ theory (Chomsky 1965).

The direction changes yet again to discuss the world of words and morphology, describing the part that morphology plays in different languages, and explaining what are considered to be irregularities in English words. These are often referred to when attempting to learn English as a second language during criticism of its incomprehensibility. But Pinker takes the discussion much further, describing the reasons for a number of these anomalies, clarifying the complexity, and often justifying it. An array of statistical information concerning natural language follows, for example, the phenomenon that children between the age of 1 and 18 learn an average of 10 words per day, and discussing how humans associate meanings to words with ease, when in fact numerous interpretations could be considered.

Pinker moves on to the mysteries of sound, how words are communicated using a complex array of muscular movements of the mouth and tongue, why quite different sentences can sound identical, and the effect that this has on automatic dictation. A moment is taken to defend the anomalies of English spelling – why do similar spellings have different pronunciations? Explaining that words are often based on the same morpheme to indicate similar meaning as "the goal of reading, after all, is to understand text, not to pronounce it." (p. 191).

Artificial Intelligence is briefly introduced, comparing the optimism of film roles such as *HAL* from "2001: A Space Odyssey", and *C3P0* from "Star Wars", to the reality of 50 years of research. A fleeting review of Natural Language Processing is presented, from the early language mimicking systems such as ELIZA to the complexities of language grammars. Pinker discusses why computer parsers are too meticulous for their own good, often identifying hundreds of legitimate ambiguities that a human would not consider.

Pinker then takes a look at the languages of the world – there are between 4000 and 6000. Comparisons and distinctions are made, describing the differences between SVO (Subject-Verb-Object) languages such as English, and SOV languages such as Japanese. He moves on to consider where languages originated from and how they develop within societies, acknowledging the fact that many languages are doomed for similar reasons that species become extinct.

Pinker considers the genius of young children and their adeptness during language learning. He describes a number of the stages involved, from single-word acquisition to comprehension. Even when children make errors they often presume sensible interpretations which adhere to grammar rules. He then raises the rather obscure question, "Why aren't children born talking?". Part of the answer is to listen to themselves during development of their articulators, but also stating that compared to the proportion of their lives that other primates spend in their mother's womb, babies are born 18 months early, in which time they are talking.

Pinker then moves on to consider whether there are specific language genes, and whether it is possible to identify a *language organ*. Although brain research is still rather primitive, the left side of the brain contains what he considers to be the *language organs, Broca's area* and *Wernicke's area*. He discusses the internal working of the brain, and Neural Networks which have been developed to simulate this process.

A discussion follows concerning language compared to the unique abilities of other creatures. Chimpanzees are considered to be second only to humans in their ability to learn. A number of experiments have been carried out and outlandish claims made, for example, on teaching them to learn American sign language. Pinker dismisses these claims one-by-one and clearly explains why the results have been so overrated. His overall summary being that animals communicate at a more instinctive level, and cannot therefore carry out intelligent processing of language.

The penultimate chapter discusses *language mavens*, those people who criticise the way language is used. They are scorned by Pinker who accepts that there are some fundamental features of language which should be taught, but changes in the use of language are a form of evolution, this is how language has progressed in the past, and will progress in the future. To conclude, Pinker returns to the original question to justify whether there is a language instinct. He discusses the Standard Social Science Model (SSSM) which explains human behavior due to culture and the innate ability to learn. Learning is reconsidered, in particular *generalisation by example*, until finally returning to the modules of the mind and the instincts that are innate.

From this list of areas covered by Pinker it is clear that he has produced a book with much depth and variety, and one which captures the reader's interest from start to finish. Criticisms of this book are few. Pinker keeps the linguistic jargon to a minimum; and when introducing concepts he offers clear explanations. Although, as the chapters progress, the complexity becomes more intense and some jargon creeps in which will, in the opinion of the reviewer, confuse a reader without the necessary linguistic background.

A wide array of considerations and arguments are examined and this is to the immense benefit of the book. Unfortunately some of the arguments put forward are insufficient: these are either difficult to comprehend due to the lack of information, or may be inconceivable because of the nature of the argument, one example being the discussion of human instincts in the final chapter. Pinker seems to leap between persuading the reader that his opinions are valid and mocking the instinct arguments put forward by other authors. The direction of this chapter is lost in places.

The book is based on an instinct primarily related to syntax and grammars. Syntax has always played an important role in language research, and it is not believed that Pinker is attempting to defend that. He accepts the need for semantics and pragmatics, but should possibly address some of the criticisms of the syntactic approach raised by the semantic and pragmatic communities.

In the opinion of the reviewer, the powerful argument presented outweighs the criticisms. This book will be fascinating for the whole spectrum of science readers, it offers an in-depth discussion of the issues for the specialist, and an excellent overview for the general reader. Pinker's book has already received a number of reviews praising its depth and quality. These being from a variety of prestigious organisations and individuals, including: The New York Times Book Review, The Sunday Telegraph, Richard Dawkins, Bill Gates, and Noam Chomsky. This is yet another, praising Pinker for a fine piece of work.

References

Chomsky, N. (1965). *Aspects of the Theory of Syntax*. MIT Press: Cambridge, Massachusetts.

Darwin, C. R. (1874). *The Descent of Man and Selection in Relation to Sex* (2nd ed.). Hurst & Co.: New York.

ROBIN COLLIER
Department of Computer Science
University of Sheffield, England
September, 1995

GPSR Compliance

The European Union's (EU) General Product Safety Regulation (GPSR) is a set of rules that requires consumer products to be safe and our obligations to ensure this.

If you have any concerns about our products, you can contact us on ProductSafety@springernature.com

In case Publisher is established outside the EU, the EU authorized representative is:

Springer Nature Customer Service Center GmbH
Europaplatz 3
69115 Heidelberg, Germany

Batch number: 10607320

Printed by Printforce, the Netherlands